"Mac Pier has produced a much needed book with a worldview of l lenses. This book will cause religious leaders, policy makers, and world leaders to recog.... beyond New York City's place in the global economy—long recognized as the secular capital of the world—there is a spiritual dimension to this global city. This is a must-read for religious leaders around the world who seek to influence the spiritual life of secular urban areas."

—REV. DR. W. WILSON GOODE SR.
National director, Amachi; former mayor of Philadelphia

"Mac Pier and I share a common commitment to our New York City, its children, and its neighborhoods. This deeply moving book documents what leaders are doing to change lives in this great urban center."

—FRANCES HESSELBEIN
Founding president and chairman, Leader to Leader Institute

"Mac Pier's understanding of the spiritual dynamics of New York City is unparalleled. In *Spiritual Leadership in the Global City*, he eloquently captures what God is doing through united prayer and through the remarkable stories of 25 urban churches. Reading it has renewed my hope for this great city and other cities worldwide."

—JOHN D. BECKETT
Chairman of the board, The King's College, New York City
Author, Loving Monday: Succeeding in Business Without Selling Your Soul

"*Spiritual Leadership in the Global City* tells the story not only impacting New York City but also the global influence of New York City leadership on the country of Rwanda."

—KOFI HAGAN
National director, World Vision Rwanda

"Dr. Mac Pier has been a proven friend and colleague for more than 25 years. He has always demonstrated an enormous passion for the people of this great, yet challenging community. As a man of tremendous integrity, intelligence, biblical scholarship, and leadership capicity, I cannot think of another individual in this Greater New York metro center, who is better equipped to relate these dynamic stories to a national and global audience."

—BISHOP CARLTON T. BROWN,
Bethel Gospel Assembly

"The urban pastor is tempted to be overwhelmed with the challenge, to lose faith, and to give up. Mac has once again shined a light on the city and revealed a cadre of servant warriors who have a high level of entrepreneurship, Christlike passion for souls, faith to move mountains, and who refuse to give up. This narrative will lift the spirit and increase the faith of all who face impossible challenges. With God nothing shall be impossible!"

—REV. DR. ROBERT JOHANSSON,
Sr. Pastor, Evangel Church and School;
Board chairman, Concerts of Prayer Greater New York

"God is at work in the city of New York. As He has done so many times in the past, He is using leaders who are committed to proclaim the good news of the gospel and to be His agents of reconciliation and transformation. In this book, Mac Pier shares with us the miracle that is happening in the lives of thousands of people in one of the largest cities in the world. There are lessons for all of us to learn and apply."

—C. WILLIAM POLLARD
Chairman emeritus, ServiceMaster
Author, The Soul of the Firm *and* Serving Two Masters? Reflections of God and Profit

"As one of New York's premier leaders, Mac is able to recognize other effective leaders involved in city transformation. The profiles, principles, and perspectives found in this book are essential to all who endeavor to empower people in the urban context. I highly recommend this book!"

—JOSEPH MATTERA
Overseeing bishop, Christ Covenant Coalition

"The supreme Lord of cities has set the pattern for redeeming cities: incarnational leadership. Mac Pier gives us the back story of 25 servant ministries that surround my home in metro New York. Each one is effectively advancing the kingdom because each is thoroughly incarnational. What Christ is doing through them, He can do with any of us. Here are compelling models that can motivate and mobilize authentic spiritual leadership anywhere."

—DAVID BRYANT
Founder, Concerts of Prayer International; president, PROCLAIM HOPE!

"*Spiritual Leadership in the Global City* is a testimony to how God has been raising up churches, individuals, and Christian-agency leaders, calling and mobilizing them with a vision for significant kingdom influence and impact. The book gives a glimpse into how obedient servant leaders are faithfully tapping into the remarkable potential and diversity of metropolitan New York and making a difference locally and across the globe through life transformation and the emergence of hope. Mac Pier has been an exceptional catalyst in this effort."

—JOHN CLAUSE
Senior regional director, World Vision

"Spiritual Leadership in the Global City shows that, to be a great leader, you must allow God to lead you!"

—HORST SCHULZE
President and CEO, West Paces Hotels; former president of Ritz-Carlton

"Mac Pier is part of an emerging generation of leaders whose lives are marked by a kingdom agenda rather than personal ambition. Mac has taken seriously the claims of Christ on his life, and has responded in such a way that his life itself has become his strongest teaching. He can say, 'Follow me as I follow Christ.' Mac has devoted his life and ministry to and offers practical, real life examples of the incarnational principles that manifest the Great Commission. I urge you to have 'ears to hear' what the Sprit is saying to us through this prophetic brother."

—ROBERT STEARNS
Executive director, Eagles Wings Ministries

"Mac's heart beats like that of a native New Yorker. He has wonderfully captured the uniqueness and the greatness of the church that is in New York. It is a story long overdue in its telling, and one that many New Yorkers may not even know. How thrilling that the rest of the body of Christ will now know what we in this awesome city have long been aware of—the church of Jesus Christ is alive."

—REV. DR. ROGER MCPHAIL
Gateway City Church

"Mac Pier was one of the first people to welcome me in 2001 when I came to Manhattan to start The Journey Church of the City. Since then he has been a consistent friend and adviser. Our friendship is based on the fact that we have three common driving interests: to lead people to pray, to start new churches, and to help church leaders see the value of the city in God's eyes. In this new book, all three of these interests come through loud and clear. I recommend this book for pastors and church leaders serving in major cities and to anyone with a heart for God's work in the city."

—NELSON SEARCY
Author; founder of churchleaderinsights.com
Lead pastor, The Journey Church of the City

"Having spent the last decade doing youth ministry in New York City while laboring diligently to continue the legacy of leadership of my great city, Mac Pier offers a bird's-eye view on the spiritual landscape of one of the most influential cities in the world. The church models set forth in this great read serve as examples and an ancient boundary stone for emerging leaders. Most importantly, *Spiritual Leadership in the Global City* documents the spiritual heroics of modern-day men and women in the faith. It reads like a modern day Hebrews 11—a city ablaze by the Spirit of God with global ramifications!"

—Rev. Adam Durso
Executive pastor, Christ Tabernacle; executive director, Youth Explosion Ministries

"God's great work in the megacities often stems from a personal story where someone dared to do something about a holy dissatisfaction. Dr. Mac Pier captures our attention by taking us on a faith-building tour of the greatest city on earth—New York City—and some of its surrounding communities. He doesn't show to us shopping centers or museums, but rather ordinary people who accomplished extraordinary feats for God. You will learn the stories of how some of the city's most powerful spiritual leaders and social architects were formed when they decided to tackle the things that made them dissatisfied. Read it! Get inspired! Grow as a leader!"

—David D. Ireland, PhD,
Senior pastor, Christ Church

"Born and raised in New York City, I have lived with a passion to unite evangelicals in our Region since I came back to plant Gateway in the mid-1960s. Many of us who shared that vision had just about given up when God raised up the Concerts of Prayer Greater New York ministry under the leadership of Mac Pier and David Bryant. God had used the unique leadership skills He gave to Mac to bring us together for united prayer and ministry. I believe God will use Mac, this book, and the New York City Leadership Center to help raise up the next generation of spiritual leaders in our region, and hopefully, in other world-class cities in our world today."

—Rev. Dr. Daniel Mercaldo
Senior pastor, Gateway Cathedral

"Mac Pier presents a view of urban leadership and the unique distinctives that allowed these individuals to have an impact on life in New York. As a lifelong resident and a ministry practitioner for more than 30 years, I see *Spiritual Leadership in the Global City* as a fresh look at how the kingdom of God has taken shape in New York. Mac offers a template for ministry that is applicable in other global venues."

—MARC RIVERA
Senior pastor, Primitive Christian Church

"*Spiritual Leadership in the Global City* provides exciting evidence that a dedicated faith in God can overcome the greatest challenges in the diverse, complex environment that is New York City. This powerful book by Mac Pier serves as a source of inspiration to anyone—whether in New York or in any city—illustrating that a focus on prayer and commitment to His higher purpose will transform any community. This transformation unites people across all cultural and societal boundaries, creed, and race to lead those who have lost hope back to a community strengthened by spiritual and values-based principles. Mac's book is a must-read for those leaders who seek to transform their community through their faith in God."

—HARRY TUCKER
President, Dynamex Consulting

"Every person—young and old, affluent and less affluent, leaders, managers, and servants—will gain something from this groundbreaking work of all the churches that are located in the center of the world—Greater New York City. Reading this comprehensive work by Mac Pier will illuminate two things: (1) God is dynamic and ever-changing and (2) His church is a reflection of who He is and the great work that He is doing to impact lives in this diverse global city."

—RUPERT HAYLES
Chief operating officer, Christ Church

"Mac Pier's *Spiritual Leadership in the Global City* reveals the ripples of a revolution occurring in New York City. Dig deep in this and find out how you can join to fight against the insidious culture that is incessantly attacking the young people across the globe."

—RON LUCE
President and founder, Teen Mania Ministries

"I have known Mac Pier for more than 16 years, and he is one of the most passionate and compassionate intercessory prayer persons—concerned about God and His people—whom I have ever met. He has extraordinary insight; understanding, addressing, and interrelating the dynamics of culture, the demographics, and needs of the people groups in the Greater New York City metro area, and incarnational faith and effectual intercession. In this book, Dr. Pier leads the reader on a journey to this understanding as he unveils a remnant in New York City that is making a difference through prayer, compassionate ministry, and leadership development."

—REV. PURA DE JESUS-CONIGLIO, ESQ.
Coordinator, Bronx House of Prayer/Pray New York! (Bronx Region)/
Operation Bronx/NYC Restoration Team

"Mac Pier and his hardworking group at Concerts of Prayer Greater New York are important leaders in the creation of the "glorious urbanism" that is replacing the old image of a Sodom and Gomorrah New York City. Because of COPGNY, the twenty-first century will likely see the rise of the archetypical image of 'Jesus the New Yorker.' And because so many people around the world identify themselves as New Yorkers in Diaspora, *Spiritual Leadership in the Global City* will be invaluable for Christian leaders of the 'extended New York City,' from the dusty lanes of Mali, Africa, to the bustling streets of Shanghai, China."

—TONY CARNES
President, Values Research Institute

"Mac Pier has been a serious student of God at work throughout New York City—surprisingly, the most collaborative and spiritually connected big city in the world. His relentless commitment to kingdom activism and his unbridled passion to serve church leaders are second to none. Mac's grasp of what God is doing across Greater New York is mind-boggling. Want to be amazed and encouraged? Read this book."

—STEVE BELL
Executive vice president, Willow Creek Association

"I have no doubt that God called Mac and Marya Pier to New York City for such a time as this. Their lives are an example of utmost integrity to a call that is catalyzing an unprecedented level of kingdom collaboration across the five boroughs of this great city. Relationships are being transformed and unity in the church is more than a concept; they are real and bringing much needed redemption and restoration to the most influential city on the planet. If you care about reaching your city for Christ, this is a must-read because this can happen where you live as well."

—JIM MELLADO
President, Willow Creek Association

"This is a fascinating read for leaders and lovers of the gospel and the cities. Most of the world lives in the megacities and each city has influence far beyond its boundaries. But New York City is unique in its global influence. Mac Pier has gifted us with a fascinating story of this city of cities— its history, personality, culture blends, and challenges and its heroes. This is not a book of statistics; it is filled with life, people, and exciting accounts of how the gospel has moved and is still moving in the Big Apple. I was spiritually and strategically affected by my first read, you will be too."

—PAUL STANLEY
Vice President - Navigators

In Memoriam

Richard D. Pier

(1931–2008)

To my father, who taught me how to love a city

OTHER BOOKS BY MAC PIER

The Power of a City at Prayer
Mac Pier and Katie Sweeting

Signs of Hope in the City
with Robert Carle and Louis DeCaro Jr.

SPIRITUAL
LEADERSHIP
IN THE
GLOBAL CITY

MAC PIER

NEW HOPE
PUBLISHERS

BIRMINGHAM, ALABAMA

New Hope® Publishers
P. O. Box 12065
Birmingham, AL 35202-2065
www.newhopepublishers.com
New Hope Publishers is a division of WMU®.

Library of Congress Cataloging-in-Publication Data

Pier, Mac, 1958-
  Spiritual leadership in the global city / Mac Pier.
      p. cm.
  Includes bibliographical references and index.
  ISBN 978-1-59669-241-1 (sc : alk. paper) 1. New York
(N.Y.)--Religious life and customs. 2. Christian leadership. 3.
Intercessory prayer--Christianity. 4. Interdenominational cooperation.
5. City churches. 6. Prayer--Christianity. I. Title.
  BR560.N4P54 2008
  277.47'1083--dc22
                              2008024676

Cover Design: Design Works, thedesignworksgroup.com
Interior Design: Glynese Northam

ISBN-10: 1-59669-241-3
ISBN-13: 978-1-59669-241-1
N084151• 0908 • 5M1

DEDICATION

Spiritual Leadership in the Global City is dedicated to Ray Bakke, Ken Blanchard, David Bryant, Bob Buford, Wilson Goode, Frances Hesselbein, Allan Houston, Bill Hybels, C. William Pollard, and Rick Warren. Your passion for Christ and His church has molded a generation of leaders.

CONTENTS

FOREWORD

I made my first trip to New York City after the tragedy of 9/11 on September 21. I was able to tour the destruction of the site. This event was one of the most horrific in American history. The decision to attack the twin towers of New York City was a leadership decision, to cut the financial nerve center of our nation to much of the world.

That same evening I spoke to a group of leaders assembled at the Marriott Marquis in Midtown Manhattan. For some it was an eerie experience, their first time venturing into Manhattan after 9/11. Concerts of Prayer Greater New York, under the leadership of Mac Pier, assembled the group. That night I spoke on the ability of the church to make a huge difference even in the face of tragedy.

In the years since that evening in Manhattan, I have been back to New York City almost annually to reconnect with many of the leaders from that event. Our team at Willow Creek has been in and out of New York City dozens of times, slowly building a relationship with some of the most passionate leaders who come from every major denomination and ethnic background. The leaders in this group genuinely love each other and love their precious city.

As I have increasingly traveled around the world to encourage spiritual leaders in some of the most difficult of places, I have grown to appreciate what God is doing in New York City more and more. My view of the church has been transformed over the years. I love the local church and I love when churches and their leaders come together. That is happening in New York City in extraordinary ways.

I have met many of the leaders written about in this book. In fact, ten of the chapters feature churches and leaders that have hosted the Willow Creek Leadership Summit since 2005. I am really proud of these churches and believe that their stories have much to teach us about leadership. I am proud of leaders like A. R. Bernard and David Ireland who have extraordinary influence in the region. I have had them both speak at our national events. I consider them friends.

I am proud of Christ Tabernacle and the Dursos. They have been a great asset to us in thinking about youth ministry. We have invited them to lead services at our Palm Sunday weekend. Bob Johansson has been a faithful leader for over four decades in Queens as well.

I am proud of Keith Boyd, Joe Cortese, Dan Mercaldo, Steve Tomlinson, Glenn Harvison, Jeff Boucher, Fred Provencher, Jeff Ebert, Scott Hoffman, and Scott Rasmussen who have all worked with us to have an impact on the broader body of Christ. The depth of relationship between the churches and their leaders is palpable.

I encourage you to read this book with an open heart to all that God can do through you as you become a stronger leader. It is important for leaders to get better. It is also important to recognize that God has an important leadership anointing on cities that will shape the world.

— Bill Hybels
Senior pastor, Willow Creek Community Church; South Barrington, Illinois

FOREWORD

New York City is arguably the most influential city in the world—perhaps in world history. The nations of the world are here and are affected by what happens here. In ways beyond our understanding, God has always been strategic in His plan to redeem humanity. He raises up leaders, often in influential places and at pivotal times, who cooperate with Him to make the history He has destined. Is it possible He is doing just that in this city now through McKenzie "Mac" Pier, the diverse leadership of Concerts of Prayer Greater New York (COPGNY), and now the New York City Leadership Center?

What is happening here has some similarities with what happened in first-century Jerusalem when God first breathed His life into the New Testament church. An unlikely group of leaders "were all together in one place" (Acts 2:1), waiting and praying for what God had promised. When God showed up and empowered them with what to say and do, "people from every nation under heaven" (Acts 2:5), were strategically positioned and ready to respond. They went from Jerusalem and literally changed the whole world.

For the past 20 years, leaders and churches from Greater New York City have been "all together in one place," united in prayer. In his introduction to Mac's book chronicling the New York City prayer movement, *The Power of a City at Prayer*, David Bryant wrote, "I tell leaders everywhere that the united prayer thrust in New York City is the most significant urban prayer movement in the world."[1] It has been fascinating to be a part of this movement, as both a local church pastor and a board member of COPGNY in recent years. My life has been changed. The congregation I serve has been changed.

So, what's the big deal? Thousands of pastors and leaders representing virtually every cultural group are "together in one place." Hundreds of churches from a plethora of both denominational and nondenominational traditions are "together in one place." Pastors' Prayer Summits, citywide prayerwalks, Concerts of Prayer, National Day of Prayer events, and years of the ongoing Lord's Watch Monthly Prayer Vigil. No purely personal agendas. Politics not allowed. Leaders of all shapes and church sizes equal on our knees. In New York City. How could this not change you?

It is wonderful to see what has grown out of this prayer and unity. We have learned that as we have prayed together the Holy Spirit has come and given us power to go do something. Special things have happened in the past few years with this unlikely group of leaders in Greater New York and especially through Mac Pier.

Mac is simply one of the most effective leaders I have ever studied, observed. or known. Under his leadership, COPGNY has inspired the sponsorship of thousands of orphans in Rwanda in partnership with World Vision. Many of us have traveled to teach the COPGNY prayer model and leadership to our colleagues there. (We've learned a lot from them as well—especially about forgiveness, reconciliation, and restoration.) We have partnered with various groups to envision planting hundreds of new churches in this region. And we've partnered with a variety of parachurch organizations like the Billy Graham Evangelistic Association around citywide evangelism and the Willow Creek Association around leadership development.

Gestating in us, though, has been a sense that God is calling us to do more, something worthy of the unique thing He has been working in us all these years. That "more" is now coming to life through the New York City Leadership Center. We assert that the church in the most influential city in the world needs to invest everything it can in leaders who can influence the world. We want to help develop leading pastors, leaders in local churches and leaders in the marketplace—the arts, entertainment, finance, media, and education. If we can dramatically raise the leadership level here, and if leaders here will skillfully leverage their influence for kingdom purposes worldwide, things could get real interesting in the coming years. We believe that the New York City Leadership Center will impact leaders who will influence the future of our world.

Over two centuries ago, God put a dream for a new nation in the hearts of some very passionate men. One of these men was John Adams, who became the second President of the United States. Adams knew that America existed even prior to the actions that brought about its formation: "But what do we mean by the American Revolution? Do we mean the American War? The Revolution was effected before the war commenced. The Revolution was in the minds and hearts of the people."[2] But neither he nor his fellows entered into the creation of the

United States without deep introspection, self-doubt, and even fear. As he traveled to the First Continental Congress in 1774, "many days he suffered intense torment over his ability to meet the demands of the new role to be played."[3] Adams wrote in the seclusion of his diary, "I wander alone, and ponder. I muse, I mope, I ruminate. . . .We have not men fit for the times. We are deficient in genius, education, in travel, fortune—in everything. I feel unutterable anxiety."[4]

This man, who became one of the great figures in history, knew the future was in him, yet he wondered if he was capable of actualizing it. He also questioned the capabilities of his colleagues—people like George Washington, Thomas Jefferson, and Benjamin Franklin. This seems unbelievable in retrospect. The great John Adams doubting himself? Doubting the abilities of Washington, Jefferson, and Franklin? Yes! This is typical of the kinds of questions honest people ask themselves as they embark on a revolutionary journey. But in spite of their self-questioning, these individuals did their duty, fulfilled their destiny, and created a future that had until that time existed only in God's mind and their hearts.

I do know that those of us (and of course there are many beyond those who hold particular positions in COPGNY, the New York City Leadership Center, or any other organization/institution) who are honored to serve this region with spiritual leadership are incredulous that God is using us. And we wonder if we are capable of actualizing the even bigger dreams that are marked by the release of this book and the launch of the New York City Leadership Center. But we do believe that God has called us to accept the responsibility to help create a future that is better than the present and past. We believe He has put a revolution in our hearts. Though it is unimportant whether history remembers those of us who are together in this place, there is no doubt that history will be better because we are. Now let's get on with it.

You will love reading what Mac has written about what Jesus has been doing through spiritual leaders in this region. This book should model for us that we can each aspire to be spiritual leaders who pray and act to make a powerful difference in our world. But please read this as a story still being written, of history yet to be made, of a God-destined future still being created. Hopefully all of us will participate in the amazing possibilities of these coming years.

—TERRY SMITH

Senior pastor, The Life Christian Church; West Orange, New Jersey

A New York City Love Affair

I am a New Yorker by choice, not by birth. Nearly 25 years ago I arrived in New York City with the expectation that within 2 years my wife, Marya, and I would return to India. After 2 years of life in Queens, New York City, we realized that the whole world was *here*. I simply fell in love with New York City.

I love the city for what it has taught my children. They have all learned cross-cultural skills. Their friends come from very diverse backgrounds. They have gained empathy toward people who are different and less fortunate.

I love the city for its ability to welcome people from all over the world. In how many other places can you have neighbors who speak Spanish, Korean, Afghani, Russian, Greek, and Taiwanese—all who live on the same side of the street? I love the sacrifice of our citizens who have left everything to start a new life and create a new future for their children.

I love the diversity of the region. Within a few hours you can be on eastern Long Island, the Jersey shore, or in beautiful Fairfield County, Connecticut. Each borough of New York has its own personality. Metropolitan New York is in many ways not a city, but a continent comprising many nations. Nearly every nation on earth is represented by the citizens in this region.

I interchange the terms *city* and *metropolitan area* in referring to the city. New York City, in its narrow sense, represents the five boroughs of Manhattan, Bronx, Queens, Staten Island, and Brooklyn. Greater New York represents the 75-mile radius around Times Square that includes Long Island, Westchester County, lower Connecticut, and New Jersey.

I love the church in all of its expression. I love the fact that we need each other and that God is bringing us together to appreciate and enjoy one another. The church is the mystery of God in the world and we get to participate in that mystery.

More than anyone else, Ray Bakke has taught me to love the urban church, and he encouraged me to write this book. Ray is Bakke Graduate University chancellor and International Urban Associates president. Billy Graham asked Ray in 1974 to study the world's cities. Ray traveled to 250 cities of a million or more.

After more than 30 years of travel and training thousands of urban leaders, Ray concludes that New York City is perhaps the best laboratory in the world to understand and study urban ministry. I was privileged to study with Ray from 1998 to 2000 as well as to co-teach doctoral students in New York City from 2000 to 2007.

Ray recruited New Hope Publishers for this book. He has met almost every leader mentioned in this book. The stories in this book are not simply great ministry models; they represent a journey with friends that has developed over 25 years.

The book has a few simple themes. The objective is to study the leadership lessons of urban ministry leaders. In each chapter you will see three predominant themes—these are leaders who take seriously a commitment to intercession, innovation, and collaboration. They understand that the church is bigger than their congregation or organization.

Another common denominator is that many of these models are host sites for the Willow Creek Association Leadership Summit. Taking on that assignment every year involves the sacrifice of time and volunteers to serve the broader body of Christ.

The underlying conviction in the book is that whenever God gets ready to do something He always raises up a leader. We need tens of thousands more leaders who embody the motivation, spirituality, and skills that are described in this book to impact our cities. My prayer is that these stories will envision a new generation of leaders to fulfill the assignment God has on their lives.

My one regret is that there are so many stories that could have been told. There are large segments of the church that are underrepresented in the book. Space does not allow me to tell all the stories that need to be told. My hope is that we will all gain a fresh perspective on how God is uniquely using leaders He has choreographed into this place and time.

ACKNOWLEDGMENTS

In many ways this book has been 50 years in the making, drawing together so many themes and relationships over a lifetime. There are several people that need to be acknowledged.

I am thankful to God for allowing me to see with my own eyes the miracle of His church in all of its expression in my lifetime in this region.

I want to thank Marya, my wife of nearly 30 years, who shares the dream of spending our lives together to make a difference here in New York City.

Thank you to Ray Bakke, who birthed the idea of this book across the kitchen table during a visit to his home in Acme, Washington, in July 2007. Ray has been a teacher, mentor, and friend to me and thousands like me for 30 years. Few people in the world embody his generosity of spirit.

Thank you to David Bryant for planting the seeds of faith in the possibilities of a movement of prayer that could impact this great region in 1988.

To my "book team," who did the research, editing, and collating, you made this book possible. Thanks to Katie Sweeting, who is an extraordinary editor and writer; Peggy Chen, whose design skills are invaluable; and to Anna Pier, whose research has brought to life the realities of our region's citizens.

I would like to thank our friends at New Hope Publishers who have worked incredibly hard to bring this book to fruition. We are indebted to the leadership and skill of Andrea Mullins, Joyce Dinkins, Kathryne Solomon, Jonathan Howe, and their team.

To Steve Bell, Jim Mellado, and Dave Wright from Willow Creek Association, thank you to those who have believed in the possibilities in New York City. I also want to thank Rick Warren and David Chrzan and the growing partnership with Saddleback Church and New York City leaders.

Special thanks to Jim Runyan, from RSI, who has been a very special friend in designing the New York City (NYC) Leadership Center. The center provides an important vehicle to communicate the message of this book.

I want to thank our leadership in the Concerts of Prayer/New York City Leadership Center. Thanks to Beverly Cook, Lauren Moy, Helen Siegel, Dee Ann Boyd, Beatrice Marcelin, Damaris Herron, Carlos Ortiz, Tom Nolan, Gary Frost, Ken Ou, and Eddie Dhanpat for their tireless efforts.

Finally, thank you to the Concerts of Prayer Greater New York Board of Directors and the New York City Leadership Center Presidential Council, whose commitment and advocacy have made it possible to serve the leaders and churches of our region. My profound thanks to

Concerts of Prayer Greater New York Board Members	Presidential Council for the NYC Leadership Center
Ronald Bailey	Lew Bakes
Craig Bates	Jeff Boucher
Carlton Brown	Daniel Buttafuoco
Roderick Caesar	John Clause
Joseph Cortese	Angelo Durso
Art Davenport	Jeff Ebert
Adam Durso	Scott Hoffman
Mike Durso	Tony Lembke
Glenn Harvison	Scott Rasmussen
Bob Johansson	A. J. Rice
Carl Johnson	John Stanley Jr.
Rodger Parker	John Stanley Sr.
Fred Provencher	Mike Toombs
Terry Smith	Dave Wright
Lloyd Syvertsen	

GREATER NEW YORK
AND THE FIVE BOROUGHS

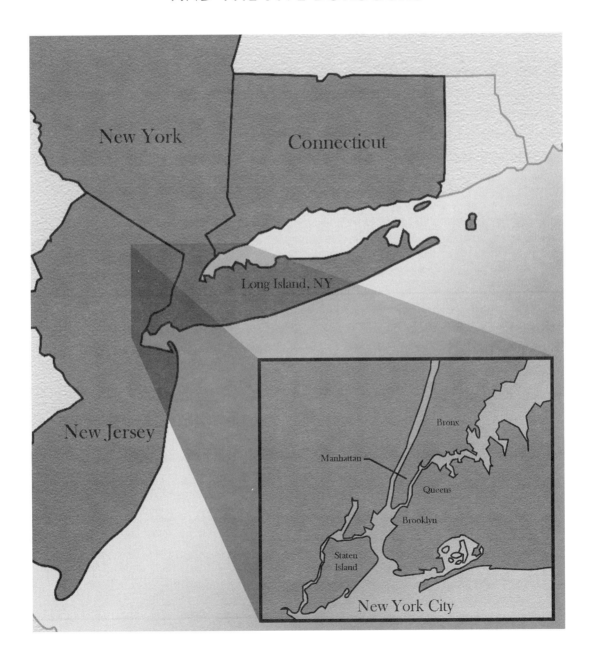

New York

Connecticut

Long Island, NY

New Jersey

Bronx

Manhattan

Queens

Brooklyn

Staten
Island

New York City

PART I:
JESUS AND THE CITY

Introduction

NEW YORK CITY AND THE
DETERMINATION OF GOD

"The astonishing fact of our time is that the majority of the world's six billion people now live and work in sizeable cities. Moreover, we live at the time of the greatest migration in human history. The southern hemisphere is moving north, East is coming West, and everyone is coming to New York! I remember well the day several years ago when, sitting in Manhattan, I read a New York Times *report that 133 nations had been found living together in one Queens zip code."*[1]

Ray Bakke, in *The Power of a City at Prayer*
by Mac Pier and Katie Sweeting

God is fulfilling His promises

Indeed, everyone seems to be in New York City. Of the more than 8 million people who speak more than 170 languages and hail from more than 100 countries, New Yorkers can be divided roughly into three types: native New Yorkers give the region its solidity; commuters give New York its velocity; and immigrants give New York its dreams. *Spiritual Leadership in the Global City* will document the partial realization of the 4,000-year-old dream given to Abraham on a starry night in the Middle East—that all the nations would be blessed. All the nations now reside in the neighborhoods of Greater New York.

God promised to bless the nations through Abraham and, as Abraham's spiritual descendants, God is blessing the nations through modern-day believers. God's promise to Abraham in Genesis 12:1–3 uses what I believe are the two most important words in the Bible uttered by God—"I will":

> *I will make your name great. (v. 1)*
> *I will give you a land. (v. 2)*
> *I will bless all the peoples of the earth through you. (v. 3)*

Modern-day New York City is at a historical crossroads between God's promise to Abraham and the ultimate fulfillment of God's plan, the New Jerusalem described in Revelation 21. The final metaphor used in the Bible to describe God's people is a city; we all have an urban future.

For those of us who are serious about biblical and world history, we need to seriously ponder these extraordinary facts about Greater New York at the dawn of the twenty-first century:

- New York City is the largest Jewish city in the world *outside of Israel.*

- New York City is one of the largest Muslim cities outside the Muslim world.

- New York City contains one of the communities with the highest density of Africans of any community in the world (Bedford Stuyvesant, Brooklyn).

- New York City contains the largest enclave of immigrants in the Western world in Chinatown (both Manhattan and Flushing, Queens).

- New York City is nearly as large as Chicago and Los Angeles combined.

- Metropolitan New York is larger than Dallas, San Francisco, Atlanta, Seattle, Boston, Phoenix, Minneapolis, Miami, and Las Vegas combined.

- New York City is one of the most international cities in human history when considering population and density.

- New York City has one of the most international churches in human history; representatives from every continent on earth worship in its borders.

How did we get here? Like all of human history, New York City is on a journey that dates back to the 1500s and the presence of the Algonquin Indians. Beginning in 1609, with the arrival of Henry Hudson, New York experienced four distinct centuries of both immigrant and spiritual history.

The events of 9/11 drew New York City into even sharper focus. In his book *Perspectives on the World Christian Movement,* Ralph Winter suggests that every 400 years there is a global shaping event that radically changes the trajectory of the church. Beginning with the Crucifixion (A.D. 33), followed by the invasion of the Barbarians and the burning of Rome (A.D. 410); the invasion of the Vikings and capturing Dublin (A.D. 834); the Crusades (A.D. 1095–1291); the missionary work of Hudson Taylor to the Inland of China (1853) and William Carey to the Indian coast (1793), each 400-year epoch represents the geographic progression of the gospel. Ralph Winter surmises in *Perspectives on the World Christian Movement* that with the exception of the Crusades, God took what was meant for evil and turned it into good by growing the church during each 400-year period.[3]

On 9/11, under the azure blue sky, 19 terrorists forever changed the way we think about our city, our nation, and the world. The extremist Muslim leadership that sent them on their mission understood something that few leaders, churches, agencies, and denominations have understood—New York City represents a spiritual battleground on a global and cosmic scale. Could 9/11 be that 400-year turning point?

A Historical and Spiritual Snapshot of Greater New York City, 1600–2000[2]

The Dutch Century   The British Century

1500s	1609	1657	1674	1727	1747	1776	1789
Algonquin tribe lives in Manhattan	Henry Hudson arrives	Flushing Remonstrance: religious freedom	The Dutch sell Manhattan to Britain	Theodorus Frelinghuysen leads New Jersey revival	Jonathan Edwards starts concerts of prayer	Francis Lewis signs Declaration of Independence	George Washington inaugurated in NYC

The Northern European and Southern Century

1790	1845	1857	1858	1863	1872	1888
Peter Williams founds first black church	Catholic Irish immigrate to NYC	Fulton Street Awakening	Cornerstone for St. Patrick's Cathedral is laid	Emancipation Proclamation	McCauley Street Mission	Student Volunteer Movement

The International Century

1891	1900	1915–1920	1939	1959	1965	1988	1991
Ellis Island opens to Southern & Eastern Europeans	Puerto Ricans begin to arrive	World War I	World's Fair	Billy Graham in Madison Square Garden	Immigration Act opens doors to world	Concerts of payer movement begins	Billy Graham in Central Park

The Strategic Nature of New York City

A 1999 PBS documentary on New York City described it as the most influential city in human history. Saskia Sassen of Princeton asks her readers to imagine a gigantic three-legged stool, a colossus of New York, London, and Tokyo, which controls huge and growing proportions of the world's resources. Of the three, Sassen states that New York is the leading global city on the planet.[4]

Like Tokyo and London, New York is a financial capital; like Toronto it is an international capital; like Washington, D.C., it is a power capital; like Paris it is a cultural capital; and like Los Angeles it is a media capital. Yet no other city in human history has been all of these things simultaneously. Five of the six most powerful media outlets in the world are in Midtown Manhattan—NBC, CBS, ABC, the *New York Times*, and the *Wall Street Journal*.

KNOWLEDGE	MORALS	AESTHETICS
A	**A**	**A**
Elite level	*Elite level*	*Elite level*
Academic think tanks	Legal philosophy and psychology	Visual arts
Elite research universities	Law schools, public policy schools	Literature/poetry
Elite opinion journals		High art music
Elite book publishers		Theater/dance
		Galleries/museums

KNOWLEDGE	MORALS	AESTHETICS
B	**B**	**B**
Popular-elite level	*Popular-elite level*	*Popular-elite level*
More selective colleges	Public policy think tanks	Public television
High-end journalism	Special interest lobbies	Public museums
Innovative churches	Innovative ministries	Film (independent)
Elite private schools	Educational reform/activism	Jazz/specialty music
Seminaries		High-end ad agencies

KNOWLEDGE	MORALS	AESTHETICS
C	**C**	**C**
Popular/grass roots level	*Popular/grass roots level*	*Popular/grass roots level*
Journalism (print/electronic)	Local activist/cause organizations	Prime-time/cable TV
The Internet	Local civic/charitable organizations	Mass-market movies
Mass-market books	School boards	Mass-market magazines
Public/private/Christian schools	Youth/recreation/neighborhood assocs	Popular music
Churches/synagogues	Moral/character education curricula	Mass advertising

- Notice that in these areas of cultural production the ideas and trends mainly tend to flow "down" from the more influential "elite" cultural institutions, though culture and ideas do flow "up" from the grassroots too.
- Where are we now? In New York City, Christians have no real foothold in any A-level cultural institutions or venues, and there is only a very, very light scattering of Christian individuals in a few B-level institutions. Most Christian cultural production is at the C popular level anywhere in the country.
- What is the vision? If our vision were realized, we would have Christians rather equally well represented at all three levels. That means there would be Christians writing and producing plays (as well as acting in them), producing literature, representing Christianity in the elite publications and research organizations and schools, and so on.

In the midst of this extraordinary influence, the church needs to regain its influence on the culture. In a presentation made to denominational leadership in February 2004, Tim Keller, senior pastor of Redeemer Presbyterian Church in Manhattan, asserted in his lecture on the church and cultural Influence that of the three levels of potential influence, the church is at the lowest level.[5]

In a 14-year period, the number of unchurched people in the United States has doubled, according to Jim Mellado, president of the Willow Creek Association.[6] The spiritual and cultural influence of the church will largely hinge on our abilities to lead, unite, pray, think, and reach out in contextually sensitive ways. There has never been a more opportune or sober moment to become countercultural in our thinking. Through our discipleship, we must work to reverse the culture's values that led so many in the past half century to leave places of influence in exchange for a big backyard and a luxury car in the garage.

This book asks spiritual leaders how they must respond to the truth about Greater New York and other world-class cities. Leaders do what leadership requires. May we pray more incessantly, may we unite as God's people more intentionally, may we labor more intelligently, and may we lay down our lives more radically.

Leadership Lessons

- Effective leadership requires an understanding of biblical promises, biblical history, and a contemporary understanding of how God is fulfilling those promises. Consider that over half the global population is now in cities compared to less than 10 percent in 1900.

- Like Jesus and Paul, leaders orient their lives and major life decisions around the most strategic places where they can make a difference. Consider your job location in light of the most influential cities in the world.

- Leaders are discontent with the spiritual and social conditions of the world and order their priorities accordingly. Nearly every city is wrestling with unemployment, homelessness, youth violence, and drug addiction. How are you engaging these issues?

Leadership Reflection Questions

1. Read Genesis 12:1–3. Identify three ways you have seen God blessing the nations in your lifetime.

2. In what ways is the city you are now living in a strategic location?

3. What is one priority you could change to be more strategically engaged in a major metropolitan community? (Have your spiritual community pray regularly for citywide concerns; find an issue that your church or network can rally around such as homelessness; build a relationship with your local political officials).

Best Practices

Consider joining the Lord's Watch Monthly Prayer Vigil. Download the prayer guide from the COPGNY.org Web site. This provides New York City, national, and international prayer requests monthly with 100 churches participating since 1995.

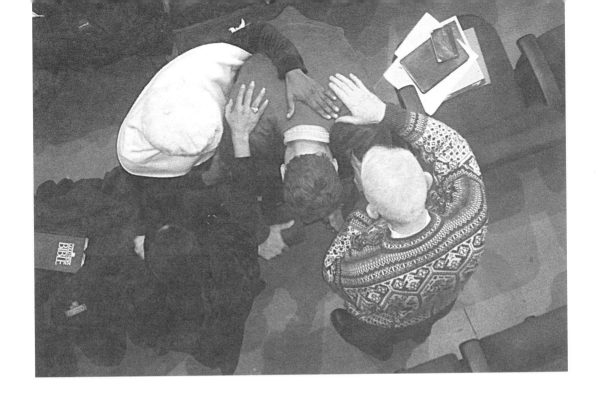

Chapter 1

THE NEW URBAN PENTECOST:
20 YEARS OF PRAYING

"They were all together in one place."

ACTS 2:1

A Conversion to United Prayer

My wife, Marya, and I were lying in bed one November evening in 1988. We heard what sounded like a firecracker in our Flushing, Queens, neighborhood. When our housemate, Maureen, came home, she told us a murder had just occurred in the neighborhood. A Chinese couple was showing their son his wedding gift, a condominium on a nearby street, when the mother was shot and killed after a bungled, drug-related robbery attempt.

Ten days after the murder, Marya drove home from her night shift at the hospital, and as she pulled into the driveway, her eyes met the eyes of a man who fit the description of the murderer. During that same time, we received the news that Marya was pregnant with our third child; we already had a four-year-old daughter and a two-year-old son. This question gnawed at us: Do we want to raise our children in this environment?

We had moved to New York City from South Dakota in 1984 to work with InterVarsity Christian Fellowship. Our original plan was to be in New York for 2 years and then return to India. We had spent the summer of 1983 in Bihar, India, with Operation Mobilization, and lived for ten weeks in a state the size of Nebraska but with a population of 100 million people. In much of Bihar the ratio of Muslims and Hindus to Christians is 100,000 to 1.

Every Friday in India, we prayed three to nine hours. This life-changing experience in India converted me to the priority of extended united prayer. In 1984, we sold our possessions and moved to New York City; Marya was pregnant and we had secured only temporary housing. Our initial plan was to stay in New York City until 1986, but it soon became obvious to us living in Flushing, Queens, that God had brought the whole world to New York City and, in particular, our neighborhood. It was no longer necessary to travel to distant parts of the world to minister among other nationalities. So we stayed in New York City.

We have lived for 20 years in a neighborhood with 100 language groups. For a season, people spoke seven languages on our side of the street alone—Russian, Greek, Spanish, Korean, Chinese, Afghani, and English. Our neighborhood is also *one of*, if not *the most*, religiously plural neighborhoods in the world. When we take a right out of our front door and travel west on Beech Avenue, within four blocks we pass a house mosque (people primarily from India, Afghanistan, and Pakistan), a Russian Orthodox Church, a traditional Buddhist temple, and a Frank Lloyd Wright–designed Confucian temple. Further down on Parsons Boulevard is Church of St. Mary's Nativity (Roman Catholic). When we walk from Parsons Boulevard to Bowne Street on Ash Street, we pass the Korean American Presbyterian Church, one of the largest Korean churches in North America and 1 of 300 Korean churches in northern Queens.

Traveling south on Bowne Street, we pass a Jewish center, then the Boon Chinese Church, a daughter church of Oversea Chinese Mission, the largest Chinese church on the East Coast. On the next block is the first Hindu temple in North America, serving the 20,000

Hindus in the area. A number of apartments have been built around the temple to form a tightly knit Hindu community in the neighborhood.

Two blocks over, near the intersection of Kissena Boulevard and Geranium Avenue, a mosque that cost $3.2 million to build and was funded by 200 families stands tall. The story of the mosque's construction was written up in the *New York Times* architectural review. A few blocks away, the Freedman's Synagogue stands on the corner of Sanford Avenue and Kissena. Interestingly, above the doorframe of the synagogue is the verse from Isaiah 56:7, *"My house shall be a house of prayer for all nations."* As one can see, within a half-mile radius of our home, every major world religion is represented.

Our home church in New York City, First Baptist Church of Flushing, celebrated its 150th anniversary in 2007. It is a multicongregational model with five services—in English, Mandarin, Cantonese, and Spanish on Sunday. It has an ESL (English-as-a-second-language) and community program reaching out to the immigrants who call the Flushing neighborhood home.

A History and Theology of Urban Prayer

The New Testament is essentially the story of two cities. It is the story of Jesus going to die in Jerusalem, the religious capital of the world. It is also the story of Paul going to die in Rome, the political capital of the world. The city-centric nature of these men's missions is not accidental.

Jerusalem has dominated the urban landscape of the Bible and the modern day since David captured the city in 2 Samuel, chapter 5. For 3,000 years, Jerusalem has been and remains the religious capital of the world. Psalm 48:2 describes Jerusalem as "the joy of the whole earth," "the city of the Great King." Isaiah 62:6–7 commands God's people to give God no rest until He makes Jerusalem a praise in the whole earth.

In the opening chapter of Acts, Jesus issues only one command in verses 1–14. The command is simply to wait. As the disciples were waiting, they were praying, repenting, and reconciling with one another. Simultaneously, God was bringing the 15 nations into Jerusalem to celebrate Pentecost. That is the biblical and historical pattern—God's people pray in unity and God choreographs the nations into the neighborhoods.

God spoke to me powerfully through Joy Dawson. She was a national leader with Youth with a Mission. She taught an important truth at a national prayer conference in Birmingham,

Alabama. If there were ever a group of people who hated each other, it was this group: Peter had denied the Lord, Thomas had doubted the Lord, and the disciples had abandoned Jesus and the women. God had to do the supernatural work of reconciling relationships across the chasm of broken trust. After He did this, the Spirit fell and the church went public.

It was in the midst of its community and life of prayer together that the early church landed on the most important truth—having God and each other, they needed nothing else. The early church was free to give away their possessions and their very lives, confident of the city that Abraham saw described in Hebrews 11. This city, the new Jerusalem, is described for us in the Book of Revelation as the final metaphor for the church.

As the Book of Acts provides the *model* of urban prayer, Isaiah provides the *content* of our prayer. In his final section (chaps. 55–66), Isaiah paints a picture of Jesus as the anointed Conqueror. He provides the following snapshots that profoundly resonate with the realities of our urban populations: build houses of prayer, rebuild broken city walls, bring good news to the poor, and give God no rest—pray continually.

In Isaiah 56, Scripture commands us to make God's house a *"house of prayer for all nations."* It speaks to the power and urgent necessity of **reconciliation**. Most of the churches in our urban centers are tribal—either by ethnicity, economic class, or denomination. Jesus quoted this passage in John 2 when He cleansed the Temple of the money lenders. The greatest barrier to spiritual impact is the enormous trust deficit between diverse Christian groups. We can only love those we know. We can only know those we trust. Here in our region, we have learned to spell love—*time*. There is nothing more powerful to build trust than simply to travel and spend time with people on their turf.

Isaiah 58 commands us to *rebuild the broken walls of our cities*, to declare a true fast of justice. Our cities are broken in so many dimensions that we are in desperate need of **reformation of society**. We live in this city with the greatest disparity between rich and poor, and as the rich get richer, the poor become even more marginalized. Over 700,000 public school students perform below grade level in math and reading—we need to pray and act. Seventy percent of children of prisoners will end up in prison unless there is some type of intervention—we need to pray and act.

Isaiah 61 commands us to *bring good news to the poor*. This was Jesus's inaugural address. It speaks of the need to proclaim the gospel so that it is accessible to the poorest of the poor as well as to the rich. Living in the most religiously plural city in the world, we need to pray desperately for people to be **reached with the gospel.**

We are not only religiously plural, but we also live in one of the most densely populated places on earth. Over 21 million people, representing 1 out of every 300 people on the planet, live within 50 miles of Times Square. During the workweek there are 250,000 people per square mile working in Midtown Manhattan.

Isaiah 62 commands us to *give God no rest*. Many churches across our region have embraced this vision of **revival**, of an awakening to Christ in all His glory through relentless, aggressive, unrelenting prayer. Korean churches are praying at 6:00 A.M. daily. Midweek prayer services number in the hundreds of thousands across the nation. Observing the church at prayer in New York City is like having a front-row seat to Revelation 5, where people will gather from every nation and tongue. The modern-day church of New York City is the closest approximation to this Revelation 5 reality in human history.

The Church of New York City at Prayer

Three distinct centuries of prayer have had an impact on New York City. In the eighteenth century, Theodorus Frelinghuysen led the Reformed church into seasons of revival through his preaching in 1727 in New Jersey. Across the Atlantic, Count Nicholas Ludwig von Zinzendorf, of the Moravians in Germany, launched Hernnhut in 1727 (the Lord's Watch), a 100-year prayer meeting that thrust 300 missionaries out around the world—many to America. You cannot understand American Protestantism apart from Count Zinzendorf's leadership. In his book *Dynamics of Spiritual Life,* Richard Lovelace said that the Moravian movement was the closest approximation of New Testament Christianity in 2,000 years.[1]

In 1747, Jonathan Edwards wrote *An Humble Attempt,* his call to visible unity and explicit agreement. This was the birthing of concerts of prayer. Concerts of prayer became the methodology of gathering quarterly to pray with other congregations for revival. This movement spread throughout New England and had an impact on the New York City region.

A century later, layman Jeremiah Lanphier launched the Fulton Street Prayer Revival on September 23, 1857. During a climate of slavery and economic devastation, 6 people gathered for prayer near Wall Street. Within weeks, the simple prayer meeting grew to 50,000 daily participants and sparked a national revival that swept 1 million converts into the churches, nearly 4 percent of the national population, in 18 months.

The revival planted the seed of the evangelical social awakening that lasted from 1865 to 1920. This awakening saw the beginning of the homeless ministry movement including the Salvation Army, Bowery Mission, and Christian and Missionary Alliance.[2]

On January 1, 1863, President Abraham Lincoln signed the Emancipation Proclamation. Baptist and Methodist missionaries teaching literacy to freed slaves saw the largest response to the gospel of any ethnic group in church history among African Americans. The first African American church in New York was started in 1790 by Peter Williams as described in *Signs of Hope in the City* (Judson Press, 1997).

In 1888, the Student Volunteer Movement came alive in New York City and, subsequently, 25,000 young people became missionaries in 40 years. The early nineteenth-century revival movement in Korea and resulting explosion of church growth can be traced to Horace Underwood and the 1857–58 revival (as described by Rev. Jimmy Lim, executive director of the New York City Council of Churches in the 2007 video *It Started with One*).

The 1906, the Asuza Street revival in California had a profound impact on New York City. The revival that spread to the Caribbean, Latin America, and Africa boomeranged back to New York in the form of incoming immigrants of Pentecostal persuasion. The fastest-growing churches in the twentieth century in New York City were Pentecostal.

The modern concerts of prayer movement began with a meeting in June 1987 between two Here's Life Inner City staff and an InterVarsity Christian Fellowship staff member. The plan was to invite 16 churches to participate in a concert of prayer on February 5, 1988, at First Baptist Church of Flushing, led by David Bryant. Bryant helped to reignite the global prayer movement by traveling to 350 cities worldwide and gathering churches in united prayer.

When the evening arrived, there were not 16 churches in attendance—more than 70 churches had gathered! By the fall of 1989, seven regions of Greater New York were participating in annual rhythms of united, congregational prayer, and more than 150,000 people have participated to date.

A Movement Matures

As the prayer movement grew, it began to take on diverse expressions. Congregations began praying together in 1988; pastors began praying together in 1989. Our first pastors' concert of prayer took place at Brooklyn Tabernacle—400 leaders participated. This evolved into the Pastors' Prayer Summit which began in 1991 with less than 100 pastors, and has met annually in January ever since, attracting more than 400 pastors and leaders recently. The themes of the summit include worship, prayer, and community. The summit has been described by many pastors as the most powerful spiritual experience of their year.

In 1995, the murder rate in New York City peaked at more than 1,500 murders, and churches began a daily prayer vigil patterned after the Lord's Watch from Count Zinzendorf. What started with 30 churches in 1995 grew to more than 100 churches and has continued unabated until today. Churches pray around the theology of Isaiah following specific prayer requests for revival in the church, reconciliation between churches and peoples of varying cultures and ethnic backgrounds, reformation of society, and reaching out with the gospel. In the next five years, the murder rate would drop by 40 percent.[3]

Timeline of the Prayer Movement in Greater New York

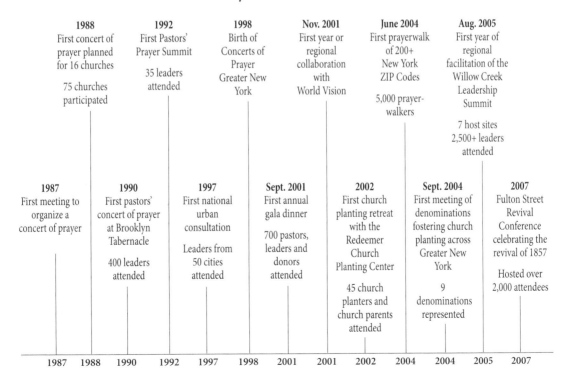

1988	1992	1998	Nov. 2001	June 2004	Aug. 2005
First concert of prayer planned for 16 churches	First Pastors' Prayer Summit	Birth of Concerts of Prayer Greater New York	First year or regional collaboration with World Vision	First prayerwalk of 200+ New York ZIP Codes	First year of regional facilitation of the Willow Creek Leadership Summit
75 churches participated	35 leaders attended			5,000 prayer-walkers	7 host sites 2,500+ leaders attended

1987	1990	1997	Sept. 2001	2002	Sept. 2004	2007
First meeting to organize a concert of prayer	First pastors' concert of prayer at Brooklyn Tabernacle	First national urban consultation	First annual gala dinner	First church planting retreat with the Redeemer Church Planting Center	First meeting of denominations fostering church planting across Greater New York	Fulton Street Revival Conference celebrating the revival of 1857
	400 leaders attended	Leaders from 50 cities attended	700 pastors, leaders and donors attended	45 church planters and church parents attended	9 denominations represented	Hosted over 2,000 attendees

| 1987 | 1988 | 1990 | 1992 | 1997 | 1998 | 2001 | 2001 | 2002 | 2004 | 2004 | 2005 | 2007 |

In 2004, we launched a new prayer initiative called Pray New York!, enlisting church members to prayerwalk the ZIP Codes around their churches. In four years, more than 20,000 people have participated, simultaneously praying in the more than 200 ZIP Codes of New York City on the first Saturday of June. This was coordinated borough by borough by local pastors and ministry leaders.

United Prayer Births Collaborative Mission

After 9/11, three collaborations emerged which have become the largest of their type in the nation. In the aftermath of 9/11, World Vision approached Concerts of Prayer Greater New York to create the American Family Assistance Fund to assist victims and their families. Largely through churches, participants raised and distributed to victims more than $6 million. Pregnant wives of the men who had been killed and suddenly unemployed workers from Windows on the World were among the hundreds of grateful recipients.

In 2002, I responded to a request to travel to East Africa to see the AIDS pandemic firsthand. Traveling to Uganda and Tanzania, I saw a few dozen of the millions of orphans in those countries. We invited local churches to help reverse the pandemic through child sponsorship and community development in East Africa. To date, local donors have sponsored more than 8,000 children and a new strategy will ensure the sponsorship of thousands more.

In 2003, COPGNY hosted the National Leadership Forum on the Gospel in the City. Tim Keller of Redeemer Presbyterian Church preached expositionally from the Book of Acts. As a result, a church-planting collaboration began with 17 denominations joining in the work. Together we identify, train, and fund church planters. Our decadal goal is 700 new church plants in Greater New York, and we are on our way with 50 to 100 church planters in training each year.

In 2004, I took a team of pastors to attend the Willow Creek Leadership Summit. We were evaluating whether or not it would be an appropriate training resource for urban leaders in New York City. We decided to partner with the Willow Creek Association and began with six training sites in 2005, expanding to ten in 2006 and 2007. Of the 8,500 participating leaders in our region in the past 3 years, more than 60 percent have been ethnic minority. This has been an incredible resource locally and globally, with the number of participating leaders globally reaching 100,000 in 2007.

In 2007, the New York City Leadership Center was incorporated to further address the leadership challenges of Greater New York. This embryonic effort will draw from the best regional, national, and global talent to train leaders in the world's leading global city. *The purpose of the center is to synergize best of class training and service opportunities to radically impact Greater New York socially and spiritually.*

The evangelical social awakening after the Fulton Street Revival parallels the movement of collaborating agencies after 20 years of praying together. God has raised up a community of intercessory organizations including Houses of Prayer, Eagles' Wings, and New York City Intercessors. The trust level is high among these diverse communities who are working toward a common goal of the renewal of our city, region, and beyond.

Leadership Reflection Questions

1. Can you identify three to five major spiritual landmarks in your city or community?

2. How can you support or stimulate united prayer in your church, community, or city?

3. Consider gathering churches on the National Day of Prayer or Martin Luther King Jr. holiday.

4. Is there a regular or annual gathering or pastors' prayer gathering in your region? Consider providing scholarship support for an under-resourced pastor to attend.

A prayer for our cities: *Jesus, we pray that You would give us eyes to see our cities in all of their potential and all of their need. Help us to love our neighbors and to see You disguised in them.*

Chapter 2

THE SOUL OF GREATER NEW YORK

"You purchased men for God from every tribe and language and people, and nation."
REVELATION 5:9

It was an unremarkable Sunday evening in the late 1980s in Flushing, Queens. I remember walking down Sanford Avenue toward our church, First Baptist. As you walk down Sanford Avenue heading west, you realize 149th Street is the dividing line between 100-year-old homes and the six-story apartment buildings that saturate the community.

Walking along Sanford, you pass a building that has become occupied primarily by Russian immigrants. Near our home, you would meet a number of Korean families. As you get closer to Main Street, Flushing, the community becomes inhabited more so by Chinese people. You might see Mexican day laborers standing on the street corner, depending on what time of day you pass by.

Back in the 1980s, First Baptist had Sunday evening church services. I remember my first visit to the church in 1984, having heard about it before leaving home in South Dakota. The first Sunday I visited, in July, the choir sang "On Jordan's Stormy Banks." I still remember. It was a powerful song sung by Caribbean, Chinese, Hispanic, and Anglo choir members. The choir director was Filipino. The song meant a lot to those of us who had left family and familiarity to come to New York City.

There was a baptismal service that particular Sunday night. The crowd was pretty small to average in size; maybe 50 to 75 were in attendance. What was remarkable was the story of those who were being baptized.

Within a handful of people being baptized were those who had begun to follow Jesus from Hindu, Jewish, and nominal church backgrounds. I was asking myself, *Where else in the world does this happen, that people from three major religious traditions are being baptized in the same service? Where else in the world or even within New York can you worship with people from 60 different language backgrounds?*

What was happening in Flushing is in miniature what has been happening in metropolitan New York—the nations have moved into the neighborhood.

Metropolitan New York Today

Approximately 21.5 million people live within 50 miles of Times Square, representing 1 out of every 300 people on the planet. The 1980s and 1990s were a time of intense immigration. According to Amanda M. Burden, in *The Newest New Yorkers 2000,* within New York City, the immigrant population increased by nearly 800,000 people between 1990 and 2000. Of those new immigrants, 86 percent landed in Queens, Brooklyn, and the Bronx. In fact, by 2000 nearly 1 percent of *all Americans* were immigrants living in New York City (2.9 million people), and 10 percent of all internationals in America were living in New York City, reports Burden.[1]

Region	% Immigrant
Manhattan, NY	29.4
Staten Island, NY	16.4
Brooklyn, NY	37.8
Queens, NY	46.1
Bronx, NY	29.0
Westchester, NY	9.3**
Rockland, NJ	9.3**
Bergen, NJ	9.3**
Suffolk, NJ	9.3**
Nassau, NY	9.3**
Fairfield, CT	9.3**
**Rounded estimate from *The Newest New Yorkers*	

A snapshot of which countries the greatest number of immigrants have come from reveals people from the Dominican Republic, China, and Jamaica have maintained their percentage rank of the first three positions. The most rapidly increasing immigrant group is Mexicans; they nearly quadrupled their presence in New York in ten years.[2]

The Hispanic Presence in New York City

While Puerto Ricans are expected to maintain a population of roughly 750,000 over the next 40 years, the Dominican community is expected to see significant growth, to reach a population of close to 1.75 million. The Mexican community is expected to explode over the same time frame, from the current 125,000 to nearly 4 million, as reported by Laird W. Bergad, Center for Latin American, Caribbean, and Latino Studies.[3]

It is easy to see the Hispanic presence by borough across New York City; Hispanics represent the largest minority group, at 28 percent of the total population of New York City.[4]

Foreign-born Population by Country of Birth
New York City, 1990 and 2000

	2000		1990		Growth, 1990–2000	
	Rank	Number	Rank	Number	Number	Percent
TOTAL, Foreign-Born	–	2,871,032	–	2,082,931	788,101	37.8
Dominican Republic	1	369,186	1	225,017	144,169	64.1
China	2	261,551	2	160,399	101,152	63.1
Jamaica	3	178,922	3	116,128	62,794	54.1
Guyana	4	130,647	6	76,150	54,497	71.6
Mexico	5	122,550	17	32,689	89,861	274.9
Ecuador	6	114,944	10	60,451	54,493	90.1
Haiti	7	95,580	7	71,892	23,688	32.9
Trinidad & Tobago	8	88,794	12	56,478	32,316	57.2
Colombia	9	84,404	8	65,731	18,673	28.4
Russia	10	81,408	*	*	*	*
Italy	11	72,481	4	98,868	(26,387)	-26.7
Korean	12	70,990	11	56,949	14,041	24.7
Ukraine	13	69,727	*	*	*	*
India	14	68,263	14	40,419	27,844	68.9
Poland	15	65,999	9	61,265	4,734	7.7
Philippines	16	49,644	16	36,463	13,181	36.1
Bangladesh	17	42,865	42	8,695	34,170	393.0
Pakistan	18	39,165	29	14,911	24,254	162.7
Honduras	19	32,358	27	17,890	14,468	80.9
Greece	20	29,805	18	31,894	(2,089)	-6.5

The USSR was ranked 5th in 1990 with 80,815 residents. If it were a single entity in 2000, it would have ranked 4th with approximately 164,000 persons.

Hypothetical Population Projections Among Puerto Ricans, Dominicans, and Mexicans in New York City

Using Annual Population Growth Rates between 2000 and 2006

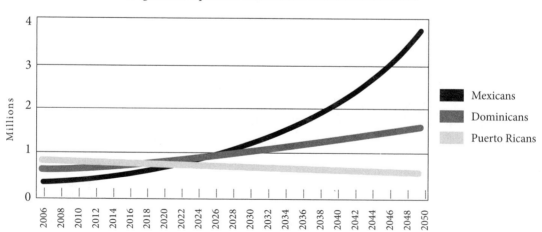

The country of origin changes dramatically from borough to borough:

- Bronx Hispanics are 78 percent Puerto Ricans and Dominicans.
- Manhattan Hispanics are 74 percent Puerto Ricans and Dominicans.
- Brooklyn Hispanics are 75 percent Puerto Ricans, Dominicans, and Mexicans.
- Queens Hispanics are 76 percent Ecuadorians, Puerto Ricans, Dominicans, Colombians, and Mexicans.
- Staten Island Hispanics are 64 percent Puerto Ricans and Mexicans.[5]

Distribution of Latino Population by Borough, 2000-2006

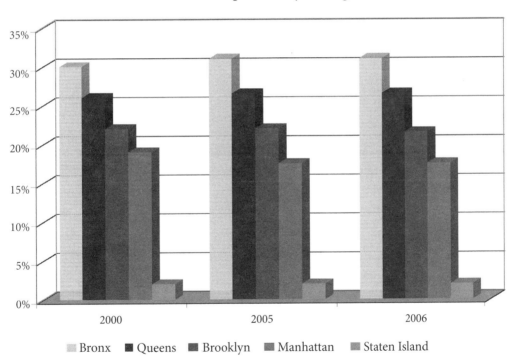

Immigration trends suggest that Dominicans will surpass Puerto Ricans and become the largest sector of the city's Latino population in 2015. Mexicans will surpass Puerto Ricans to become the second largest Latino national group by 2023. Mexicans are expected to surpass Dominicans to become the largest minority group in the city by 2029—in two decades.[6]

Asians in New York City

According to 2006 census figures, approximately 1 million Asians now live in New York City. Chinese immigrants were the second largest group in the 2000 census with an addition of 100,000 immigrants since 1990.[7] Chinese residents are the largest Asian immigrant group in each borough with the exception of the Asian Indians in the Bronx. Chinese New Yorkers represent nearly 50 percent of the Asians in New York, while Asian Indians number about 20 percent. Koreans comprise a little more than 10 percent of the total Asian population, but almost 20 percent of the Asians in Queens. Queens is home to 50 percent of the Asians in New York City, according to the US Census.[8]

**Major Asian Subgroups
New York City and Boroughs, 2000**

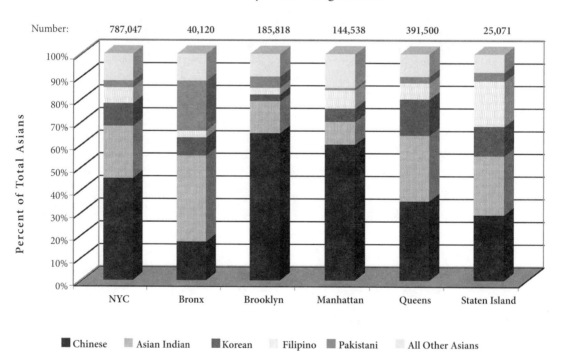

Tony Carnes, of the Values Research Institute, and Pei-te Lien of University of California, Santa Barbara, have indicated that almost 50 percent of all Asian immigrants moving into the United States are Christian. Carnes also believes that 80 percent of the Buddhists immigrating into New York are spiritually open.[9] In northern Queens, 300 Korean churches populate the landscape, with several congregations surpassing 1,000 regular attendees. More than 400 Korean pastors have joined a metropolitan Korean pastors' association. Asian Christians are changing the face of the church in New York City.

Africans in New York City

In each of the past two decades, the African immigration population has doubled, reaching 95,000 Africans by 2000. The actual number of Africans is probably higher, because the count does not include more recent arrivals and the numerous illegal immigrants. The population is expected to grow even more this decade, according to Peter Lobo, the deputy director of the Population Division of the Department of City Planning. He describes the new arrivals as "overwhelmingly highly educated and professional."[10]

In 10 years, more than 100 African congregations have been established in New York City. Combined with the huge influx of Asian and Latin Christians, these figures reveal the dramatic growth of Christianity in the Southern Hemisphere across Asia, Africa, and Latin America. It would be fair to say that much of the growth is rooted in the Pentecostalism that began on Asuza Street in California a century ago, spread globally, and has boomeranged back to New York City through the immigrant communities. Leaders like Tim Keller, senior pastor of Redeemer Presbyterian Church, Manhattan, have concluded that we have an opportunity to see our city filled with faith that we have not seen in 100 years.

The African/African and American/Caribbean communities comprise nearly 2 million people in New York City and nearly 25 percent of the total population. New York City has the largest population of people of African descent in the US, despite a trend of New York–born African Americans leaving the city in significant numbers.

Jews and Muslims in New York

The United Jewish Appeal-Federation of New York 2002 report states that 972,000 Jews lived in New York City in 2002. This represents a slight increase from the 1980s and 1990s, but is half the total of the 1950s, when 2 million Jews lived throughout the five boroughs of New York City.

Since 1980, over 300,000 Jewish immigrants from the former Soviet Union have settled in New York City. Their arrival was accompanied by a rise in the level of poverty within the city's Jewish population. Today, one out of five Jewish families in the neighboring counties of Westchester, Nassau, and Suffolk are on the verge of poverty.[11] New York City remains the largest Jewish city in the world—Brooklyn, Manhattan, and Queens County hold the three largest Jewish populations by county in America.

According to Peter Awn, dean of Columbia University's School of General Studies, and co-principal investigator of a study on Muslims in New York City, the Muslim population in the city has grown to an estimated 600,000 people.[12] Of all American counties with the highest density of Muslims, 9 of the top 25 include 4 NYC boroughs and 5 New Jersey counties.[13]

Muslims have been understandably feeling uneasy since 9/11. Our neighbor Mohammed, from Afghanistan, put a US flag in his window immediately after the attacks. There was 24-hour police surveillance at the house mosque a block from my home for several weeks after 9/11 as tensions remained high in the city and Muslims felt the brunt of the rage.

Two years after 9/11, I attended an open house at the local mosque on Geranium Avenue in Flushing. The men I met in the foyer were what I expected—men from Pakistan and India. What surprised me were the two young men assigned to talk with me—both native New Yorkers—one was Italian and the other Puerto Rican. Both of these young men were lapsed Catholics. The former director of ministerial services at Riker's Island Correctional Facility was Imam Luqman Abdush-Shahid, a Baptist who converted to Islam. The current director is also an imam. Muslims are no longer easily identifiable, but can be from any cultural or ethnic background.

The Spiritual Trends of Greater New York

With immigrant populations pouring into Queens, Brooklyn, and the Bronx, we have seen correlative growth in the establishment of new churches. Many of these new churches are established in languages other than English to meet the needs of New York's newest immigrants.

While the newly planted immigrant churches tend to thrive, throughout the rest of the region in traditionally English-speaking populations, especially among Anglos, there is a sense of rapid decline. I know of *only one* self-ascribed evangelical church in New York City that has more than 1,000 people and is primarily Anglo. Interestingly, the least likely person to attend church on a Sunday morning in New York City is an Anglo male between 40 and 50. The spiritual demographics outside of Queens, Brooklyn, and the Bronx mirror Western Europe, while in Midtown Manhattan, one estimate is that the evangelical population is .5 percent. It is a city of dual spirituality.

In a 1998 survey done among the religious communities in Flushing (Jewish, Muslim, Hindu, Buddhist, and Christian), the one common theme was this: everyone was losing their youth. Even in the immigrant churches, it is estimated (especially among Asian churches) that a majority of second-generation immigrants attending church leave after high school. Forty percent of New York City college students who come from Buddhist homes leave the Buddhist faith by their freshman year.[14]

The spiritual and ethnic demographics suggest that Greater New York is in a time of intense religious struggle. Secularism is hammering away at religious values held by families for centuries. Immigrants' sense of being uprooted leads to weakening long-established ties to family religious traditions among the next generation. Naked consumerism attempts to persuade our children that happiness lies in the material world, external to traditional spiritual commitments. Both new immigrants and native New Yorkers are bombarded with the same negative messages from the media, where the house you live in, the car you drive, the cell phone you talk on, and the clothes you wear are more important, and certainly more easily measurable, than the state of your soul.

The antidote to and strategy for these challenges/opportunities is effective spiritual leadership. If we can incarnate the truth of Jesus through our united prayer, our innovative efforts to meet real needs, and our collaboration to work together, the world will be changed. An unprecedented, unified effort is needed to effect significant, long-lasting transformation.

Leadership Reflection Questions

1. How have you seen the demography in your city or community change in the past 10 to 20 years? Who are your "new neighbors" from across the ocean?

2. With changing neighborhoods, what new spiritual opportunities have opened to your community?

3. What are the trends among young people in your church and community? What is being done to attract young people?

Chapter 3

THE NEW YORK CITY LEADERSHIP CENTER

"All the believers were together and had everything in common."

ACTS 2:44

Bill Hybels was sitting in a college classroom as a student at Trinity International University in Deerfield, Illinois, in the 1970s. He had his future mapped out to take over his family business. The lecture that day challenged him to consider what an Acts 2 church could look like—a church where people would literally turn the world upside down with their devotion to God, commitment to each other, and passion for people far from God.

He left the classroom with his world turned upside down, knowing he would have to reconsider his future options. He and a few friends decided to start the Willow Creek Community Church. Beginning in a movie theater, the young church sustained itself through efforts such as selling tomatoes door to door.

The Willow Creek Community Church has been described as the most influential local church in the United States. Now more than 30 years later, with a vision to reach the unchurched, it has grown to more than 20,000 attendees and birthed the Willow Creek Association (WCA). The WCA has expanded its influence around the world to have an impact on more than 100,000 participants in the 2007 Global Leadership Summit.

The WCA began with the recognition that leadership development is the critical success factor in helping leaders and churches change their communities. The WCA mantra is "*Change a leader and you change a church, change churches change a community, change communities change a city, change cities change the nation*." Like no other modern-day city on the planet, if you change New York City, you change the world.

We at Concerts of Prayer Greater New York (COPGNY) began partnering with the WCA in 2004 to bring the Leadership Summit to New York City. A common zeal to envision and train leaders across cultural and denominational lines characterizes our partnership. Interaction with the WCA forged and informed the organizational "DNA" of the New York City Leadership Center. In January 2006, the initial concept paper was written and outlined the rationale for the center, just 18 months after COPGNY had begun the journey with the WCA.

October 20, 2006, Bill Hybels addressed the audience at the Concerts of Prayer Greater New York Gala Dinner at the Hilton Hotel, in Midtown Manhattan. He described formative moments in his life: witnessing the burial carriage of Senator Robert F. Kennedy roll by in 1968; seeing the launch of the space shuttle *Challenger* that exploded in Florida in 1986; and watching the wreckage of a small plane at the White House during the Clinton administration. When one sees what is happening in New York City today, one sees history moving from the tragedies Hybels described to the hope he sees now.

As Hybels looked across the ballroom at this gathering of ministry leaders, denominational executives, marketplace leaders, and pastors from every imaginable ethnic group, he said, "I have never seen anything like this in my lifetime. All of us are witnessing history. You may be too close to it to appreciate it, but you are witnessing history. I have traveled around the globe and what is happening in New York City with the body of Christ is unprecedented in my lifetime."[1]

An opportunity comes along once in a lifetime, or perhaps once in a century, to participate in something historic. In my own 25-year journey in New York City, I have had a sense that the New York City Leadership Center is poised to make an important contribution to the incredible move of God across the city in unimaginable ways. You will read in the following chapters expressions of this movement from distinct lenses: united prayer and networking; ministry to children and youth;

church planting and mission; and impacting culture and community. This book is all about leaders doing what leadership requires—and the resulting impact on lives and communities.

The New York City Leadership Center in Historical Context

New York City has played a central role not only in recent years, but also it has *historically* shaped the nation and the world in the arenas of politics, social movement, and faith. Over each of its four centuries dating back to Henry Hudson's discovery in 1609, New York City has played a distinctive role.

In the seventeenth century, the Dutch Century, the Flushing Remonstrance was written by local citizens to protest the imprisonment of John Bowne, a Quaker. A group of citizens led by Edward Hart protested the decree of Governor Peter Stuyvesant, denying his order that they "should not receive or entertain any of those people called Quakers because they are supposed to be, by some, seducers of the people."[2] The Flushing Remonstrance outlined the rationale for religious freedom and became a building block for free religious expression in the United States.

In the eighteenth century, the British Century, the nation's first capital was in New York City as George Washington was inaugurated on a balcony. Many of the Founding Fathers made New York their home, including Alexander Hamilton, who is buried in the cemetery outside Trinity Church on Wall Street.

In the nineteenth century, the century of Western European immigration and freed slave migration, the Emancipation Proclamation played a defining role in the establishment of the African American church. From the confines of slavery, African American churches in urban America, and especially New York, grew to become the most important urban institutions in America. African American churches pioneered many of the incarnational ministries so important to its citizens, meeting both spiritual and social needs—from prayer meetings to prison ministry, fellowship to feeding the hungry.

The twentieth century became the International Century, beginning officially with the opening of Ellis Island in 1892. It also represented the dramatic shift of New York from being a historically Protestant city to becoming a Catholic and Jewish city. St. Patrick's Cathedral became the symbol of Irish Catholic strength as the second most well-known church in the world, after the Vatican. In the 1990 census, 43 percent of New Yorkers described themselves as Catholic. The first half of the twentieth century was dominated by the emergence of New York as the largest Jewish city in the world. The Immigration Acts of 1965 and 1990 opened the shores of New York to Africans, Asians, and Latinos. These incoming immigrants, and subsequent dramatic shifts in population, continue to ignite a resurgence of Evangelical/Pentecostal presence in the city.[3]

Organizational Context

The concerts of prayer movement in New York City has gone through four distinct phases in the 1987–2007 time period. The first phase, 1987–1994, was the *informal, grassroots phase.* Initially, leadership from InterVarsity Christian Fellowship and Here's Life Inner City served this prayer movement. We worked collaboratively to bring churches together to pray. Resources were limited so we all worked as volunteers.

The second phase was the *organizational phase,* 1994–1997. I left InterVarsity to work full time with churches, and employed one full-time staff member. We were able to grow the prayer initiatives and began to expand our thinking about the urban dimension of our work. Our work in New York City was the urban strategy division of Concerts of Prayer International, under the leadership of Rev. David Bryant. We held two urban consultations with Ray Bakke, renowned urbanologist and author, and contributed to *Signs of Hope in the City,* published by Judson Press in 1997.

The third phase was the *indigenous phase,* 1998–2001. With an indigenous board of pastors, COPGNY launched as an independent ministry. The staff had grown from two to six team members. The primary benefit for me during this season was to study with Ray Bakke, traveling with him to global cities such as Manila, Philippines, and Vancouver, Canada. I left his graduate program in 2000 understanding New York City ten times better than I had before 1998. The programs of COPGNY continued to grow as we hosted two more national urban consultations.

The fourth phase of the movement arrived suddenly on 9/11. Between 2001 and 2007 we entered the *collaborative phase* of the movement. The pressure associated with 9/11 forged three incredible partnerships: with World Vision, the Willow Creek Association (WCA), and Redeemer Presbyterian Church. Each partnership grew to be the largest of its type in the nation. The soil of united prayer for 13 years was bearing extraordinary fruit.

Globally, 8,000 children were sponsored by local Christians through the ministry of

World Vision, 200 church planters were trained and funded through the partnership with Redeemer Presbyterian Church, and 8,500 leaders were being trained at the WCA Leadership Summit—we began to sense that the ministries God was burgeoning were larger than the wineskin Concerts of Prayer could contain.

The incorporation of the New York City Leadership Center in 2007 is the fifth phase of the movement, the *institutional phase*. It comes at an opportune moment in the life of the world's leading global city, where there is a desperate need for skilled and faith-filled leadership. The leadership center will partner with existing institutions (seminaries and agencies) and both incubate and birth new opportunities to expand the kingdom of God. The pervasive needs of the people in New York City require innovative approaches by cutting-edge leaders willing to create new molds of ministry in the twenty-first century.

Why the New York City Leadership Center?

Tony Carnes, of the Values Research Institute, conducted a survey of 800 leaders in summer 2007. When asked if there was a need for a leadership center, the conclusions were overwhelming. The following distinct groups believe there is a definite need for a leadership center:

- 86 percent of overall respondents
- 90 percent of immigrant church and ministry leaders who are very dissatisfied with their leadership skills
- 91 percent of church and ministry leaders who are very dissatisfied with their leadership skills
- 93 percent of African American church and ministry leaders
- 97 percent of Brooklyn church and ministry leaders
- 100 percent of denominational leaders[4]

Why is there such a strongly felt need? One respondent said this, "The most educated people in the world are in New York, and you have [many undereducated] clergy."[5]

It is no wonder that both clergy and marketplace leaders feel overmatched by the enormous challenges of reaching secular New York. Missions agency leaders are also often ill equipped for the cost of doing business in one of the most expensive regions in the world.

A 2002 report by Carnes indicated that two-thirds of clergy in New York City had not finished seminary and one-third had not finished college. There is both a huge hunger, and an apparent need, for both formal accredited education and skill-based training. In the report, these areas led the demand for training:

- Motivating others
- Developing leaders in my ministry
- Communication skills
- Vision casting and strategic planning
- Collaboration with other ministries

Building on the foundation of 20 years of incarnational ministry through Concerts of Prayer Greater New York, the New York City Leadership Center seeks to address these needs.

What the Center Provides

The purpose of the center is to synergize best of class training and service opportunities to radically impact Greater New York socially and spiritually.

1. Educate leaders in the art of result-producing leadership

We will educate in four dimensions: conferences, training in leadership communities, curriculum development, and courses with partnering seminaries. Crucial to our strategy is measuring results.

We will continue to utilize the annual leadership summit as a place for vision casting and training. Seminaries will offer courses through the center for graduate credit, and online curriculum will be developed to support local churches and agencies that want to access best practices.

2. Collaborate through outreach

We are not developing leaders for the sake of developing leaders. Given the enormity of the spiritual and social needs of our region and world, we will bring best practices together to innovate for greater results; in the first year, establishing partnerships around outreach to at-risk youth in the 20/20 strategy. This strategy brings together a network of young leaders and national agencies to partner with churches. Outreach to children of prisoners and urban youth is part of the anticipated parcel to this collaboration.

3. Replicate the vision in other cities

As the center matures, opportunities are created to cast vision in other cities, as well as to host leaders from around the world. The center is an advocate for incubating and implementing citywide movements of united prayer and collaborative outreach. Our commitment is to partner with other local and global organizations who are like-minded in impacting global cities.

Progress

The rationale draft for the center was written in January 2006. In the following two years much was achieved:

- Formation of a National Advisory Team, including the following participants:

Ray Bakke	Floyd Flake	Bill Pollard
Steve Bell	Wilson Goode	Marc Rivera
A. R. Bernard	Rupert Hayles	Tim Schmidt
Ken Blanchard	Frances Hesselbein	Horst Schulze
Bob Buford	Allan Houston	Paul Stanley
David Epstein	Bill Hybels	Harry Tucker
Tony Evans	David Ireland	Gary Veurink
Priyan Fernando	Jim Mellado	Rick Warren

- Formation of a presidential council from Greater New York with 15 members.
- The center incorporated as its own 501(c)(3).
- Collaborative outreaches put in motion, involving youth and marketplace leaders.

You will read in the following chapters about some of the leaders and their stories that provide a collage of what God continues to do in Greater New York. These are indigenous leaders who will have much to contribute to emerging leaders in the New York City area and beyond in the coming years.

Leadership Reflection Questions

1. Can you identify a leader whose courage changed your life?

2. How did that leader change history?

3. What dream has God put in your heart that will require you to exercise courageous leadership?

Chapter 4

Pray New York!

"My house will be called a house of prayer for all nations."
ISAIAH 56:7

A Defining Moment

During the mid-1970s, the South Bronx averaged 12,000 fires a year. The area lost 40 percent of its housing stock, and 300,000 people fled. In the burned-out zone that remained, police fought a losing battle against junkies and murderous teenage gangs.

"*The New York Times* commented that the South Bronx was 'as crucial to an understanding of American urban life as Auschwitz is crucial to an understanding of Nazism.' . . . By 1981, the *Los Angeles Times* could declare that the South Bronx was 'both a place and a scare-word.'"[1]

Against this backdrop, Bishop Gerry Kaufman of Love Gospel Assembly on the Grand Concourse of the Bronx had a vision. He saw the churches becoming a voice that would cry out in prayer for the city. In 1975, he was searching for a remnant that would stay in the Bronx, pray, and help the borough to recover. Love Gospel was at the forefront of a revival of prayer among the churches.

Bishop Kaufman said at a Pastors' Prayer Summit in the Bronx, "You will never learn to pray until you have learned how to weep." Shortly before his death, he told me over lunch in his office, "I have waited a long time to see with my own eyes this kind of coming together across the body of Christ and the region to pray together." Within six weeks, he died suddenly and was succeeded by Bishop Ronald Bailey.

Churches Begin to Unite

Pastors and congregations began praying together in concerts of prayer gatherings in 1988. In the 1990s, the March for Jesus had taken root in New York City under the leadership of Vince Fusco, Edith Stranges, and Nick Savoca. There were several borough marches in Brooklyn, Queens, and the Bronx along with a citywide march. Thousands gathered from hundreds of churches in a united expression of worship, celebration, and prayer.

In 2004, Concerts of Prayer Greater New York (COPGNY) birthed the idea of Pray New York! The idea was simply to have churches take responsibility once a year on the same Saturday in June to prayerwalk the ZIP Code of their churches. Building upon the foundation of March for Jesus and its leadership, the first Pray New York! was scheduled for June 3, 2004. More than 5,000 people participated in each of the five boroughs across the more than 200 ZIP Codes of the city. The metropolitan coordinator for Pray New York! for 2005 and 2006 was Katie Sweeting. In 2007, the role was assumed by Beverly Cook, both of whom worked on staff with COPGNY. Carlos Ortiz also played an important role for Pray New York! supporting multiple sites as a COPGNY staff member.

In Pray New York! congregations typically would gather together at the church and begin with a time of prayer and orientation. They would receive direction as to where they should walk and pray. The essence of the experience is to have people pray for their neighborhoods as they walk, with their eyes open. This powerful experience fully engages the eyes, the mind, the heart, and the soul of the participant.

The Bronx

Pura Coniglio is the fruit of Bishop Kaufman's vision. She joined Love Gospel Assembly in 1980 and has remained there for decades. Licensed to minister in 1999, Coniglio has been the minister of prayer. Puerto Rican, Minister Pura also is a practicing lawyer, admitted to the bar in 1992. Her legal focus has been to assist churches with their needs and also family law.

Minister Pura leads an initiative called Operation Bronx NYC Restoration. She gathers every week with her regional team of 13 intercessors. Every month a group of 150 intercessors representing as many as 75 churches gather. The monthly gathering is called the Bronx Household of Prayer.

Pray New York!

Prayer Walker Attendance from 2004 to 2007 for Each Region

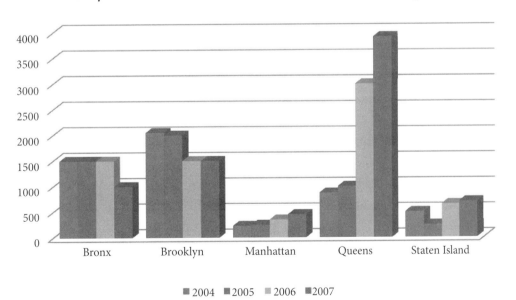

Pray New York!

Participating Churches from 2004 to 2007 by Region

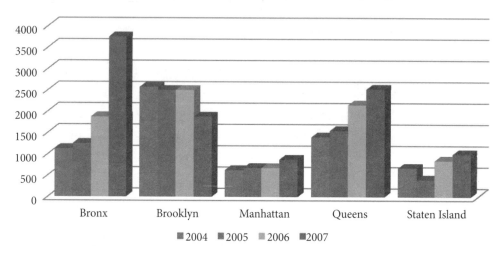

The context of the Bronx demands intensive intercession. In his book about the Mott Haven section in the South Bronx, Jonathon Kozol described a public school where only 7 out of 800 school children did not qualify for free lunches.[2] Kozol also went on to state that in 1995 the odds of an African American male graduating from college versus being in jail were 1 in 100.[3]

Minister Pura coordinates Pray New York! as well as the annual Bronx Prayer Summit, now a joint event. Pray New York! now includes more than 100 churches and 1,500 people. In 2007, the prayer summit included participation from Adolfo Carrion Jr, the Bronx Borough president. Minister Pura's vision for Pray New York! in the Bronx is to see unity grow between the Hispanic, African/Caribbean, Asian, and Anglo populations. Her desire is to see a deeper covenant relationship among the churches and leaders.

What have been the answers to prayer?
• Betting parlors, centers of witchcraft, and a cultic temple have been closed down.
• People encountered in the walk have been introduced to faith and have joined churches.
• Churches like Van Nest Assembly of God and Ecclesia Church International have jointly adopted their ZIP Code and prayerwalked their communities.

From a leadership perspective, Minister Pura has learned

- not to be judgmental or take offense but rather to be gracious in doing the hard work of building unity;
- to make sure motivation is kingdom-minded and not one of self-promotion.[4]

Brooklyn

Brooklyn is known as a city of churches. If Brooklyn were a city all by itself, it would be the fourth largest city in the nation. The center of gravity for the churches throughout Greater New York is the African American church in Brooklyn, due to its numeric strength.

Roger McPhail and his wife, Teresa, started Gateway City Church in 1990, formerly New Hope Fellowship Church. Pastor Roger has moved effectively in diverse theological circles including both the charismatic/Pentecostal community and the Evangelical traditions. He served as the Brooklyn coordinator for pastors with the 2005 Billy Graham Crusade. Pastor Roger also serves as the chancellor of the regional Wagner Leadership Institute. He travels and speaks regularly for Ed Silvoso in Latin America. Pastor Roger was also a promotional strategist with the Willow Creek Association for the Brooklyn site in 2005 and 2006.

Pastor Roger and his wife, Teresa, have also established four Christian schools over the past 25 years. Teresa is currently writing a book entitled *The Five Anointings of Children in Intercession.*

Pastor Roger's leadership involvement with Pray New York! grew naturally out of his leadership with March for Jesus. As a local congregation, Gateway City Church also had been applying prayer and evangelism principles for approximately one year prior to 9/11. He attributes the peace in their multiethnic neighborhood, in which 20 percent of the residents have a Middle Eastern background, to four weeks of prayerwalking in August 2001.

Pastor Roger also convenes one of the largest monthly pastors gatherings under the banner of Mission New York. He has an extraordinary ability to affirm the pastors in this network. At a recent Christmas party, Pastor Roger provided more than $15,000 in giveaway items for these leaders.[5]

Answers to prayer in Brooklyn have included the following:

- a change in the spiritual climate as evidenced by the peace after 9/11 and the uncovering of criminal activity within the community;

- a spiritual renaissance in Brooklyn as declared by Ed Silvoso and Harvest Evangelism in a new video describing the transformation;
- the presence of national leaders and ministries in Brooklyn such as Cindy Jacobs, Harvest Evangelism, and the Wagner Leadership Institute;
- branching out to other cities and states with the Pray New York! strategy;
- birth of other efforts to transform lives through healing services in 50 churches following Pray New York!
- the establishment of School Reformation Day in which the public and private schools of Brooklyn are prayerwalked.

The leadership lessons Pastor Roger has modeled come from Luke 10:5–9:
- Bless: Speak peace to the people and the systems. (v. 5)
- Fellowship: Listen to their concerns. (v. 7)
- Minister: Address their felt needs in the name of the Lord. (v. 9*a*)
- Proclaim: Let it be known that the kingdom of God is nearby. (v. 9*b*)

Manhattan

Manhattan is arguably the most influential island in human history. During the workweek, nearly 4 million workers commute to Manhattan. In Midtown there are an estimated 250,000 people working per square mile, making it one of the densest places on earth during the workweek.

The spiritual landscape of Midtown Manhattan is daunting. With only a handful of thriving churches between Central Park and Wall Street, the need for spiritual renewal is urgent. While there is greater church strength in Harlem, nearly 75 percent of those churches are storefronts (small in space and congregational size). In Chinatown the churches are overwhelmed by the ratio of immigrants, representing the largest immigrant enclave in the Western Hemisphere, compared to the number of congregations.

Charles Simpson arrived in New York City in 1980 from Tennessee as a bivocational church planter. In 1990 he met and married his wife, Lynn, who grew up in Washington Heights, Manhattan. Pastor Charles served as the pastor of prayer at Times Square Church from 1990 to 1993. He led a Thursday night prayer meeting that grew to over 300 and he oversaw ten other weekly prayer meetings. He adopted the model of Charles Spurgeon of having a prayer group praying for the preacher during Sunday worship, establishing a group in 1991 that continues today at Times Square Church. Since then Charles has planted five churches and assisted in the birthing of two Bible colleges.

While working in the Metropolitan New York Baptist Association office in 2006 with the executive director, Gary Frost, Pastor Charles assisted him in coordinating Pray New York! (more about Gary Frost in chap. 8). In 2007, he coordinated the Manhattan effort, which has involved 36 churches and more than 400 participants prayerwalking the more than 100 ZIP Codes of Manhattan. In June 2007, there was a celebration service to end the prayerwalk at Trinity Baptist on 61st and 2nd Avenue.

Pastor Charles's vision for Pray New York! is that it might serve as a catalyst for adopting prayerwalking as a lifestyle for New York City believers. He also sees the prayerwalk as an instrument to develop a lasting friendship between Manhattan churches.

Answers to prayer in Manhattan are many:

- The united prayer in Manhattan has been the forerunner of the success of emerging church plants. Participants have been praying large prayers to see church growth. Churches like the Journey have already exceeded 1,000 people within five years.
- The restraint of evil since 9/11, with no successful large-scale attack on the city in the following years.
- Neighborhoods like Harlem and Washington Heights have experienced an economic renaissance.

The leadership lessons Pastor Charles has modeled:

- Have genuine concern and love for the local pastor.
- Make a commitment to enhance what the local pastor is already doing.
- Be bold and genuine in articulating your passion.
- Believe 100 percent in your cause.[6]

Queens

Queens is the largest of the boroughs geographically with 76 neighborhoods, and it represents the most international county in the United States. Some of its neighborhoods are among the most diverse religiously and linguistically in the world. As much as any other region in the world, it is a microcosm of the world.

In 1998, Joel Sadaphal had a defining moment. He was looking at the lives of people in the sanctuary of Living Word Christian Fellowship in South Ozone Park and saw the sheer difficulty they were having living out their faith. He would see an initial breakthrough at church among congregants but see them return to an environment where they would feel harassed. Pastor Joel concluded that the environment must change.

His next step included meeting with other pastors. After earning an engineering degree, Pastor Joel entered the pastorate to assist his father at Deeper Life Christian Fellowship in 1982. He planted the new church, Living Word Christian Fellowship, a few miles away in 1993. The church mirrors the sheer diversity of Queens with people from 53 ethnic groups.

Pastor Joel began to give leadership to the March for Jesus in 1998. During 1999–2003, there were 4,500 citywide participants and 1,800 participants in Queens. In just three years of Pray New York! the number of participants grew to 3,900 intercessors representing more than 100 churches.

In addition to the annual Pray New York! Pastor Joel hosts monthly pastors' gatherings that have involved 60 pastors. They meet for breakfast, worship, prayer, and a topical discussion. The aggregate impact of this commitment to care for pastors and churches has resulted in far greater trust, a changing environment toward church collaboration, and a clear sense of the dawning of a great day when the unity of the church will be testimony to the unchurched.

Pastor Joel thanks God for the answers to prayer:

- Political leadership has begun to pay attention to this community of united churches, resulting in requests by local civic boards to have leaders come and pray.
- A commitment has been made to launch a post–Pray New York! festival with a gathering of churches in partnership with local corporations.
- There is a growing consensus to pray for teachers in the school system and eventually to have an impact on every major sector of society through prayer.

The primary leadership lesson that Pastor Joel embodies is that while having a great vision is important, it is paramount to work with God's servants and to appreciate their unique abilities.[7]

Staten Island

Staten Island is the smallest borough by population but also one of the most challenging boroughs in which to work. Staten Island has been predominantly an Italian Catholic community undergoing rapid ethnic and socioeconomic change in the past several years.

The island and the churches tend to be divided geographically and culturally. The Staten Island Association of Evangelicals has been an important instrument in faithfully bringing leaders and churches together for many years.

A lay leader, Hans Wiesner, emerged with a burden for intercession and unity in the churches. Hans's family owns a landscaping business, and his professional skills and spiritual passion equipped him to have an effective leadership role for Staten Island. Hans and his wife, Lori, were very effective in building bridges into diverse church communities across Staten Island.

Nearly two years before assuming a leadership role with Pray New York!, Hans and his wife, Lori, caught the vision for reaching a lost world through a revived church in their three years of studies at the College of Prayer in Atlanta. Hans said, "When Mac came and asked me to lead Pray New York! on Staten Island, I saw it as an opportunity to implement all that my wife and I had learned, and to put our faith into action."

His leadership, not as ordained clergy, but as a layperson, was an encouragement to intercessors. Even boat owners offered to use their boats to pray as they cruised the circumference of the borough. Some of the most significant answers to prayer in the borough came through men and women who were dedicated to seeking God's heart for the borough, and responding in faith as God called them. God honored their obedience in many ways, including restoring the marriage of one of the boating couples in 2006. A greater sense of awe was experienced by intercessors in 2007 when their divinely orchestrated efforts coincided with media reports of a thwarted terrorist plot the same day as Pray New York![8]

Leadership Learned

Here are some of the leadership lessons Hans Wiesner learned:

- As a mobilizer, one needs to recognize that you can't do the work of the Holy Spirit. You can communicate your passion for and need for an initiative, but it is the Holy Spirit that gives the burden to those being mobilized.
- A divine coordination between those in public authority (pastors) and those in private authority (intercessors) helps to move regional initiatives forward with greater success.
- Regional initiatives are more effective when the focus is on building a kingdom mind-set, lifestyle, and culture; moving away from an event mentality.

The answers to prayer that Hans saw revealed led him to conclude:

- God honors our efforts when we come out from the church and pray on-site with insight.
- Many people came to salvation to Christ, healings occurred, and at least one marriage was saved as a result of Pray New York!
- The words of Jeremiah 33:3 are true today: "Call to me and I will answer you and tell you great and unsearchable things you do not know."

Leadership Reflection Questions

1. Can you find a small group of people from your church or fellowship to prayerwalk your block, campus, or workplace? Can you do this monthly, quarterly, annually?

2. What churches in your neighborhood (or campus groups) should you be praying for to see God prosper?

3. For what dangerous influences in your community do you need to pray?

Chapter 5

FROM SAN JUAN TO STATEN ISLAND: CONNECTING HISPANIC CHURCHES IN GREATER NEW YORK

"You will fill me with joy in your presence."

PSALM 16:11

On a Saturday afternoon, I attended the celebration service of Luciano Padilla in Bay Ridge, Brooklyn. Others were recognizing him for his leadership among the Hispanic community regionally and globally. Pastor Padilla's impact also extended to Africa and the Caribbean.

I had two memories from that day. Toward the end of the service, Pastor Padilla had Mama Leo come to join him on the platform. Pastor Padilla took the robe given to him and placed it on the shoulders of this diminutive woman, revered as a "Puerto Rican Mother Teresa" in New

York City for her work among the poor and addicted. He was celebrating her in the midst of his own celebration, as one of the spiritual mothers for the Hispanic church in New York City.

Pastor Padilla turned to the congregation and said, "Mama Leo deserves this recognition as much as myself for her lifetime of labor among us." The Saturday afternoon event was an extraordinary festival of recognizing God's work in this church and among God's people.

My second memory was the celebration banquet. Pastor Padilla gave me a ride in the new car that the congregation had given him. At the banquet, in the middle of everyone eating their salad, a joyous dance erupted in the midst of the meal. I had never seen anything quite like it—the pure sense of joy from belonging to God and to each other. I felt I was receiving a rare glimpse as a non-Latino into the beauty, power, and energy of the Hispanic church.

In 1993, I met Robert, a Puerto Rican student studying engineering at Stony Brook University located on Long Island. By attending a university, Robert was valiantly trying not to become another statistic, like some of his friends in the Bronx who were making $2,000 a week selling drugs in Washington Heights.

However, he was failing his courses and the prospects for successfully graduating seemed dim. His friends' choices seemed to be limited to either working at fast-food restaurants for minimum wage or selling drugs. Like many Hispanic young men, Robert was struggling to build his life in New York City. I have not seen him since and I do not know what has happened to Robert.

Puerto Ricans are the largest Latino group in the New York region, part of a growing, vibrant Latino community from numerous countries. A majority of Puerto Ricans living in New York City earn less than $30,000 per year in one of the most expensive cities on earth.[1]

Puerto Ricans, Dominicans, and Mexicans comprise three of the largest Spanish-speaking groups in New York City. Puerto Ricans began arriving on the shores of New York City in 1900 after the Spanish Armada was defeated. Today, the nearly 1.1 million Puerto Ricans in the New York region are largely divided between the Bronx, Brooklyn, and New Jersey (70 percent), with another 20 percent living in Manhattan and Queens. The Dominican community is concentrated almost equally between the Bronx and Washington Heights (62 percent total) with another 30 percent living in Queens and Brooklyn. The rapidly growing Mexican community is evenly distributed between Queens, Brooklyn, and the Bronx (70 percent), with another 20 percent shared between Manhattan and Westchester County.

From every Latino community, many immigrants arrive with nothing more than the clothes on their backs and the dream of a better future for their children. Hispanic leaders have said, "Many of our people are trying to survive in a place where they don't know the language. It takes years for many to adjust to a new place and a whole new way of life."

A majority of Ecuadorians and Colombians live in Queens, while the Salvadoran community is located largely on Long Island, in Suffolk and Nassau Counties. The Guatemalan community is spread evenly between Queens, Nassau, and Suffolk County (58 percent), with 31 percent living in Westchester.[2]

Economically, the median income for Puerto Rican immigrants in the Bronx, Manhattan, and Brooklyn is $23,000–$27,000 per year. For Mexicans, it is $25,000–$30,000. For Dominicans in the same three boroughs, it is less than $20,000–$25,000 per year. Puerto Ricans, Mexicans, and Dominicans represent 86 percent of the Bronx Latinos; 57 percent of Brooklyn Latinos; and 40 percent of Manhattan Latinos.[3] As stated already, the Mexican population is expected to grow to close to 4 million by 2050, while the Dominican community will near 2 million. These are extraordinary demographic trends that require our attention.

Concurrent with the growth of the Latino communities has been the powerful growth of the Hispanic church. One estimate is that there are now more than 2,000 Hispanic churches in the metropolitan area, with 250,000 active worshippers, making it the largest non-English body of Christians in Greater New York.

The paradox of the Hispanic churches is this: they are numerically strong but economically challenged. The pastors within the Hispanic churches are acutely aware of their parishioners' needs for food, adequate housing, health, and education.[4] A high percentage of households attending Hispanic churches are headed by single mothers. Accompanying financial hardships is a sense of isolation from the broader culture. Manny Ortiz, in his book *The Hispanic Challenge*, states that the likelihood of a Puerto Rican establishing a relationship with a Anglo is only 20 percent.[5]

A Vision Is Born

Rev. Hector Bonano was sitting in his office in the Bronx in 2001, and he felt like he was sitting in a fishbowl. Although he had a successful pastorate over many years and broad influence in his denomination, he was looking forward to retiring.

On that day, some young Hispanic men visited him to talk about the need for evangelizing the Hispanic community. Rev. Bonano was moved and began to enter into a completely new world. He took on the burden of mobilizing Hispanic churches in a coordinated outreach with Carlos Annacondia in August 2003. The outdoor outreach was held in the Bronx in a park near Lehman College. To make the event possible, Rev. Bonano advanced $25,000 of his own money.

During the four-day event, 10,000 people attended; there was a significant response to the preaching of the gospel. Not only were people being born again, something else was being birthed—a calling on Rev. Bonano's life to step into a coordinating role with CONLICO (Confraternidad de Líderes Conciliares), the network of Hispanic Pentecostal churches that includes 4,000 churches across the Northeast from Pennsylvania, to metro New York, and into New England.

Rev. Bonano's preparation for the role included his serving as a residential supervisor. In the early 1980s, there were 12 churches in the Council of Missionary Churches of Christ. Under his leadership, the number of churches expanded to 65. His duties included oversight of the building of churches and reorganizing the region into four districts (Pennsylvania, Metro New York City, Upstate New York, and New England).

The accomplishments during this 24-year period included the purchase of a 21-acre camp for the denomination, the establishment of a 5-year plan to plant 50 new churches, and the ordination of bishops. His denomination subsequently named Rev. Bonano a bishop.

In 2003, Bishop Bonano took on the coordinating role with CONLICO. CONLICO had begun in 1998 as the result of the vision of Dr. Kittim Silva-Bermúdez and Radio Visión Cristiana. As the Hispanic church community rapidly grew, both the radio station and CONLICO were seen as vehicles to unite and mobilize the diverse Hispanic population.

Radio Visión Cristiana has been one of the most powerful instruments of the Hispanic church, with an estimated daily listening audience of up to 500,000 people per day, including listeners in the Caribbean and South America. One of the highlights of the radio broadcast was a letter received from then Cuban president Fidel Castro, indicating that he had heard the broadcast.

The station is fully paid for by listeners in the Spanish churches—who often send in donations of a few dollars at a time, wrapped in aluminum foil. Radio Visión Cristiana has partnered with hundreds of churches—many of the leading Hispanic churches in the tristate region. It was a natural extension of Radio Visión Cristiana to give birth to CONLICO.

The Vision of CONLICO

CONLICO exists to support the Pentecostal churches.
- Partners with agencies to address the needs of the poor.
- Partners with civic and political leaders on behalf of the needs of the Hispanics.
- Partners with the business community to address the economic realities of the Hispanic community.
- Prays together and speaks with one voice on the moral and ethical issues facing the culture.
- Builds the kingdom of God by partnering across ethnic and language lines with the broader body of Christ.

According to the Milano Graduate School Center for New York City Affairs:
- Immigrants in New York City are nearly three times as likely to worry about food or be hungry than the overall population; one-third of children with immigrant parents live in families that have difficulty affording food.
- Recent immigrants tend to be very poor; their children usually live in two-parent families, but 40 percent of legal permanent residents entering New York after 1996 had incomes in 1999–2000 below the federal poverty line—a rate double that of the city as a whole.
- Limited ability to speak English is closely linked to poverty. More than one-third of adult immigrants with limited English in New York City had incomes below the poverty level in 1999–2000. Mexican immigrants have the highest percentage of poverty among adult immigrants in New York City at 60 percent.[6]

In his unpaid role as the CONLICO coordinator, Bishop Bonano has sought to mobilize the churches and build partnerships that span the lingual, organizational, and denominational spectrum. His own church has partnered with World Vision to feed 1,000 families per month.

In March 2005, under Bishop Bonano's leadership, CONLICO rallied 30,000 Hispanics and other citizens to address the sanctity of marriage on the steps of the supreme court in the Bronx. Jewish rabbis also attended this rally, the largest of its kind in the nation. CONLICO also has taken a leadership role by traveling to Albany to appeal to state legislators on the necessity of having traditional family values reflected in their governance.

An Extraordinary Community of Hispanic Leaders in New York City: Adolfo Carrion and Ray Rivera

An important ally has been the Bronx Borough President's Office. Adolfo Carrion Jr. has been an extraordinary partner with the church community, along with his liaison officer for faith-based initiatives, the late Hermes Caraballo. The borough president has dedicated staff and resources to partner with the church community to address some of the great challenges facing the Bronx, especially in the Hispanic community.

Since borough president Carrion took office in 2001, more than $2.2 billion has been invested in residential real estate—resulting in 25,000 new units being built. He has directed 40 percent of his 2007 capital funding to housing development. Carrion created the Bronx at Work Housing Series to address critical housing needs in the borough for both consumers and developers. The Bronx has seen a development pace never before experienced in the borough's history. Total investment in the borough has increased from $400 million in 2001 to almost $1 billion invested in 2005, a whopping 236 percent increase. Since Carrion took office in 2001, more than $3 billion has been invested throughout the borough.[7]

Bronx Borough president Carrion was raised and nurtured in the church. His father, Rev. Adolfo Carrion Sr, was district superintendent for the Spanish Assemblies of God. He oversaw churches along the eastern seaboard, from Maine all the way to Puerto Rico. Borough president Carrion Jr. served on the church staff of Crossroads Tabernacle prior to his entrance into politics.

In partnerships between churches and the president's office, creative, cutting-edge programming addresses the needs of at-risk youth, the poor, and the homeless. Another extraordinary partner is the Latino Pastoral Action Center (LPAC), under the leadership of Rev. Raymond Rivera. LPAC has become one of the most progressive community development models in the nation, serving both Latinos and the broader community. Rev. Rivera has incubated several programs that have addressed the needs of inner-city youth and people living with HIV/AIDS, and he created a charter school for children in the community. The work of LPAC has been so evidently successful that it is being replicated across the nation in cities like Miami and Chicago.

The fourfold pedagogy of LPAC is rooted in a theology of liberation in both personal and structural terms; healing both inwardly and outwardly, rooted in Isaiah 53; community in

God and with one another knit together in love expressing itself in service; and transformation in our Christlikeness as well as in being agents for communities. This pedagogy has spawned several life and community-changing programs:

- Association of Church-Based Community Ministries which networks 55 organizations to receive technical assistance
- Center for Emerging Female Leadership, begun in 1996
- Family Life Academy Charter School in partnership with the board of education, training children kindergarten through fifth grade where they learn about character, family, and social issues such as justice, in addition to a regular academic curriculum
- Greater Heights Program, which assists young adults with college and career decisions as well as provides a late-night alternative to the streets[8]

Leadership Development in the Hispanic Community

Another extraordinary leader in the Hispanic community for more than 30 years has been Bishop Luciano Padilla. His church in Bay Ridge, Brooklyn, is one of the pioneer models of a bilingual church with services in both English and Spanish. Bishop Padilla helped to pioneer the establishment of Radio Visión Cristiana. He was the first Hispanic board member of Concerts of Prayer Greater New York, and the first Hispanic pastor from New York City to attend the Willow Creek Leadership Summit in South Barrington, Illinois. He traveled as part of an entourage of nine New York City leaders to evaluate whether this event would speak relevantly into the Latino church context in New York.

Bishop Padilla has hosted annual leadership conferences in his church for thousands of leaders from across the Latin world. He has been an extraordinary source of encouragement to Latino pastors in some of the most exciting areas of church growth, as well as some of the most daunting contexts globally. His missions efforts have spanned Latin America and Africa.

With his encouragement and partnership with CONLICO under Bishop Bonano, the first New York City Leadership Summit sites were held in 2005. Translation into Spanish was made available in the Bronx site at Crossroads Tabernacle. In the first three years, nearly 200 Hispanic leaders participated.

When asked what the impact of this experience was, Bishop Bonano responded, "I have waited all of my life to be invited to participate in events that Hispanic leaders could only dream about. We would never have the resources to travel to large Christian leadership events. This partnership with Willow Creek, Concerts of Prayer Greater New York, and the Hispanic churches has been nothing less than a miracle."[9]

A Vision for the Future

Bishop Bonano envisions a day when there will be large-scale collaboration between the broader body of Christ across theological and language barriers. He has a passion to see the whole body of Christ come together in prayerful dependence on God to speak into our city and culture. His son Philip has become a church planter, and is a symbol of hope for the future, representing emerging leaders. Bishop Bonano believes that up to half of the Hispanic clergy are entering the twilight of their ministry, bequeathing an urgent need to replace their leadership in the coming decade.

Leadership Reflection Questions

1. Can you identify a Hispanic faith community in or near your church or home? Have you taken a first step to get to know this community?

2. Can you seek out the opportunity to do something practical with a Hispanic congregation— such as an outreach to their neighborhood, a food drive, or outreach to a newly immigrated family?

3. Will you pray for Hispanic young people to become part of the fabric of the leadership of the church in your city?

Chapter 6

COLLABORATING IN JAMAICA, QUEENS

"So the wall was completed on the twenty-fifth of Elul, in fifty-two days."
NEHEMIAH 6:15

In 1932, Roderick Caesar Sr., an immigrant from St. Lucia, West Indies, worked as a taxi driver in Manhattan. A lay leader in a Pentecostal church in Harlem, he felt called to plant a church in Jamaica, Queens. Fifty percent of his original congregants came from a nearby Baptist church in Queens. The church had the makings of an extraordinary DNA to blend people from diverse backgrounds and theological traditions.

In 1946, Roderick Jr. was born. Roderick Jr. remembers attending meetings as a young man with his father in the 1950s and 1960s; Pastor Caesar met with the leadership of national organizations like the Billy Graham Evangelistic Association and the Oral Roberts Evangelistic

Association. As he watched his father interact with Anglo leaders, Roderick Jr. began to absorb the important truth that the gospel transcends skin hue and culture.

Rev. Roderick Caesar Sr. planted Bethel Gospel Tabernacle, and, from its early years, Bethel attracted people from diverse backgrounds. Though situated in an African American neighborhood, in the early years Norwegians began to attend, and later on the church attracted people from a Jewish Messianic background.

When Roderick Jr. was born in 1946, the church made two important decisions. Bethel Bible Institute (BBI) was launched. It still trains and educates emerging leaders. At its peak, the school attracted 600 students. The influence of the school is so pervasive that the Church of God in Christ in the New York City area attributed up to 15 percent of its pastors as having been trained by BBI.

The second decision was to begin having a regular presence on the radio. For more than 60 years now, Bethel has been on the radio, providing a regular presence in the minds and hearts of Christians across the region. Bethel and its 75-year Caesar pastorate has been an incredibly important asset in building unity across the sheer diversity of the church in metro New York.

It was in this environment that 14-year-old Roderick Jr. received a calling to ministry. His father did not influence his decision, nor did he make any promises as to his eventual placement in the church. After attending college in 1966, Roderick Jr. began pastoring another church in the late 1970s and early 1980s, and by 1984 Rev. Roderick Caesar Jr. became the senior pastor at Bethel Gospel Tabernacle.

The Growth of Bethel Gospel Tabernacle

The church grew steadily in the 1960s and had 500 regular attendees. Bethel invited evangelist John Lawrence to come in the 1960s to preach for one week. He ended up staying for three months, and the church doubled to 1,000 people. The heartbeat of Bethel has always been the message and work of evangelism, demonstrated on a weekly basis in the altar call presentations, as well as work on the missions field around the globe.

Bethel is active in six African countries, Haiti, and other parts of the Caribbean. Roderick Caesar Jr. and his wife, Beverly Caesar, joined a vision trip I took to East Africa in 2003. Together we saw the devastation of HIV/AIDS across the continent. As spokespersons for World Vision over the past five years, their influence and advocacy has been enormous; along with others, they have had an impact on churches that have sponsored more than 8,000 children.[1]

The Role of Prayer

In 1973, Sister Mildred Williams approached Roderick Caesar Sr. about a burden she had. She felt God leading her to begin an early morning prayer meeting. Her desire was to pray at the church, 7 days a week, 365 days a year, at 6:00 A.M. for one hour. Sister Williams showed up at the church faithfully, day after day, year after year, even when she was the only one there. The prayer meeting grew over the years and is now one of the hallmarks of the church. For decades, thousands of church members have gathered in the predawn dark of the church to seek God.[2]

The church also has two seasons of consecration every year when people from the congregation shut themselves in for 60 hours of prayer and worship. This provides an opportunity for the congregation to fully enter into the prayer burden they have for their children, the needy in the community, the prisoner, and the broken of the world.

A Citywide Leader

Rev. Roderick Caesar Jr. is unique among the spiritual leaders in Greater New York, demonstrating an ability to move in and out of incredibly diverse theological and ethnic cultures. Oftentimes he will find himself the only person of color in an all-Anglo setting, and he handles this with complete ease. When Roderick Caesar Jr. participated in my ordination in 1992 in South Dakota, he was the only person of color present.

Like his father, he has moved in and out of diverse organizational settings as well. His unique abilities as an emcee, worship leader, and teacher have provided an extraordinary platform to bring diverse groups of people together. It is no accident that Roderick Caesar Jr. and Bethel have been planted in Queens, New York City—the most diverse county in America—for the past 70 years.

It is also not accidental that in 1984 Roderick opened his home to my wife, Marya, and me while we searched for housing. Brand-new to New York, with a wife that was five months pregnant, Roderick and Beverly Caesar extended themselves and their home to us. Our first Christmas in New York was spent having dinner at Bishop Caesar Sr.'s home—the first outing for our 11-day-old daughter Anna.

As the friendship grew over time, Rev. Roderick Caesar Jr. played a major role in the formation of the concerts of prayer movement, along with Rev. Bob Johansson of Evangel Church and Rev. Russell Rosser of First Baptist. His credibility and leadership was a key factor in the exploding movement that started in 1988, and by the fall of 1989 included every major region in the metropolitan area.

A New Neighbor Arrives in 1976

Just a few blocks away from Bethel Gospel Tabernacle is the Greater Allen AME (African Methodist Episcopal) Cathedral of New York. While Bethel is from an independent Pentecostal tradition, Allen AME Cathedral is part of the historic African Methodist Episcopal tradition, the oldest African American denomination in the nation.

Floyd Flake arrived in Jamaica, Queens, in 1976 as the new pastor, after his tenure as chaplain at Boston College. "The 31-year-old Flake answered what he felt was the call of God. 'I felt that it was time to take my skills in marketing, sales, social work, and education, and utilize them within the church,' Flake recalled."[3] In his 32-year pastorate, Allen AME Cathedral has become one of the most powerful models of local church community development in the nation. Building on the fundamentals of solid preaching, weekly Bible study and prayer, and a commitment to evangelism, Allen AME Cathedral has reached out into the community in dozens of ways, transforming the community. Recognizing in 1976 that the community of Jamaica, Queens, was in decline, Rev. Flake set out to implement change.

His leadership over the past 32 years has included the establishment of senior housing for more than 600 elderly. When I asked one of the church leaders what percentage of the seniors attended Allen AME Cathedral, I was told about 10 percent. He quickly added that because of the senior housing and other initiatives, the reputation in the neighborhood was so strong, that the church grew from 1,000 in 1976 to its current population of 20,000.

The annual budget for Allen AME Cathedral and its corporate operations is $34 million, which includes the following enterprises:

- 750-student private preschool and grade school
- Real estate projects, including hundreds of new homes
- Charter bus service
- Incubating locally owned businesses
- More than 800 people on staff since 1999, making it the third largest private sector in Queens[4]

Rev. Flake served as a congressman for 11 years, actively serving as a member of the Banking and Finance Committee, and the Small Business Committee. He established a reputation for drafting innovative, bipartisan legislation to assist urban communities. He won two regional facilities for Queens: the Federal Drug Administration and the Federal Aviation Administration, which generated more than 2,000 jobs while also upgrading the stability and the aesthetics of the district. Rev. Flake and Greater Allen AME Cathedral of New York have been featured on CNN, CBS, BET, PBS, and in *Time* magazine.[5]

Rev. Flake is not only an innovator in faith and economic development. In December 2000, he was considered the front-runner for the position of secretary of education under the incoming administration of President George W. Bush. Though he declined the position, he still retained his title at that time as president of Edison School, which was operating 113 schools nationwide through local boards of education. A $250 million company, Edison is the largest publicly traded education company in the world. According to Rev. Flake, education and the presence of places like York College provide the stability needed for southeast Queens to grow.[6]

As an undergraduate, Floyd Flake arrived at Wilberforce University in 1961, from Houston, Texas. Rev. Flake has now taken on the presidency of his undergraduate alma mater, the flagship school of the AME denomination. In his first 2 years, Rev. Flake reduced the university's debt from $5.5 million to $300,000.[7]

In another expression of commitment to young people, Floyd Flake and his wife, Rev. Elaine Flake, established Shekinah Youth Chapel (now known as Shekinah Youth Church) in 1992. Shekinah has a youth congregation of more than 1,200 and is led by Minister Din E. Tolbert, a graduate of Cornell University. The scope of offerings of Shekinah includes Youth Ambassadors—young persons trained to exhort, teach, and peer mediate; Thank God It's Friday services and activities; Bible study fellowship; afterschool program; celibacy ministry; and college preparation.[8]

Friends in Ministry

Though they come from different traditions and different programmatic expressions, Roderick Caesar and Floyd Flake have worked closely together for 30 years. While it would be quite reasonable for both of them, with their demanding national and global assignments, to do little together, they have been making time to work together for three decades.

An initial point of collaboration took place in 1976 during Campus Crusade's I Found It campaign. In this mass outreach, churches used different types of surveys, billboards, and training resources to reach out with the gospel. As lead churches in southeast Queens, Bethel and Allen worked together for training and follow-up.

In addition, both churches have collaborated closely with InterVarsity. When I arrived in New York City in 1984, as a staff worker with InterVarsity, we held our student discipleship conference every fall at the newly opened Allen Senior Citizens' Housing Complex. As the training event grew every year, we were moved into the Allen Christian School. Joining the Sunday worship service with students from Asian, Hispanic, African American, and Anglo backgrounds was a glorious experience. Bethel Gospel Tabernacle has hosted missions training, as well as a summer internship program.

Through the years, Caesar and Flake have spoken at each other's retreats and conferences. Bethel has even had some of its best leaders become staff members at Allen AME Cathedral. Currently Rev. Roslyn Gross Hall, a former Bethel member, is giving leadership to the Allen AME Cathedral music ministry. Their reciprocity in ministry is a shining example in a too-often territorial church community.

Two years in a row Allen AME Cathedral hosted the nationally broadcast concert of prayer on the National Day of Prayer. It was thrilling to see leaders like Bill Bright come to New York and attend a reception hosted by Bethel Gospel Tabernacle. That same evening, Dr. Bright was part of the platform at Allen AME Cathedral as thousands of churches across the country got to witness the unique unity of urban churches from incredibly diverse churches meeting and praying together.

A Commitment to Leadership

Both Rev. Caesar and Rev. Flake have a strong commitment to developing leadership for the next generation. Not only has Flake spoken at numerous events around the country, he also has established an annual training event at Allen AME Cathedral to educate and motivate grassroots leaders to pursue the principles he has developed in 31 years. Rev. Flake was one of the eight speakers at the Willow Creek Association Leadership Summit in 2007, with more than 50,000 participants in North America and nearly 100,000 participants globally.

Rev. Roderick Caesar Jr. is also a sought-after speaker for denominational gatherings of pastors and conferences across the nation. He recently gave leadership during the national gathering in New York on the 150th anniversary of the Fulton Street Revival at the Christian Cultural Center. He also shared the platform with Billy Graham and others in Graham's final crusade in New York, which took place at Flushing Meadows Corona Park in Queens in 2005.

Leadership Reflection Questions

1. Can you identify one or two leaders in your city or community who have demonstrated a desire to bring other churches or ministries together?

2. What is a common community need that faith leaders could rally around (needs of the public school, safety, at-risk youth, needs of seniors)?

3. Would you consider asking respected leaders to initiate a conversation about how the faith community is working together or could work together?

Chapter 7

Back to the Future: Ocean Grove Camp Meeting Association

"Will you not revive us again, that your people may rejoice in you?"

PSALM 85:6

Prominent US pollster Scott Rasmussen was living in North Carolina in 2001, but he had spent his summers growing up in Ocean Grove, New Jersey. In an interview with Scott, he described his start with Ocean Grove in this way: "Since the time I was one month old in 1956, I had experienced a unique Acts 2 community with extra sets of grandparents, sang my first solo in Thornley Chapel, and learned the Bible as a young man. I made a faith commitment at Ocean Grove as a teenager in the 1970s. God had a plan for me that began at least 100 years before with the creation of the place known as Ocean Grove Camp Meeting Association."

91

In 1869, William Osborn searched by the sea to find a place to worship Christ. Two years later, he traveled to New York for the express purpose of discussing a bold new plan of action with fellow Methodist pastor, John S. Inskip. Osborn walked into Inskip's study and firmly declared, "I feel that God would have us hold a holiness camp meeting!"

The idea became a reality four months later as Methodist holiness advocates held the first specifically holiness camp meeting in Vineland, New Jersey. Immediately following this encampment, the leaders formed the National Camp Meeting Association for the Promotion of Holiness. Osborn originally came to Cape May and concluded that he had found the destination for which he had been searching. Deciding to stay the night there, he was nearly "eaten alive" by mosquitoes. In great discomfort, he continued his search and came to Ocean Grove—the only place in the entire region without a mosquito population!

The first formal spiritual meeting in Ocean Grove was July 31, 1869—a holiness camp meeting. The Ocean Grove Camp Meeting Association of the Methodist Episcopal Church was founded at Christmastime in 1869. In the original charter, as granted by the state of New Jersey on March 3, 1870, Ocean Grove was set aside as a place of perpetual worship of Jesus Christ. This charter is unique for any US community.

The group elected Ellwood H. Stokes as the association's first president. With his leadership, Ocean Grove grew until it became what Delbert Rose has called the Mecca of Methodism, or as others would have put it, Ocean Grove was God's Square Mile.[1]

Historical Context of Ocean Grove

Ocean Grove was established 12 years after the Fulton Street Revival, which held its first prayer meeting September 23, 1857, just 50 miles to the north in Manhattan. Before the Civil War, the majority of the Protestants in America were either Baptist or Methodist, with one-third being Methodist.[2] After the Emancipation Proclamation, more African Americans became Christians in the 1865–1900 period than any other ethnic group in the history of North America.[3] This was largely the result of Baptist and Methodist missionaries teaching freed slaves how to read.

During this turbulent time in US history, the church was at the forefront of great spiritual and social change. From 1857 to 1859, on the wave of the Fulton Street Revival, Protestant denominations grew by 474,000 people.[4] In New York City there were 10,000 conversions weekly for a season, and a million conversions in an 18-month period.[5]

Welcoming the burgeoning number of believers, Ocean Grove saw itself as a place for spiritual, emotional, and physical restoration. It is strategically located on breathtaking beachfront property. The association's commitment to important social issues such as women's rights, suffrage, temperance, and civil rights also expressed the association's concern for wholeness. Ocean Grove was part of the Wesley brothers' legacy in their application of practical holiness, and was a destination for national leaders in the spiritual realm and also in the political. Several US presidents have come to Ocean Grove, including Ulysses S. Grant, Teddy Roosevelt, William McKinley, and Richard Nixon. Billy Graham and other world-renowned evangelists have preached in the Great Auditorium.

Worship is an important theme woven throughout the association's 140-year history. Hymn writers Fanny Crosby and Thomas Chisholm penned their famous hymns at Ocean Grove. The practice of Sunday worship was so important that blue laws up until 1980 allowed no cars to be visible inside the town from Saturday midnight until Sunday midnight. The town was also alcohol free. Beaches remained closed until after 12:30 P.M. on Sundays.[6] These last two items remain in effect today!

Committed to both holiness and wholeness, in the 6,000-seat Great Auditorium in Ocean Grove, built on the 25th anniversary of the association, the stage is flanked by electric signs that read *Holiness to the Lord, So Be Ye Holy*.

Ocean Grove Today

Scott Rasmussen today appears regularly on major television networks, especially during national elections. Despite his demanding work and family life, he felt a tug to return to Ocean Grove not just for the summer, but as a resident. One day he heard a message from Charles Stanley entitled "Success God's Way." Stanley described a man who had an irrational love for a place. His question was, "Why do you think God gave that to you?" Scott Rasmussen completely identified with the man in the story, as it described how Scott felt about Ocean Grove. He and his wife, Laura, moved to Ocean Grove later that year.

In 2006, Scott Rasmussen was elected president of the board of trustees for the Ocean Grove Camp Meeting Association. His vision is to see an organizational renewal at Ocean Grove that will contribute to a larger cultural renewal in the region and nation. Ocean Grove is located equidistant between New York City and Philadelphia. One out of every six Americans is within a day's drive of the association, and the current network of churches in contact with Ocean Grove numbers more than 1,000.

Scott Rasmussen views Ocean Grove as a place to hear from leaders and experience programs that will help people encounter Christian love. Between Memorial Day and Labor Day, the camp meeting hosts some of the most prominent national speakers and musicians, and the annual choir festival attracts thousands of people and hundreds of churches. The cultural program of Ocean Grove also includes weekly organ concerts, a summer band, and Saturday night concerts in the Great Auditorium. Every Saturday, nationally known artists—from Garrison Keillor to Ronan Tynan—hold all the summer concerts.[7]

Fresh Leadership

Scott Hoffman and his wife, Nancy, joined Rasmussen and the other leaders of the Ocean Grove Camp Meeting Association in 2006 and 2007, after relinquishing a fashion accessory business. They lived in Chester, New Jersey, and began attending Ocean Grove more than 20 years ago.

Attending a session in the Great Auditorium in 1989, Scott Hoffman listened to a message from Dan Betzer. In the middle of his message, Betzer stopped and said he had been prompted to say that someone in the audience was being called to full-time ministry. Scott knew immediately it was him. He was advised to run away from the calling, but after 2 years of running, Scott surrendered to that call. He accepted the unusual call in 1992 to pastor the church he had been attending, First Congregational Church in Chester. The church was 252 years old and had not changed its worship style in 50 years. The average age of the congregation was over 60, and the 280 members from 1979 had dwindled down to 30 members when Scott Hoffman assumed the pastorate in 1992.

Hoffman used his leadership skills to grow the church from 30 to 250 before he left in 2007 to work full time for Ocean Grove as chief administrative officer. Nancy Hoffman joined the Ocean Grove staff as well, giving oversight to operations and administration. Scott and Nancy Hoffman bring an important set of skills and experience, and alongside Scott Rasmussen, they bring fresh growth to the Ocean Grove Camp Meeting Association. Scott Hoffman has seen his new assignment as an opportunity to use his gifts to help churches work together.[8] With a renewed vision to embrace Ocean Grove's heritage as a place set aside for spiritual birth, growth, and renewal, he also comes alongside local churches to help them accomplish what they could not do alone. The long-term vision also includes the purchase of property to expand the housing capacity for the association's program offerings.

A Vision for Leadership Development

As Scott Rasmussen and Scott Hoffman look to the future, they envision an Ocean Grove Discipleship Center to provide a combination of summer opportunities as well as year-round training resources to include the following elements:

1. A Full Menu of Summer Offerings
In August 2007, Ocean Grove hosted the Willow Creek Leadership Summit for the first time. This event serves hundreds of leaders in the south Jersey and metro Philadelphia area. Speakers included Bill Hybels, Colin Powell, and Marcus Buckingham. Plans include accredited courses with Nyack College and Alliance Theological Seminary and Somerset Christian College; Crown Financial Training; and Community Cable Network satellite programming will also be available.

2. Pastoral Resources
Ocean Grove provides Professional Life Coaching for pastors who want to have an on-site experience, including one-on-one coaching. Also, sabbatical opportunities exist by the ocean for pastors needing directed time with the Lord. Ocean Grove also provides in-house retreats for church and organizational staff who want to have midweek experiences on-site.

3. Youth Worker University Concept
Ocean Grove has an outstanding youth program. Under the leadership of David Burke, Ocean Grove will partner with such entities as *Group* magazine, *Children's Ministry* magazine, Teen Mania, and Youth Specialties to host training and outreach experiences. Several institutions will host satellite programs at Ocean Grove including undergraduate and graduate programs.

4. The New York City Leadership Center

Fully developed, the partnership between Ocean Grove and the NYCLC is designed to provide off-site training resources for churches, agencies, and marketplace leaders throughout Greater New York. With only a handful of retreat resources available to the more than 10,000 churches in the metro NYC area, Ocean Grove provides an incredibly important resource for churches and leaders.

The NYCLC will incubate training programs and initiatives that will require volunteer mentor development. Ocean Grove provides the perfect setting for potentially hundreds of leaders to train in an environment conducive to spiritual reflection.

Why the Ocean Grove Camp Meeting Association Is So Important

Pastors today face perhaps the greatest challenges in the recent history of the church, as explained by *Pastor to Pastor, Focus on the Family, Ministry Today,* and *Charisma* magazines:

- More than 60 percent of pastors polled say that they have no one to talk to when it comes to the challenges they're facing in ministry.
- More than 55,000 of the 365,000 pastors in the US are in transition every year, moving from one ministry to the next.
- Half of all ministry leaders are so discouraged that they say they would leave the ministry if they had another source of income.
- More than 85 percent of pastors' wives wish their spouse would choose another profession.
- Seventy percent of pastors polled constantly fight depression.
- For those pastors that finished well, 50 to 60 percent said that they had a mentor or coach.

The need for innovative and dynamic leadership in Greater New York is staggering. Ocean Grove provides an incredible resource for leaders to seek personal renewal and to access much needed training.[9]

Leadership Reflection Questions

1. In this story, how did you see God prompt the leaders of Ocean Grove, both in its beginning and in the present, to take decisive action?

2. How do you see God renewing His purposes in this story over a 140-year period?

3. What is your vision for creating a place of rest and renewal for your own benefit away from the routines of your own life?

PART II:
JESUS AND THE CHILDREN

Chapter 8

20/20 VISION FOR THIS GENERATION

"Jesus said, 'Let the little children come to me.'"

MATTHEW 19:14

The Journey of Two Leaders

Gary Frost grew up in Youngstown, Ohio, during the 1960s and 1970s. His father's community leadership as director of the McGuffey Community Center helped to mold Gary's life. For almost 20 years, Gary's father, a role model in the ethnically mixed neighborhood, was like a "community dad" to scores of young men.

He brought discipline and purpose into their lives. The 24 Eagle Scouts who emerged from the center show part of Gary's dad's legacy. Mr. Frost helped to organize athletic teams that built a sense of community. Many young African American men became doctors and lawyers through the power of a mentoring relationship. His legacy also lives on in his son Gary. Gary's brother Neal was one of those young men who became a doctor, with a specialty in obstetrics and gynecology.

After they married in 1976, Gary and his wife, Lynette, became foster parents for a 17-year-old girl. She became the first of more than 40 foster children the Frosts would gather under their roof. His burden for the fatherless compelled Gary to make six journeys to Africa, including stops in South Africa, Kenya, Rwanda, and Uganda. In Africa, nearly 6,000 children are orphaned daily by the HIV pandemic.

I traveled with Lynette on her first trip to East Africa with World Vision in 2003. I saw her envelop in her arms Robert, a young Ugandan who had headed his household since he was 11 years old; her compassion for youth was obvious. While traveling together, Lynette told me of a memorable conversation she had 8 years prior with Gary.

They had been foster parents for several years and she asked her husband if that season of their life was over. Gary told her that God had a special gift for them and his name would be Benjamin. Lynette was incredulous, as children had always arrived already named by their parents. Shortly thereafter, Lynette got a call from the hospital about a newborn child available for adoption. The child was yet to be named. Lynette called Gary to see if he might be interested, and Gary said without hesitation—bring him home; his name is Benjamin.

Gary Frost had pastored in Youngstown, Ohio, for 18 years when he took a position as a vice-president with the North American Mission Board outside Atlanta, Georgia. He moved to New York City in 2004 to serve as the executive director of the Metropolitan New York Baptist Association, a fellowship of more than 200 Southern Baptist churches.

Gary Frost also has an impact on youth and adults by taking teams of churches to connect with the inmate population at Riker's Island Correctional Facility in Queens. The vision is to build a bridge between churches and prisoners' children that they might fulfill their God-given potential. The desire is to pilot this effort with 250 mentors.

Gary transitioned into a new role with the New York City Leadership Center in fall 2007. As director of the Emerging Leadership initiative, his assignment is to link like-minded leaders, churches, and agencies that share a common passion to see children excel.[1]

One of those leaders is Jeremy Del Rio. Jeremy's father and mother provided him with a life-transforming example of ministry leadership. The Del Rio family had moved into the

Lower East Side in Manhattan to live among the gang members and the poor. Rev. Rick Del Rio also was one of the first to arrive at ground zero on 9/11—on his motorcycle. As one of the first pastors on-site, he joined others climbing through the rubble looking for survivors. For days he lived on two or three hours of sleep, returning to the rubble to pray and search.[2]

Jeremy became a campus leader at New York University, boasting a student body of 50,000. He formed the Christian Inter-Fellowship Council, which consisted of nine campus groups, also serving on his father's church staff leading the youth. He eventually formed Generation Xcel, a youth center in housing projects on the Lower East Side.[3]

In 2003, Jeremy facilitated a national discussion on the topic of urban youth during the National Leadership Forum: The Gospel in the City. The leaders that emerged from the forum founded the Coalition of Urban Youth Workers with Jeremy as its initial chairperson. In 2005, Jeremy and Dimas Salaberrios, a ministry colleague in New York City, led the youth coalition for the Billy Graham Crusade in Flushing Meadows Corona Park.

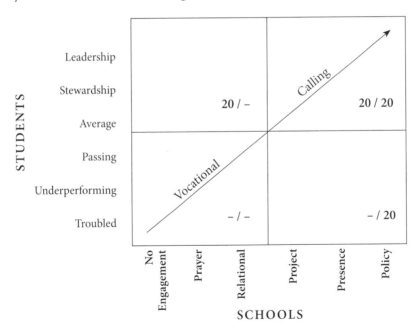

*The methodology of 20/20 is to change churches' perspectives on both students and schools from an adversarial one entrenched over decades of hostility and mutual mistrust to one of partnership and service.

The horizontal axis on the adoption matrix represents the congregation's engagement with a school.

The 20/20 churches make a commitment not only to the schools but also to nurturing student leaders who can be change agents within and for their own generation. The matrix's vertical axis captures this commitment.

A Paradigm Shift on Reaching Youth

The coalition hosted a breakfast in 2005 in preparation for the Billy Graham Crusade in Manhattan. There were 787 youth workers in attendance. "One of the presenters asked how many of the 787 youth workers in attendance get paid to do youth ministry. . . .The three-dozen mostly para-church hands that went up vividly captured both the state of youth ministry in the city and the picture Jesus painted of a plentiful harvest and too few laborers. Relying on several dozen vocational ministers to reach 2 million youth in the five boroughs and 5 million in metropolitan New York would remain an exercise in futility."[4]

Here is a partial profile of youth in New York City:

- With an enrollment total in the 2002 school year of 1.1 million children, the school system is the largest in the nation. Tony Carnes, of the Values Research Institute, observed, "If it were a city, the student body would be the tenth largest city in the nation with populations larger than Seattle, Boston, and Washington, D.C."[5]
- Nearly 60 percent of public school students still cannot read at grade level and nearly 70 percent still cannot perform basic math, according to the 20/20 Vision Web site.
- In 2000, Hispanics were the largest racial/ethnic group in the public school student population (38 percent), followed by non-Hispanic Blacks (35 percent), non-Hispanic Whites (15 percent), and non-Hispanic Asians (12 percent).
- New York has great disparity between many of the top schools in the nation including Bronx High School of Science and Stuyvesant High School, and local schools like Morris High School in the Bronx, with an entering class of 1,400 and a graduating class of only 24.[6]
- In New York State, 85,000 children have parents in prison, including 12,000 children with mothers in prison according to *New York Amsterdam News* writer David Jones's article, "Saving Children of Prisoners."[7]
- African American Images publisher Dr. Jawanza Kunjufu asserts in his book, *Raising Black Boys*, "In 1980, one of every ten African American males was involved in the penal system. In 2007, one of every three African American males is involved in the penal system. It is projected that in 2020, two of every three African American males will be involved in the penal system."[8]

- New York records on kids' well-being show the following percentages of children lived below the poverty line in 2003: 37 percent of those in the Bronx, 33 percent of those in Brooklyn, and 31 percent of those in Manhattan.[9]

Youth pastor Edwin Pacheco, a leader in the Coalition of Urban Youth Workers, describes the implications of such staggering failure: "If a child cannot read, he cannot complete a job application or engage an information economy (or study Scripture). If she cannot do math, she cannot balance a checkbook or determine why last month's fashions don't have to be replaced (or calculate tithes). Our students are ill equipped to become who God created them to be."[10]

"Pacheco has redefined youth ministry beyond the old paradigms of youth group altar calls and pizza parties both in his home church of Bay Ridge Christian Center and among the bi-vocational youth pastors he networks through Youth Rock. 'Youth ministry is not about ministering to youth. It's about empowering them to minister.'"[11]

Kevin Young, area director for Student Venture, the high school ministry of Campus Crusade, was one of the few "professionals" at the Billy Graham breakfast. He has been one of the architects of 20/20. In order for an outmanned and under-resourced labor force to stand a chance, he reasoned that "reinforcements would have to come from within our congregations. He began calling for churches 'to redefine "youth minister" to include any believer who maintains any meaningful contact with youth, such as parents, mentors, teachers, custodians, health care workers, entrepreneurs who hire teens or market sneakers at them, and especially other students.'"[12]

20/20 Vision

The incoming kindergarten class of 2007 will graduate high school in 2020. Think of the historic impact of the identified 7,100 evangelical and charismatic churches in the five boroughs if they were invited in a simple way to engage the 1,400 public schools in New York City. The same template could be applied in other cities.

Mobilizing congregations for prayer and scalable engagement requires a plan, and for two years, the Coalition of Urban Youth Workers has experimented with a grassroots model for how to adopt a local school. Pacheco describes what has emerged as "a matrix designed to move congregations through seven levels, from no engagement to holistic, 20/20 engagement."

"The strategy of 20/20 is to solicit 10% of the city's 7,100 churches (710) to adopt 50% of its 1,400 schools (700) by 2010 for holistic engagement, service, and advocacy. More short-term, 20/20 is recruiting 10% of that goal, or 71 churches, to officially launch in September 2008."[13]

"Adoption begins by identifying a specific, neighborhood school for intentional and consistent prayer. It continues as congregations overcome generational mistrust by cultivating personal relationships at the school, what Pastor Ray Parascondo of Staten Island calls building a 'resume of trust.'"

"Beyond relationships are meaningful acts of service, where congregations themselves become answers to prayer and offer tangible value to the school. Next is a ministry of presence, where church members meet ongoing needs by volunteering as coaches, lunchroom monitors, or tutors. . . . Finally comes the credibility to speak into policy decisions both at the school and systemic level. A church holistically engaged in this way is a 20/20 church."[14]

Three Models

Paint the Town

A Southern Baptist initiative known as New Hope New York was engaged in the city in 2004. Gary Frost introduced this project to the late Hermes Caraballo, who linked them with Middle School 80 in the Bronx. Five hundred volunteers were recruited to paint 73 classrooms in two months; also sports camps were offered to students in the school. Within a three-year period, the Paint the Town (PTT) initiative assisted 35 public schools. More than 5,000 volunteers from outside New York City have come to the city to paint 1 million square feet of public school property. Gary Frost believes that PTT has become a doorway into the soul of the city.[15]

The fruit of this effort is seen on Staten Island at Crossroads Church. In two years they participated in the painting of four schools, simultaneously planting a church on Staten Island. The school eventually opened its arms to allow Pastor Ray Parascondo to hold services on school property after inviting Pastor Ray to address student assemblies.

Under Gary's leadership, the Metropolitan New York Baptist Association offered total grants of $100,000, divided among congregations to work directly with neighborhood schools. Almost 30 percent of grant recipients were non-Baptist churches, as funds were given without regard to denominational affiliation. The final result was 11 PTT projects in all five boroughs and New Jersey. These projects opened hearts and minds that produced what Walter Sotelo of Manhattan Christian Church called "crazy glue" connections between schools and their sponsoring churches. Jannie Wolff of Abounding Grace Ministries described how the influx of volunteers prompted onlookers to ask who they were and why they kept coming. As word spread, individuals approached them, looking for prayer. Pastor Ed Perry of Bethlehem Church described how PTT helped restore confidence in the faith community.[16]

Abounding Grace Church and School Adoption

In July 1996, 13 youths from Abounding Grace Ministries (AGM) established Generation Xcel as a neighborhood youth center. Despite drawing 75 to 80 percent of its students from the public elementary and middle schools across the street, Xcel's attempts to formalize a relationship with the school "pretty much failed beyond the fact that we shared so many students and prayed consistently for the school," says Xcel cofounder Jeremy Del Rio."[17]

Then, in 2006, Jonathan Del Rio and former Xcel program director Dorothy Rivera joined the middle school's faculty as math teacher and dean. Jonathan, the youth pastor at AGM, had applied for a teaching fellowship specifically with the goal of being placed in the school as an extension of his youth ministry. Six months later, AGM received a PTT grant, and for the first time had something tangible to offer the school.

All summer, PTT volunteers helped beautify the building's interior. Then in July, six artists immortalized everything that Xcel represents in the school's playground on four walls and six column surfaces—ten paintings in all. Collectively, the murals communicate the mission, values, and opportunities that Xcel empowers kids to realize.

AGM's adopt-a-school experiment came full circle, when Middle School 34 invited Xcel to present the meaning behind the murals at the first middle school assembly ever conducted by an outside group. Four of the artists and two former students shared about the power of creativity in pursuing one's dreams—a message inspired by "in the beginning" when "God created."[18]

Amachi

Wilson Goode, the executive director of Amachi and former mayor of Philadelphia, tells a poignant story. He introduced a grandfather, a father, and a grandson to each other for the first time in prison. His research has indicated that, without some form of intervention, 70 percent of all children of prisoners will end up in prison. Amachi is a faith-based initiative which seeks to find mentors from local churches who will mentor one child with an imprisoned parent for one hour for one year. Amachi seeks to link people of faith with children of promise in a weekly one-hour mentoring relationship. Nationally, 100,000 mentors have been recruited to connect with children across the nation, according to Goode.[19]

Leadership Reflection Questions

1. Can you identify the public schools within your ZIP Code and their population?

2. Are there any coordinated efforts among local churches to reach children in the public school through any outreach efforts?

3. Could you start by drafting a prayer guide for one school in your community?

4. Is there a public service opportunity that would serve your local school?

Chapter 9

CHILDREN IN THE CROSSROADS

"Whoever welcomes one of these little children in my name welcomes me."
MARK 9:37

Aimee Cortese was standing in the kitchen of a family friend in California in 1982 when she was confronted with the voice of the Lord. This is how Aimee relayed the incident to me:

> "'Aimee, it is time to go back to the Bronx.' I had been away from pastoral ministry from some time now. It seemed like corrections and evangelism would be my role the rest of the way through. But God said it again . . . 'Aimee, back to the Bronx.' I said, 'Lord, how about sunny Florida, Puerto Rico, even California?' And, right there in Pastor Sam's kitchen, God said it a third time. 'Aimee! . . .' and I said, 'Yes, Lord.'"[1]

Aimee Cortese was the first female prison chaplain at Sing Sing Correctional Facility, a maximum security prison in Ossining, New York, located approximately 30 miles north of New York City—the Corteses made their home in nearby Spring Valley. She served at the prison for ten years, 1973–83—an intense classroom setting for Aimee where she met people who had been imprisoned for drug addiction and murder. A burden developed, deep within her soul, for people who need to know the powerful forgiveness of God. Aimee was serving the prison population during the very troubled decade of the 1970s in the Bronx, a time when 300,000 people fled and more than 40 percent of the Bronx burned to the ground.

In an original play written by her son, Joseph Cortese, *Rooftop*, performed at Crossroads Tabernacle, actors enacted stories depicting typical Bronx residents in the 1970s. One story showed a single mom who went to prison after throwing her baby down an apartment garbage chute in order to keep her drug-dealing boyfriend from leaving her. Aimee Cortese met and led people like that to faith in Christ.

While living in Spring Valley, Aimee and her husband, Joe, would take their four children on the four-hour round-trip commute to Brooklyn Tabernacle three times a week. The prayer life of the church and the pastoral leadership of Jim and Carol Cymbala significantly marked the whole family. All four musically talented children were involved with the church. The three sisters formed a singing trio and the son became a drummer. Joseph Cortese began drumming at Brooklyn Tabernacle at age eight. The model of music and prayer would later deeply shape the life of the new church.

Preparations for a Church Planter

Before her decade as a prison chaplain, Aimee Cortese distinguished herself as both an evangelist and a children's worker. Puerto Rican by ancestry, she had married into the Italian Cortese family. Aimee was the pastoral associate of her father, Rafael Garcia, of the Spanish Eastern District, for 16 years. An extraordinary preacher, Aimee Cortese was the keynote speaker at the 1977 Assemblies of God English convention—and the first woman to speak at that convention.

Aimee developed a strong Vacation Bible School (VBS) in the 1950s and 1960s, building the VBS to 1,000 children in Thessalonica Christian Church in the Bronx. She also traveled throughout Latin America as a Billy Graham delegate.[2] Aimee's three passions of evangelism, children's ministry, and compassionate concern for at-risk youth formed the foundation of the new church, Crossroads Tabernacle, established in 1982.

Now that the decision had been made to start the church, a location was needed. Aimee had been told of a storefront church just under the apartment of a friend, Monin Santiago, in the Castle Hill section of the Bronx. After a quick phone call, a lease was negotiated. The owners of the building had never wanted this particular building to be anything but a church. The owners believed in that little house of prayer; there was a remnant there.

The new church eventually moved to 1246 Castle Hill Avenue. The church was located at the crisscrossing of several highways: Cross Bronx Expressway, Bruckner Expressway, and Hutchinson River Parkway. It was aptly named Crossroads Tabernacle, reflecting the influence of Brooklyn Tabernacle. Aimee Cortese reflected on the significance of this storefront church: "How precious is our God; I started my walk with Him in a little storefront church at age 12. I've come full circle around and back to my beginnings: a little storefront church."[3]

Reaching Out

Aimee Cortese's heartbeat is evangelism. The church's first outreach on the streets of the Castle Hill projects had a special emphasis on children. Joined by the Brooklyn Tabernacle choir and by Soul Liberation, a popular choir from Texas, the church gave a standing-room-only concert. The church grew quickly. Leadership in the church included Luis Rivera; and Adolfo Carrion Jr., who later became Bronx Borough president, was an active choir member. The church continued to grow and needed to find new places of worship. By 1996, the church had grown to 800 people.

The current place of worship on Castle Hill Avenue, purchased for $1 million, is the former RKO theater used by the Three Stooges during their New York City stage career. The church is located just off of the number 6 subway line and the number 22 bus to Castle Hill. The purchase and renovation into its current 1,000-seat structure is a miracle. Having received a purchase price way below market value, the largely Puerto Rican and African American church was able to build the space into some of the most attractive church space in the city. The current facility also has a state-of-the-art recording studio, described in a *Bronx Times* article as one of the "largest and most sophisticated theatres and recording studios in the borough."[4]

Leadership Transition

Joseph Cortese graduated from high school and traveled to California for training as a percussionist. He had a promising future in music in the mid-1980s and was traveling around the world with popular singer Roberta Flack. In 1987, at the age of 20, Flack told Joseph she would not need him for her performance on the *Tonight Show*. She had decided to use older musicians. Joseph had been wrestling with his future. He interpreted that experience as a sign to return to Crossroads Tabernacle to assist his mom in the fledgling church. Joseph Cortese completely dropped music for the next five years. His first assignment was to serve his mom and the church in the area of maintenance.

As the church grew, Joseph Cortese became head of the Youth Department in 1989, expanding the already strong outreach to children and teens. Aimee was passionate about preventing youth from falling into a life of drugs, violence, and incarceration. For six years Joseph helped shape the outreach of the church, which also included recovery groups for those with addictions.[5]

Joseph Cortese led the Music Department and served as choir director from 1995 to 1998. His music and artistry launched the Upper Room Music Company, whose assignment was to write and compose original Christian music. The group has since produced four highly acclaimed CDs. In 1997 The Storytellas was formed as a collaboration between six Christian hip-hop artists who participate in street-corner outreach throughout the New York City area. The purpose of the ministry is to evangelize and reach inner-city youth and adults who are not drawn to conventional church outreach efforts.[6]

On a Sunday night in 1998, Joseph Cortese was surprised to see a number of older Anglo men in the audience. As it turned out, they had arrived as part of his ordination from their oversight group, Fountainhead Ministries. Joseph Cortese, now Rev. Joseph Cortese, transitioned into the senior pastor role to succeed his mom, Aimee Cortese.

A Decade of Collaborative Leadership: Prayer, Mission, Children, Arts, and Leadership Development

Prayer

The past ten years have seen the continued growth of the church as well as its influence throughout the Bronx and surrounding region. Currently, 1,000 people worship at Crossroads in the two Sunday morning services. Under Pastor Joseph's infectious leadership and desire to learn, the church has become an increasingly important voice.

Part of the legacy of Brooklyn Tabernacle has been its strong prayer emphasis. Cross-roads has a dynamic Tuesday night prayer meeting attended by several hundred members. The men gather to pray every Saturday morning. There is time set aside for midday prayer daily. Regionally, Crossroads has hosted several boroughwide National Day of Prayer observances in partnership with the Urban Youth Alliance. The vision for and commitment to regular sustained prayer cannot be overlooked when considering the more than 25-year impact of the church.

Rev. Joseph Cortese recently joined Concerts of Prayer Greater New York (COPGNY) as a board member. His participation in the worship team for major COPGNY events, such as the Pastors' Prayer Summit and Fulton Street anniversary has made a rhythmic contribution! Crossroads also mobilizes its people to participate in the annual Pray New York! effort throughout New York City.

Mission

The mission of Crossroads Tabernacle is to be a united and caring community of believers, living in authentic relationships, having an impact on the Bronx and beyond through Christlikeness. The church supports 30 missionaries throughout the world and also supports an Assemblies of God missions project that includes a dozen missionaries. The vision of the church is to strengthen its Bronx expression, particularly in the realm of HIV/AIDS, under the leadership of Rosa Caraballo. The leadership of the church has learned much globally about HIV/AIDS in the past few years through its World Vision involvement.

Children

Crossroads maintains a strong Sunday School program as well as midweek offerings for children. Annually, more than 200 children attend the Vacation Bible School. Through 1996, the church also hosted 150 children each year for Sleep-Away Camp in the Pennsylvania mountains. Most of the children attended for free. Melissa Cortese, Joseph's wife, joined the church staff and has given oversight to this outreach after a career in medicine.

In 2005 and 2007, Joseph and Melissa traveled to Rwanda, East Africa, as part of World Vision trips. In response to the needs of more than 1.3 million orphans in that country, Crossroads' members sponsored 200 children on a Hope Sunday—one Sunday set aside to promote and recruit child sponsors. In 2006, Crossroads pioneered a Hope Campaign by mobilizing 100 volunteers to talk to their friends about child sponsorship with World Vision. The campaign recruited 400 new sponsors to assist children living in HIV-impacted communities in Rwanda.

Crossroads became a charter member of the Hope Church Alliance, a community of 50 churches in Greater New York committed to working collaboratively together in countries affected by HIV. Crossroads and several other churches have now sponsored more than 3,000 children from Rwanda.

Arts

In January 2005, Aimee and Joseph Cortese saw the fruition of a 22-year-old dream. The Boden Center was launched at Crossroads Tabernacle with a Friday night, January 7, performance—*A Higher Standard*. Aimee had the original vision for an urban performing arts center. The vision was to have a place where young people and adults could come and study the arts.

Aimee was determined that her four children would study music in their home—music was as much a priority as brushing your teeth. Joseph Cortese Sr. is a classical pianist, and the three daughters—Damaris, Deborah, and Joanne—received piano and voice lessons at Carnegie Hall under the tutelage of the late Mary Louis Cooper and Emelia Delterso. Joseph Cortese graduated from Musicians' Institute in Hollywood.

The Boden Center launch was produced by Joseph Cortese and included artists from the Alvin Ailey American Dance Theater. The audience was treated to Tony Award–winning talent. The Boden Center began offering lessons on January 31, 2005, in instrument, including piano, bass, guitar, drums, vibraphone, and woodwinds, and in dance.[7]

Leadership Development

Rev. Joseph Cortese has a deep commitment to leadership development within the congregation. Every quarter, the church hosts a pastor or professor to spend a Saturday morning with the leadership of the church for educational and spiritual development. The church provides a breakfast for the 50 to 60 who gather. This has been an important staple for the church.

In 2005, Crossroads agreed to host the Leadership Summit for the Bronx. More than 1,000 leaders from dozens of churches have participated in the training in the past few years, including

Spanish-speaking leadership in the Bronx. Translation has been offered in partnership with CONLICO, which has recruited members of its own leadership to participate. Given the enormous spiritual and social needs of the Bronx, Crossroads has become a regional center for hosting many of the boroughwide events. The church is trusting God to raise up an army of prayerful, educated, and passionate leaders to lead Bronx churches in the mid-twenty-first century.

Leadership Reflection Questions

1. Can you describe a time when you felt called to do something by God that radically changed your life's direction?

2. Who have been three or four people in your life who have shaped you? How have they done that?

3. If you were to narrow your primary spiritual passion down to one or two emphases, what would they be?

Chapter 10

Building Church, Children, and Community: The Story of Evangel Church

"Now to him who is able to do immeasurably more than all we ask or imagine."

EPHESIANS 3:20

Pastor Bob Johansson loaded up his only possessions into a trailer to return to New York City from Rochester in 1965. Pastor Johansson and his wife, Jan, along with their three small children left a successful pastorate to assume the church his grandfather Rev. Evan Williams had started. The church had dwindled to a very small congregation—and Pastor Williams had been praying for God's man to take up the mantle.

Pastor Johansson is part of a family with a powerful spiritual legacy. God called Evan Williams to become a church planter in 1933. Though Williams had a successful building business, he responded to God's call. He also had a passion for missions. In fact, he eventually died in Haiti while working with an orphanage and building churches.

His father also was a faithful leader and elder of the church. At his father's funeral, Pastor Johansson commented that his father had not missed a single Sunday in his 35 years as the Sunday School superintendent. The legacy his father left behind is lived out in the lives of his extended family.

Pastor Johansson's wife, Jan, is the Evangel Christian School's counselor. His son Brian is now the executive director of the Bowery Mission. His daughter, Carolyn Marko, is principal of Evangel Christian School (pre-K–12th grade). His son Stephen, with a degree in music, leads worship in his church in New Jersey. Pastor Bob Johansson's lifetime passion has been the discipling of young men and women in the principles of prayer, education, and missions.

He was struggling with the challenge of coming to New York City to restart his grandfather's church—especially knowing that his twin brother, Paul, a missionary to Africa, had a great and thriving work in Africa, a Bible school, and a large correspondence school. Pastor Johansson was convinced that it would take 3 to 4 years to get the church moving, and he knew it would require a mighty measure of entrepreneurship. The church did not progress very quickly.

Pastor Johansson remembers standing outside the church and looking across the street at a massive wall of five-story apartment buildings that stretched the entire block. He thought to himself, *This is impossible.* As he stood outside of his small church in 1966, the Lord said to his heart, "If you will be faithful, the walls of Jericho would fall. If you will humble yourself, I will exalt you."[1]

Almost 40 years later, that promise was fulfilled as Pastor Johansson was honored with the 2007 Extraordinary Leadership Award by the Council of Churches of the City of New York. Pastor Johansson, who holds a master's degree from New York University, has also been honored with honorary doctoral degrees by Alliance Theological Seminary and received citywide recognition at the Concerts of Prayer Greater New York gala event in 2003.

Today, Evangel Church in Long Island City, Queens, has grown to nearly 1,000 people and has established the largest Evangelical elementary and high school in New York City with more than 500 students and staff. The church ministers in a context where 45 percent of its members are Hispanic, 15 percent are African American, and 82 nations populate the church, hailing from every major continent on earth. What has happened over the past 42 years to transform this church and this leader from a meager storefront church to a thriving church led by a great spiritual father who has had a tremendous impact on the city?

The Early Years

Whenever Pastor Johansson gets the opportunity to address a group of seminary students, he will always tell them, "You can always negotiate the timeline, but you must never negotiate the vision."[2] In the early days of Evangel Church (formerly Community Gospel Church), the timeline was constantly being negotiated. It wasn't until 1973 that the anticipated growth began to appear—4 years after the church was restarted. The church labored to build a community within the young transient population of Queens. Concurrently, aggressive evangelism took place through street outreach, tract distribution, and "rap" sessions.

In 1973, the church had grown to 150 people and a new building was purchased. Several more years of growth resulted in the building of an educational annex in 1980. A revival among young people, likely an outcome of the Jesus movement that had been sweeping the nation, influenced church growth. The church raised funds to add space. Every time the church had a building campaign it never returned to pre-expansion giving levels but continued to increase its giving.

The Building Years

As the congregation matured, Pastor Johansson began to recognize a disturbing reality. The church-friendly culture of the 1950s and 1960s was disappearing. It was becoming more difficult for parents to only have the option of placing their children in public school. By the 1990s, the hostility toward people of faith became apparent in much of US culture. He also began to realize that the traditional tripod of church, home, and school to nurture a child into adulthood was crumbling. With the rapid increase of single-parent homes and the spiritually unfriendly environment of many public schools, an alternative had to be created.

In the interview in his office, Pastor Johansson concluded, "A local church may have, at best, 3 to 4 hours a week to shape the minds and hearts of its people, especially children. I have a burden to mold young people's minds 30 hours per week."[3] In 1984, a burden to establish an academically competitive and spiritually strong Christian school began to dominate his vision. The school was birthed in September 1985.

Parallel to this discerned need was the need for sufficient, long-term space for both the church and the Christian school. In 1986, the church began to fast and pray every week for the location of a suitable property for their vision. In 1987, the property was found—Public School 4 in Long Island City, a short distance from the East River that separates Manhattan from Queens.

For the next two years, hundreds of volunteers came every Saturday to clean and renovate the school so that it would be presentable for Sunday morning worship as well as usable for the school. During these same two years, for every $2.00 donated, $1.00 was saved. In 1989, the congregation moved in and began worship services. During this period, more than $3 million was saved toward the building of a new sanctuary.

The following year, the church broke ground for the new building, a breathtaking 1,800-seat sanctuary, gymnasium, and office tower (measuring together with the school building 125,000 square feet) between Crescent Street and 27th Street in Long Island City. The architecture and landscaping carefully create important themes often missing from the urban landscape—space, light, community, and greenery. The first service was held in June 1999, 12 years after the congregation had fasted and prayed for the location and expansion of space.

Pastor Johansson continues to be a visionary with a deep love for the city. On the drawing board is a new high school building and an international prayer tower with a glass wall overlooking Manhattan. Churches will be invited to spend the night in prayer, calling upon God for revival.

Today the school and the church building are attached. The school, rapidly expanding in enrollment, offers an academically challenging environment to nurture students 30 hours a week. Through their high school studies, students are eligible to graduate with as many as 20 college credits. The students are also eligible to participate in the National Honor Society. Evangel Christian School prepares students to pass the New York State Board of Regents before graduation. Evangel has recently received authorization to offer I-20 documentation so that foreign students can get a student visa to attend. Pastor Johansson has concluded that many pastors would not have stayed in New York City had it not been for the resource that the school provided for their children.

The church and school were meeting important needs in the community, but a glaring need for training was evident to Pastor Johansson and his twin brother, Pastor Paul Johansson, which led them to plant the New York School of Urban Ministry (NYSUM) in 1984. They developed the vision behind NYSUM: to provide a place for people to live while immersing themselves in urban studies and street ministry. Rev. Paul Johansson left Elim Bible Institute to run NYSUM, and in 1987 Peter DeArruda stepped into the executive director role. From 1984 to 1997, NYSUM's home was a small building that provided housing for its students and some programming space.

As the ministry grew, so did the need for space. In 1997, NYSUM purchased a hospital on the corner of 31st Avenue and 46th Street in Long Island City for $3 million. The hospital required mammoth renovation to meet NYSUM's needs. One month after 9/11, in October 2001, NYSUM also became the landlord for Concerts of Prayer Greater New York.

During its 24 years, NYSUM has hosted and trained 35,000 people to accept the challenge of urban ministry. NYSUM offers a compassionate street outreach, including food distribution and the development of an urban theology, which some have sought to duplicate in their hometowns. The underlying purpose of NYSUM is to expose dedicated Christians to the challenge of New York City and convert them into lifelong servants both in the city and in their hometowns. For many it has been a life-changing experience.

The Evangel Journey by Period

Year	Attendance	Church and School Development	Citywide Involvement
1965	15	Upgrade facilities.	
1970	150	Building relational community	
1976	200	Built 16,000 square feet of new space; had spent six years doing aggressive evangelism.	Participated with Here's Life Inner City in the I Found It campaign. Participated in the citywide leadership of Here's Life Inner City.
1980	300	Moved into new building.	Established NYSUM as a training resource.
1988		Fasting and prayer weekly. Found property and moved into PS 4. Purchased PS 4 and held 4 services. For every $2.00 raised, $1.00 was saved for building expansion.	Launched Concerts of Prayer.
1990	650	Established Evangel Christian School with 150 attendees.	
1995		Broke Ground for new sanctuary and held first service.	Board chair of Concerts of Prayer Greater New York.
2000	800	Established Christian High School with 500 attending K–12.	
2005			Billy Graham Pastoral Chair.

A Citywide Spiritual Father

I first met Pastor Johansson through our involvement with the Here's Life Greater New York Board of Directors. Under the leadership of Ted Gandy and Glen Kleinknecht, Here's Life pioneered the 1976 I Found It campaign, linking churches for greater evangelistic impact. After the campaign, Here's Life also offered time management and leadership courses for pastors.

When we planned our first Concert of Prayer in 1988, Pastor Johansson was involved in helping to lead the event. He has a riveting understanding of Jesus's prayer in John 17, that the world will believe when the church is one. Perhaps more than any other leader I have known in 24 years in New York City, Pastor Johansson has had the commitment to be *present*. There are larger churches in Greater New York, but I know of no leader whose influence is larger and more admired than Pastor Bob Johansson.

Pastor Johansson has shown up at book signings, special church concerts, and anniversaries of leaders all throughout Greater New York. On occasion he is the speaker, but the majority of the time he is not. He is especially intentional when it comes to affirming leaders of different cultures. He states, "In order for the church to be united, I will go the extra mile to affirm leaders of different cultures."[4]

Part of his influence is embodied in the values his church models. In the prayer movement, Evangel Church has played a central role. Aida Force, a member of Evangel and the matriarch of the prayer movement, leads the Lord's Watch for Evangel—200 people have been praying monthly for 48 hours, the first Thursday and Friday of every month. Aida has been on staff with Campus Crusade, along with her husband, Greg Force, for more than 30 years.

Rooming with Pastor Johansson at the Pastors' Prayer Summit is a highlight of my year, as we have the opportunity to share our dreams and pray with other leaders. He has been a spiritual father to hundreds of leaders over the years. Despite the demands of his own church and school, he has the paternal instincts of knowing when to simply be *present*. We have also roomed together in Bihar, India, traveling to see the emerging church network in northern India. Though our spiritual traditions are quite different, our common heart for the city and the church has woven an important friendship.

I will never forget when in June 1995, after the New Era Foundation collapsed, it was Pastor Bob Johansson and Rev. John Smucker, another spiritual father, who gathered together to pray with me. My church had just lost $1 million in funding and my two-person organization had lost $90,000. I was discouraged that more had not come out to pray. Pastor Johansson reminded me that Jesus promised that He would be with us when two or three were gathered. Pastor Johansson said, "That puts us on the heavy side."

On November 1, 2007, Pastor Johansson called for a prayer meeting of the Concerts of Prayer Board to intercede over the emerging New York City Leadership Center. We spent the afternoon praying at Rev. Terry's Smith church offices in West Orange, New Jersey. Pastor Johansson's conclusion from that season of prayer was that it paralleled the significance of the nineteenth-century Haystack Prayer Meeting in Massachusetts when several college students met to pray in a rainstorm. In that meeting, as Samuel Mills and the others prayed under that haystack, they committed themselves as career missionaries and changed the face of missions. Pastor Johansson was challenging Concerts of Prayer and the involved churches to renew their commitment to Isaiah 62:6–7—to give God no rest and give ourselves no rest until He accomplishes His purposes in all the earth. The New York City Leadership Center represents a new paradigm for collaboration and mission just as Concerts of Prayer did 20 years ago.

Leadership Reflection Questions

1. When have you had to wait longer than anticipated to see God fulfill His purposes in your life or calling?

2. How might you go the extra mile to strengthen the unity of the church in your city or community? Who should you encourage with your presence?

3. What would the impact be of your staying at your mission for 30 to 40 years?

Chapter 11

Youth Explosion!

"And the Lord added to their number daily those who were being saved."

ACTS 2:47

Christ Tabernacle was planted in 1985 by Michael and Maria Durso. Their unforgettable journey to faith provides an important window into the nature of a God who transcends tragic circumstances for His larger purposes. Christ Tabernacle has emerged in New York City as an invaluable model for engaging the next generation.

"For years, Maria Durso thought that life had played a cruel trick on her. Her mother died when she was just five months pregnant with Maria. No one thought the baby—just two-and-half pounds at birth—would survive." No one even bothered writing a name on the birth certificate—a nurse later named her Maria. As her dad was suicidal, Maria grew up in a boarding school, where she was beaten and sexually abused. Maria was told that the devil lived inside of her because she was left-handed. By the preadolescent age of 11, she was already abusing drugs and alcohol. Maria eventually tried committing suicide by overdosing on heroin—not once, but three times.[1]

"In 1975, Maria was 24 years old and living with Michael Durso, her boyfriend. The couple traveled to a lavish resort in Mexico to kick back and party. One night while Michael went out for a walk, Maria stayed in the hotel room and reflected on her life—she had money, romance, and everything else the world said she needed to be happy, yet she was angry with God. She started to curse His name and shake her fist at Him. 'In the beginning of my tirade, this gentle God spoke my name,' says Maria Durso. 'When He said the name "Maria," oh, it wasn't an audible voice; it was an internal voice. That voice filled up the void. Immediately I felt this great conviction of sin, but at the same time, I felt this great sense of hope and worth.'"[2] After their Mexico trip, they visited a church where Michael also was converted. Maria and Michael were soon married.

For the next 10 years, Michael and Maria Durso took on leadership roles at Brooklyn Tabernacle. Michael Durso's evident leadership potential in his roles at the church caused the leadership to encourage him to plant a new church—in 1985, Christ Tabernacle was born. In little more than 20 years the church grew to 4,000 members and a staff of 60. The church has one of the most well attended weekly prayer meetings in the city, extraordinary youth programs, and a musical choir with multiple recordings. What led to this dramatic growth?

A Dual Crisis

In 1996, 11 years after the successful planting of Christ Tabernacle, Michael Durso was contending with two crises. Though having grown up in the church, his son Adam was far from God. Adam had finished high school and attended a year of college, but seemed aimless. The concept of fasting and praying for youth at the church specifically started when Maria Durso took a very public and passionate decision to fast and pray in direct opposition to Adam's rebellion, drug pushing, and blatant disrespect toward the things of God. An entire prayer band would often put the names of their children on a bull's-eye bulletin board and spend hours fasting and praying. It was because of Maria's position and mantra—"a life for a life"—that members later became full of faith and hope that prayer could change anyone! This subjective experience, combined with the theological truth that prayers of the righteous accomplish much, made for a one-two punch in the Spirit! The prayer band experienced the truth of James 5:16, that the prayer of the righteous is powerful and effective.

The second crisis, related to the first, was the church's inability to involve young people meaningfully. In a church of 500 people there were only 18 youth. This all changed dramatically when Adam Durso experienced a radical surrendering to God in 1996. The truth that had been sown into his life finally took hold of his heart and he completely surrendered to Jesus. While he was vacuuming the church office in August 1996, he proposed an idea to his dad. Adam asked his dad to allow him to hold a one-time youth meeting during Thanksgiving weekend. The meeting would reflect the culture the young people of the neighborhood were familiar with—hip-hop.

Before that meeting occurred, nothing contemporary had ever been tried in the church. Adam Durso and his team of 18 regular youth-group attendees, including 7 leaders, carefully planned the meeting. Pastor Michael Durso joined the young people as they fasted and prayed for the success of that meeting. They promoted the event to their network of friends. To appeal to the youth and their gravitation toward hip-hop, they designed their event to have more of a club feeling. When they opened their doors for this event on the Friday after Thanksgiving of 1996, 1,000 young people attended! At the altar call, 60 young people gave their lives to Christ, more than triple the total number of regular church attendees before the event. Living up to its new name, Youth Explosion was born.

Youth Explosion

The next year, the regular Friday night youth group grew to 60; in two years, attendance averaged 250. Since 1998, the regular attendance of Youth Explosion has ranged from 500 to 700 young people each Friday night. Major events attract as many as 1,200 young people. The rapid growth of Youth Explosion also spurred the growth of the entire church. There were many nonchurched young people converted to Christ, and they were bringing their parents to church with them. The parents, amazed at the personal transformation taking place in the lives of their children, found themselves blessed as well.

A regular experience at the close of Youth Explosion meetings (called Aftershock) is inviting young people to come forward and dedicate their lives to God. Young people serious about committing their lives to God are invited to surrender not only their hearts, but also any possessions that would hinder their spiritual walk with God. A large box is kept at the front of the altar and young people routinely turn in knives, guns, and illicit magazines. The transformation of lives has been not only individual but also community-wide. The local crime rate began to decline as a direct result of the lives of changed young people, and the local police were happily surprised at the impact this one youth group was having on the community.

The leadership of Christ Tabernacle has a vision to change young people not just spiritually, but also psychologically, emotionally, academically, and behaviorally. Pastor Michael Durso takes his youth leaders seriously and fully participates in the major events of Youth Explosion.[3]

Christ Tabernacle

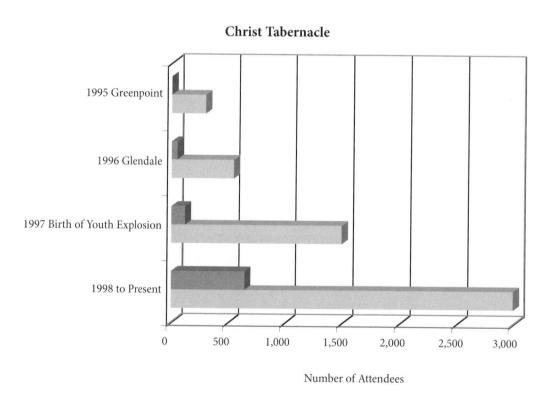

Number of Attendees

Innovation and Growth

The church has experienced two major geographical moves and dramatic growth spurts. When the church relocated in 1996 from Greenpoint, Brooklyn, to its current location in Glendale, Queens, it grew quickly from 250 to 500. Youth Explosion began within a year after this initial move; by January 1997, the church had 1,300 to 1,500 regular attendees. This growth was largely attributable to 65 percent of the young people attending Youth Explosion bringing their parents to church.

A second move took place when the church began a satellite campus in Bushwick, Brooklyn, for ten months. This move allowed the church to expand by adding a Spanish service. The satellite campus eventually returned to the Glendale location, but it evolved into the addition of a Saturday night service. Attendance has jumped again to 3,500 regular worshippers on a weekend.

Starting in 2003, Youth Explosion has hosted an annual outreach in partnership with Great Adventure Amusement Park. Each June, young people are given discounted tickets to attend the theme park—the day ends with a concert and an altar call. The outreach peaked at 35,000 participants, and continues to be an important part of the journey of Christ Tabernacle extending its influence across the region with innovative outreach.

Vision, Influence, and Innovation for the Future

The vision that Christ Tabernacle has for its future includes the preaching of Christ, building up of the saints through the use of their gifts, and a deliberate strategy to reach out to the community. In the past few years Christ Tabernacle has taken on the assignment of reaching out to every Angel Tree child in its ZIP Code by providing them a backpack with supplies for school. Angel Tree is an outreach of Prison Fellowship to children of prisoners. The church has also adopted an entire grade school and provided backpacks with supplies for the 600 children in grades K–6.

The strategy going forward includes the creation of a community development center called the Legacy Center to provide the following:
- Afterschool tutoring
- Crisis intervention with family and financial counseling

- English as a second language
- A gymnasium to provide sports leagues and tournaments
- Educational courses
- Arts and music

The church plans to convert a neighboring four-floor building for the center. The center will provide an independent structure from which the church can pursue funding for the programming of the center. Part of the funding strategy for the Legacy Center is an opportunity to purchase a local gas station. The anticipated revenue stream from the gas station will provide a reliable funding base to staff and implement the diverse programs for the center.

In addition to the creation of the Legacy Center, Christ Tabernacle is planning to establish a food court. This cafeteria will provide a much-needed resource for the thousands of regular attendees on the weekend, while also providing an income stream for the church. As many urban churches are discovering, there needs to be an intelligent marriage between meeting the practical needs of their congregants and the economic realities of a growing church.[4]

The church continues to extend its influence by hosting Queens churches for the Willow Creek Leadership Summit in August. With a leadership team of several hundred and dynamic world-class speakers, the Leadership Summit has become a great asset to hundreds of churches in the region. Christ Tabernacle has formed an important partnership with Willow Creek as they have exchanged learning about youth ministry and congregational leadership development. Bill Hybels spoke at their weekly prayer meeting in April 2007 in an unforgettable event.

The church has a growing desire to connect with other churches around the region. Michael and Adam Durso have joined the Concerts of Prayer Greater New York Board of Directors. Their commitment is to serve regional events as well as their own local ministry. Adam Durso has played an important role in the efforts of Teen Mania to make inroads into the metropolitan area with major outreach events in 2008 and 2009.

Back to the Basics

The heartbeat of the church in the midst of all the growth, opportunity, and change is the corporate prayer and worship life of the church. Every Tuesday night the church is filled with

1,000 praying people. The church is predominantly Latino, with a large number of African Americans and many other nationalities. Many in the church face economic challenges—the sense of dependency on God is an immediate reality when confronted with time stresses, limited resources, and a city that is not always friendly to faith.

What God Has Done in 30 Years

Who could have imagined 30 years ago that a young couple living together would develop a church that would have an impact on thousands of people on a weekly basis? The journey of Michael and Maria Durso, along with Adam Durso and Youth Explosion, is reflected in Paul's prayer in Ephesians 3—God can do immeasurably more than we can ask or imagine. The longing of the church leadership is that from the womb of forgiveness, faith, and vision, hundreds of churches would be established to live out the legacy of Christ Tabernacle and the broader body of Christ.

The legacy of Michael and Maria Durso, and their heart's desire to see youth love and serve Christ, is also demonstrated in the lives of their other two children. Jordan Durso and his wife, Vaness, with their three children, are missionaries in Lima, Peru. Recently they were asked to give leadership as regional director of 700 Club/Operation Blessing Latin America Division. Christopher Durso recently transitioned into the role of youth director, as Adam now serves as executive pastor of Christ Tabernacle. As you can see, this story is about 30 years of successful ministry, but it also speaks to the importance of the next generation . . . and the fruit of their labor could not speak more eloquently!

Leadership Reflection Questions

1. Can you identify an unlikely person in your life through whom God might speak (a family member, neighbor, co-worker)?

2. What can you do to specifically encourage young people in your church or community?

3. What would it look like to grow the discipline of corporate prayer in your life and local church?

Chapter 12

Touching the World from Wyckoff

"Go and make disciples of all nations."
MATTHEW 28:19

Jeff Boucher came to work at Wyckoff Baptist in New Jersey in 1990. He had experienced success from 1985 to 1989 working with young people as a Campus Life staff member, and arrived to work with a youth group of 9. For three months Jeff did everything he could imagine to reach out and grow the group. However, three months passed and the group was still stuck at 9 kids. He found himself praying a prayer of desperation: "God, is this the right fit?" In response to his prayer, God spoke to Jeff's mind, *Take them to a place where they have to trust Me.*[1]

    The next week Jeff announced to the group that they were going on a missions trip to an Indian reservation in Canada. The week after the announcement, 2 new kids showed up asking to go on the trip. In July 1990, 19 kids and 6 adults participated in the trip, raising $13,000 in the process. The trip included three days of training, followed by constructing a building on the reservation. By November 1990, the youth group had grown to 60 attendees.

Wyckoff Baptist Church and Touch the World

Wyckoff Baptist, located in Bergen County, New Jersey—an affluent northern suburb of New Jersey on Route 208 just outside New York City—was struggling in 1992. The church membership leveled off at 180 and church leadership traveled to the Navigators Presidential Conference in Colorado Springs to gain help in deciding whether or not they had the right pastoral leadership. Paul Stanley, vice-president of Navigators and brother to congregational leader Gordon Stanley, challenged the team not to complain, but to pray.

In 1994, after a season of extended congregational prayer and spiritual wrestling, the senior pastor decided it was best to leave. This was the first time in church memory that a pastor had left on good terms. The climate was ripe to do innovative thinking and strategic discussion regarding the future direction of the church.

Fred Provencher arrived at the church in 1996, as copastor with Jeff Boucher. By that time, the church had grown to 240 people. Since the first missions trip with the youth in 1990, the church was riding the crest of the wave of new involvement of young people. The response was so powerful from the missions trip that Touch the World—a unique missions-oriented ministry to youth—was incorporated as a separate 501(c)(3) nonprofit. Church leader Ed Gallenkamp understood that one local church could not contain the vision of a missions movement among young people. The church leadership recognized that people wanted to give to what kids were doing.

Jeff Boucher maintained his dual role on staff with the church and as president of Touch the World for a decade, until 2000. The vision of Touch the World was to turn kids from apathy to energy. Given the middle-class and upper-class context of the area, Touch the World provided an important discipleship vehicle for kids who had it all materially. Participation in the missions trips grew exponentially in the coming years, reaching 1,000 participants in 2007. Touch the World is the most effective youth missions mobilization movement in the northeastern US.

As Touch the World grew rapidly, it also expanded its local outreach. Demonstrating its fluency with youth culture, Touch the World moved innovatively into a coffeehouse outreach, a skate park, and an outdoor activity program. The staffing has continued to grow and departmentalize around all of these initiatives.[2]

Year	Missions Trip Attendees	Ministry Activity
1990	19	
1995	85	
2000	150	Joined by Hi BA.
2001	200 (Started Scotland work.)	Started Holy Grounds Coffee Lounge.
2002		Started Solid Foundation Skatepark.
2004	Sites developing in Uganda, Cuba, and Mexico.	Started Pathfinders Outdoor Recreation Outreach.
2006		Started OFX (sound and light ministry).
2007	300 summer missionaries. 100 youth in Scotland. 1,000 trip attendees year-round	

Concurrent with the growth of Touch the World, Wyckoff Baptist was experiencing growth and innovation as well. The church went through major structural change, transitioning by 1996 into an elder-led congregation. The constitution was rewritten to expand the philosophy of ministry to include small-group leaders called shepherds, and to make them the ones who chose the elders.

The philosophy of mission changed to include the percentage of missions giving as a part of the whole budget, at 20 percent. This created the funding base to build the staffing necessary to serve the growing congregation.

The church experienced a sustained period of growth for more than ten years, due in large part to the growth of the youth group.[3]

Cornerstone Christian Church (formerly Wyckoff Baptist)

Year	Congregational Size	Youth Group Size
1989	180	9
1992	240	
1997	300	100
2000	450	
2002–2003	560	160
2004	670	
2007	1,200	300

During this period of remarkable growth, the church built an additional building and launched multiple services. A distinguishing feature of the new services—young people helped lead the worship. The youth group programming broadened to include specific groups for 6th–7th-graders; 8th–9th-graders; and 10th–12th-graders. Four staff members were assigned to work with this youth population.

The church also changed its name to Cornerstone Christian Church, adopting a more neutral name that fewer people in the North Jersey religious culture would reject, as opposed to being perceived as a traditional Baptist church. The church has never had a denominational affiliation.

After Fred arrived in 1996, the church reworked its vision: "We are reaching families through youth and children." As the church has continued to grow and mature, the vision has been modified: "Our vision is to reach individuals and families by ministering to children and teens. This is fulfilled when a person has become a maturing, worshiping, serving disciple of Jesus in a community of believers."[4]

Both Touch the World and Cornerstone Church have reached a core conviction that young people are a way to renew existing churches as well as birth new opportunities. Their language and purpose is very focused on the potential of young people. By investing in young people and making them the highest missional priority, adults have also experienced significant renewal.

Both Fred Provencher and Jeff Boucher have demonstrated innovative and collaborative leadership. This is incredibly important given the assignment of leading in the North Jersey context, which has been described in the following ways:

• A time-starved culture where a seeker-sensitive approach to ministry is ineffective.

• A small number of evangelicals in a largely Catholic culture.

- A highly educated population affects the way people hear preaching.
- An environment where the spiritual leadership from the 14 churches in Wyckoff is not engaged with the broader community.[5]

A Church Is Planted

In 2004, Jeff Boucher also felt a burden to plant a church for people who did not have a church home. He began in April 2004 with a group of 20, and by November the group had grown to 50. Since then, the church has grown rapidly, approaching 400 regular attendees. The church moved into a new building in 2007. This church, named Powerhouse Christian Church, reflects the conviction that when a person is following Jesus, he or she will experience God's power. The church plant grew out of the opportunity to leverage the summer- and Christmas-break missions experiences into the life of a congregation, for those not already involved in another congregation. The new church also sees training people for prayer as foundational to its mission. Every week, 20 intercessors pray in teams of 2. The church also believes in the power of a deliverance ministry, as modeled in the life of the early church.

In another role that complements his roles at Powerhouse and Touch the World, Jeff Boucher serves as a community chaplain and is called upon to intervene in moments of upheaval among the youth.

Touch the World outreaches such as Holy Grounds Coffee Lounge (a coffeehouse), the Solid Foundation Skatepark, and outdoor sports adventure also provide a relevant way for nonchurchgoing young people and their families to connect with the young church.[6] All three of these models—Touch the World, Cornerstone Church, and Powerhouse Church—teach us that, with a spirit of innovation and leadership development, it is possible to experience historic growth, even in a very difficult context.

The Traits of Effective Leadership

Both Fred Provencher and Jeff Boucher, demonstrating a spirit of collaboration, partnered with other youth group leaders in a 1992–95 Northern New Jersey Youth Alliance, comprised of a core group of 10 leaders and a broader participant group of 15 to 20. This team of career youth workers collaborated on joint programs, which grew to include the 500-person Mega Night outreach. By the late 1990s, they realized that youth were retreating from mass events and longing for more intimate community. This cultural shift coincided with the rise of Touch the World.

Pastor Fred Provencher made his first trip to Africa with World Vision in 2004. On his return, he motivated Cornerstone Christian Church to significantly engage a community in southern Uganda, near the ground zero of the AIDS pandemic. Cornerstone has helped to sponsor more than 200 African children and undertake projects such as the church's involvement in the support of an African national from Uganda, who is employed by the Navigators.

Outreach from the church has extended both nationally and globally. A local ministry partner is Star of Hope Ministries in Paterson. Paterson is one of the five neediest cities in the US. The church has invested resources in Star of Hope programs and provided scholarships for Paterson pastors to participate in Willow Creek Association's annual Leadership Summit.

Cornerstone Christian Church hosted the leadership summit in 2006 and 2007 for churches in North Jersey, building one of the largest sites in the Northeast. Under the leadership of Rob Parker, dozens of churches came together to participate in the training experience. Now Rob Parker is extending the ministry of Cornerstone even further by planting a new, missionally minded church in North Jersey scheduled to start in fall 2008.

Fred Provencher has also served on the board of directors for Concerts of Prayer Greater New York, helping to shape the thinking and direction of the organization as it launches the New York City Leadership Center. Fred Provencher has been working closely with John Stanley Sr. and John Stanley Jr. to design an outreach to businessmen working in downtown Manhattan.

Jeff Boucher has agreed to host the 2008 Willow Creek Leadership Summit, demonstrating his ongoing collaboration and desire to see training provided for the body of Christ in North Jersey. Boucher has also joined the presidential council for the New York City Leadership Center. He has done an effective job of advocating for the center, even as he continues to build the church and missions agency he is a part of. He has a "view of plenty." There are enough resources to go around to accomplish all that God intends to do.

Leadership Reflection Questions

1. Have you ever taken a missions trip to get yourself outside of your comfort zone? If not, when could you do this?

2. Are there young people in your sphere of influence who need to be encouraged to use their gifts in new ways?

3. Are there youth groups and youth ministries that could be encouraged to collaborate together in your region?

PART III:
JESUS EXPANDING HIS CHURCH

Chapter 13

THE CHURCH MULTIPLICATION ALLIANCE: REDEEMER PRESBYTERIAN CHURCH AND CONCERTS OF PRAYER GREATER NEW YORK PARTNERSHIP

"All the Jews and Greeks who lived in the province
of Asia heard the word of the Lord."

ACTS 19:10

In 1999, I had a breakfast meeting in Manhattan with Tim Keller, Dick Kaufmann, and Glen Kleinknecht. Tim Keller had come to New York City in 1987 to do some initial research on planting a church in Manhattan. I remember talking to Keller from our Flushing apartment by phone when he called to introduce himself. This was about the same time we were planning the first concert of prayer with Glen's colleagues at Here's Life, Ted Gandy and Aida Force.

The reason for the breakfast was to share a vision that Tim Keller and Dick Kaufmann had. They envisioned a movement of churches being planted across denominational, economic, and geographical boundaries. They believed that the Concerts of Prayer network was the place to partner such a vision.

Redeemer had grown quickly in the ten years since it had begun. The church began in 1989 with a prayer group of 15 people in an Upper East Side apartment. The first service was held on April 9, 1989. By that, fall a second service was added and attendance was already at 250. The church moved to its worship location at Hunter College by spring 1993. The initial congregation clearly sees the early days of Redeemer as a time of revival as all kinds of diverse people were being added to the church.

By 2000, Redeemer had begun to plant churches in other parts of New York City, and eventually in other global cities. Over the next ten years, Presbyterian Church in America (PCA) churches were planted in Greenwich Village, Rye, Harlem, and Oyster Bay. In New Jersey, churches were started in Teaneck, Hoboken, and Montclair. Beyond the metro area churches were started in Palo Alto, California; Toronto; Budapest; Sao Paulo; and London.[1]

Church Multiplication Alliance Meeting Attendance

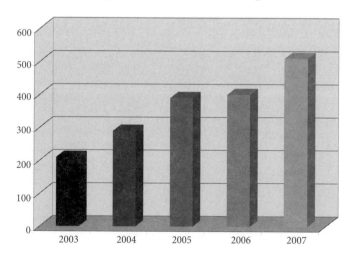

*From 2002–2007, nearly 1,700 have attended church planting meetings, 180 have participated in Church Planter training programs, and nearly 100 new churches have been planted in Greater New York.

Before Redeemer

Terry Gyger, current director of the Redeemer Church Planting Center, was a founding committee member for the PCA. While sitting in a home missions agency meeting for the PCA, it dawned on the leadership that the only way to do multiplication church planting would be through flagship churches. Across the country 75 percent of all PCA resources came from 50 churches. Terry Gyger came every quarter to New York City to help lay the foundation for the church planting center after Dick Kaufmann relocated to plant a church in San Diego. Gyger recruited a Brazilian colleague, Osni Ferreira, to come and lead the center.

The PCA had been effective in suburban church plants but was ill equipped to plant churches in the large cities of the Northeast. Terry Gyger then approached Tim Keller about coming to New York from where he was teaching at Westminster Theological Seminary in Philadelphia.[2]

Manhattan is largely composed of single professionals, and there was at that time few churches to which they could bring their nonbelieving friends. According to Terry Gyger, the secret to Redeemer's rapid growth was Tim Keller's articulation of the gospel to a secular mind-set. Keller had developed an apologetic to secularism.

Another foundational building block for establishing Redeemer Presbyterian Church was a denomination-wide commitment to pray for its success. When Redeemer launched in 1989, there were few healthy and growing churches in Manhattan. The investment to establish a healthy congregation would be substantial.

It is not coincidental that Redeemer's growth paralleled the rapid growth of the New York City prayer movement. Thousands of people and hundreds of churches were praying on a monthly basis for the rapid expansion of the gospel in the region. There seemed to be a convergence of focused spiritual attention on New York, even as God attracted gifted thinkers, leaders, and evangelists to Redeemer.

Redeemer's vision is to spread the gospel, first through its own congregation, and then through the city by word, deed, and community. Redeemer's vision is to bring about personal changes, social healing, and cultural renewal through a movement of churches and ministries that change New York City and, through it, the world.[3]

Redeemer aspires to be a church for the city that seeks the welfare of the city more than its own good. The transcendent aspiration is not to build a great church but to build a great city.

This has expressed itself in a balanced approach to ministry in an outworking of the kingdom through evangelism, social ministry, cultural renewal, corporate worship, and decentralized small groups. Efforts like Hope for New York were started to mobilize volunteers to assist the poor through partner agencies.[4]

Redeemer expanded to a multisite model by 1997. While the Hunter College site remained the larger of the congregations, other sites developed on the west side of Central Park. By 2007, a fifth service was added to accommodate the 5,000 regular attendees.

Currently, 225 small groups meet at Redeemer on a regular basis. This is the primary strategy for Redeemer attendees to experience community. The incredible pace of Manhattan life makes this an important lifeline to the church.

Redeemer's commitment to mercy and justice is expressed through Hope for New York led by Mike O'Neill. Volunteers spend thousands of hours annually to assist agencies and sister communities serving in poorer communities. Hope for New York helps to make that vital link.

Katherine Leary leads the faith and work dimension of Redeemer's outreach. She oversees seven full-time coordinators. Specialized groups lead entrepreneurial efforts to help marketplace leaders integrate their faith and work. Part of the vision for faith and work is to incubate small business ventures.

Demographically the church is 45 percent Asian, with the majority of the rest Anglo. The church is also 70 percent single young adults, though more families have become a part of Redeemer life.

The preaching and worship at Redeemer continue to be its foundation. The church has a carefully articulated commitment to be outward-faced. Redeemer has been extraordinarily effective in providing a safe place for people to come and consider the reasonableness of faith.

The Church Multiplication Alliance

The partnership in building the alliance was rooted in Redeemer's credibility as a rapidly growing church committed to the good of the whole church. The partnership was also rooted in Concerts of Prayer's commitment to knit together as many diverse traditions in the Bible-believing church world as possible. As the alliance began to take shape in the 2000–2004 time period, the alliance committed to identifying, recruiting, training, and funding church planters.

Mark Reynolds came from the Philippines in 2003 to become the associate director of the Redeemer Church Planting Center. Mark has overseen the training of the center for a number of years. He also leads the day-to-day operations of the Church Multiplication Alliance (CMA) on Redeemer's behalf.

Lauren Moy, chief operating officer for Concerts of Prayer (COPGNY), has been the day-to-day liaison for COPGNY for more than five years. She has given primary leadership to coordinate the quarterly meetings, mobilize prayer for planters, maintain communication with the denominations, write and send the enewsletter, and write foundation proposals. Together, the leadership of Redeemer and COPGNY found some initial partners in the foundation community that financially supported the vision. The idea was to provide small seed grants to church planters that would motive other funding sources to help launch these church plants.

The National Leadership Forum that Concerts of Prayer cohosted with Mission America in 2003 was a turning point for the alliance. Tim Keller did three expositions from the Book of Acts for the leaders attending from 50 cities. Keller drew largely from Acts 8 and Acts 16 to address the necessity of contextualizing the gospel. He highlighted six major themes:

- *Knowing the importance of the city*—The early church was both multiethnic and international. The Apostle Paul's strategy was to go to cities of major cultural influence.

- *Knowing the centrality of the gospel*—Understanding that the gospel is neither license nor legalism. We are in desperate need for the Holy Spirit to change us and articulate the gospel in a clear way.

- *Relating Christians to culture*—Christians should live long-term in the city and create a dynamic counterculture in the city.

- *Having a church planting mind-set*—Apostle Paul planted churches everywhere he went. For 200 years, all churches were house churches. New churches are the best way to reach new generations, new residents, and new people groups.

• *Knowing how to contextualize*—The necessity of articulating the gospel in a way that those who hear it can understand it. We need to learn the difference between essential and nonessential.

• *Practicing the fullness of ministry*—The gospel must express itself in word, deed, and community to be heard.[5]

One thousand leaders attended the forum from 50 cities, including more than a dozen denominations. The church planting track motivated new interest on the part of denominations and organizations to join the alliance. In February 2004, we had a follow-up meeting with denominational leaders to map out the structure of the alliance.

Jared and Ann Roth emerged during that time period as national champions for the CMA. Jared Roth had a national vice-presidential role with the Foursquare denomination while Ann was the national church planting coordinator for the denomination. They helped to form the structure around which denominations could join the alliance.

By 2007 numerous denominations and organizations participated in the alliance:
• Assemblies of God
• Baptist General Conference
• Brethren in Christ
• Christian Reformed Church
• Concerts of Prayer Greater New York
• Evangelical Free Church of America
• The Foursquare Church
• Grace Brethren North American Missions
• Missionary Church USA
• Nazarene Church
• The Orchard Group
• Presbyterian Church in America
• Reformed Church in America
• Southern Baptist

These denominational partners have shared best practices, recruited planters, assisted with strategic planning, and mobilized prayer for planters.

The Components of the Alliance

United Prayer

We are very deliberate in promoting a united prayer theme around church planting. Beginning in January each year, we gather nearly 100 pastors and ministry leaders to pray for new church plants. Every quarter an eprayer letter is circulated to our database, asking for specific prayer for church planters, church plants, and communities they reach.

In June we ask the approximately 8,000 participants in Pray New York! to include church planting efforts in their prayers as they walk. We want every ZIP Code and every block in our city to be prayed over, asking God to bring laborers as well as to soften the hearts of people in the city toward Himself. A church planting prayer guide by borough and ZIP Code is developed and distributed to nearly 300 participating churches to mobilize prayer for church plants.

Vision Casting

Four times a year, the alliance convenes 100 to 200 leaders to cast vision for church planting. We host different presenters to come and share their stories in church planting. Speakers also present the theological and methodological rationale for church planting. This has been a powerful place to connect like-minded leaders. One year, a Foursquare leader told the story of how his church plants a new church every year. He was convinced that churches that are less than ten years old are eight times more effective than churches ten years and older in planting new churches.

Training and Assessment

Prior to the initiation of the training, a thorough assessment takes place to determine the match between the temperament of a church planter and the demands of planting a church. This helps to assure the likelihood of a long-term fit.

Redeemer Church Planting Center provides one-year training modules for church planters in both English and Spanish languages. The church planters agree to attend for half-day training ten months per year. At the end of that period, church planters are trained in doing demographic analysis, core-group development, and creating both strategic and business plans to successfully launch and sustain their new church plants.

Funding

The alliance provides a small grant once a church planter has successfully demonstrated that he or she has a viable strategic and business plan to launch the church plant. Often the grant will assist the church planter in securing rental space and other out-of-pocket expenses to get started. The funding also provides credibility to church planters who need to attract other sources of support.

One of the remarkable legacies of the alliance is to see a Presbyterian church and a parachurch organization funding church planters from denominational and independent church backgrounds. It is a sign of the kingdom.

The Impact of Redeemer Church Planting Center and the Church Multiplication Alliance

- **New Church Plants.** Combining the efforts of Redeemer Presbyterian with the Church Multiplication Alliance, nearly 100 churches have been planted. Of those churches, 60 percent are from metropolitan New York and 40 percent are from other national and international sites (the national and international churches are Redeemer church plants). Redeemer has assisted new churches in Los Angeles, San Francisco, Boston, Vancouver, and Philadelphia in the United States. Globally new cities/nations include Belgium, Paris, Amsterdam, and London.

- **Vision Casting.** Vision has been cast in the past five years to more than 2,000 leaders, at such venues as the National Leadership Forum and the quarterly meetings.

- **Intercessors Mobilized.** More than 100 churches have been praying for church planting through the monthly Lord's Watch newsletter and more than 8,000 have participated in prayer through Pray New York! and the eprayer letter.

- **Training.** Redeemer Church Planting Center has trained more than 100 church planters.

- **Funding Given.** More than $1 million has been raised and given to church plants in the alliance. This does not include funding given to the PCA church plants.[6]

Leadership Reflection Questions

1. What would it look like to see churches and denominations in your community collaborate to start new churches?

2. Are there leaders you know who could be brought together with whom this vision could be shared?

3. What would it mean for the gospel to completely permeate your community and city?

Chapter 14

FROM FLUSHING TO THE FAR EAST:
FAITH BIBLE CHURCH

"Those who had been scattered preached the word wherever they went."

ACTS 8:4

John Hao arrived on a college campus in the Philippines in 1978. He was an atheist, having grown up in Hong Kong with no religious exposure. Warmly welcomed by the Chinese Christian Fellowship on campus, he was converted to Christ and became a radical follower. Pastor Hao said, "My eyes were opened to reality of Jesus in a new place. It was an incredible transformation."

In 1982, John Hao traveled to California to attend Christian Witness Theological Seminary and experienced an internship in a Chinese church in San Francisco. From 1982 to

1985, he helped this Chinese church to plant a Chinese church in San Jose. He traveled every weekend to do the planting ministry.

John met Rosie in the seminary and they married in June 1985. After they graduated from the seminary, they served in a church where Rosie interned for two years. They received a call to come to New York City in November 1985, so they left their home, their friends, and their two old cars. They decided to rely on God alone.[1]

The call came from Oversea Chinese Mission (OCM) in Chinatown, New York City, to plant a church in Flushing, Queens. OCM is the largest Chinese church on the East Coast and the church meets in a nine-story building on Hester Street in Chinatown, offering multiple services in multiple languages.

Boon Church was started in November 1985. Rev. Hao started his ministry in February 1986. Under Rev. Hao's leadership, Boon grew from 30 to 600 people in the next nine years. At the five-year point of the pastorate, the church expanded into a two-story building to include room for Sunday School and children's programs. In 1990, Rev. Hao became the seminary-extension director of Christian Witness Theological Seminary in New York.

He experienced God's power in an unusual way in his life and in the lives of the students. He saw a union of students and faculty not only from his own church but also from other Chinese congregations.

By 1995, John Hao's vision had been enlarged to reach out to the Chinese community and to the rest of the world. He longed to plant more ministries and realized that the traditional church framework would not allow him to do what God had put in his heart. Convinced that church planting, the training of workers, and establishing evangelical programs should grow simultaneously, Pastor John started to pray toward this end.

A Vision Born

In March 1995, the vision had become clearer—Rev. Hao wanted to plant a church whose DNA would be committed to four things:
- Church planting wherever possible
- Seminary training
- Missions to the Chinese people around the world
- Community service

By the beginning of 2008, Faith Bible Church was hosting seven services in six languages; it has planted seven churches around the world; and it has planted five seminaries around the world. It also hosts several powerful community services and is birthing a new $4 million community center. How did this happen?

The Context of Flushing, Queens

As a result of immigrant legislation over the past 40 years, Chinese immigrants have poured into New York City from around the Chinese world. Three Chinatowns have emerged in New York City: Chinatown, Manhattan; Main Street, Flushing; and 8th Avenue, Brooklyn. In the decade from 1990 to 2000, more than 100,000 Chinese immigrants moved into New York City.[2] This along with the additional impact of Korean immigration, transformed Flushing in 7 years from being 10 percent Asian to 50 percent Asian. There are 100,000 Chinese living in the Flushing area, mostly from mainland China, and speaking Mandarin. The remainder come from Taiwan, Hong Kong, Malaysia, and Singapore.[3]

In addition to Faith Bible Church, there are a few other prominent churches in Flushing—such as First Baptist Church and Queens Alliance Church—that reach out to the Chinese community. However, these few churches are insufficient to penetrate the large Chinese immigrant population. Some estimate that there are hundreds of thousands of factory workers, restaurant laborers, and dry-cleaning personnel who work seven days a week, with little access to anyone in the church community.

Faith Bible Church Is Born

In April 1995, without any access to resources, Rev. John Hao and his wife, Rosie, decided to purchase a warehouse building in Flushing. A real-estate broker in Boon Church pointed them toward a warehouse building for sale in downtown Flushing. The building owner was willing to lower the price, so with $18,000 in the seminary-extension account, John Hao, by faith, told the owner he would buy the property for $385,000.

John and Rosie Hao gathered with ten others, students of the seminary, for five days a week from 7:00 A.M. until 8:00 A.M. for three months. Rosie kept a record of all the sources of funding that came in locally, and from Hong Kong, Taiwan, China, and Canada. Letters with money came in almost daily. By October, $300,000 had been raised for the down payment on the property. Rosie Hao kept a journal in which she wrote, "God provided supernaturally for the new church through friends who mailed in contributions. We received just enough money at just the right time."[4]

Services began in November 1995 with 100 worshippers. The vision was to be a thriving church, but also much more than a church. Faith Bible Ministry was incorporated under the name Faith Bible Incorporated/Association. The role of new ministry was to train faithful and suitable pastors to build up churches according to biblical principles. Faith Bible Seminary was also established under this ministry.[5]

During the first ten years, Faith Bible Church baptized 700 people. *New York Times* writer Michael Luo quoted Billy Graham and described the church in a June 21, 2005, article:

"'No other city in America—perhaps in the world—presented as great a challenge to evangelism.' . . . It is evident at a warehouse in Flushing occupied by Faith Bible Ministry, where six services are held every Sunday, in English and three dialects of Chinese, for more than 700 congregants."[6]

The church has done effective missions in its own backyard, now offering services in Cantonese, Mandarin, English, Wenzhou, and Fuzhou. Each of the seven services has its own dedicated shepherd.

To sustain its growth, Faith Bible Church converted to a cell group format in 2007. Before launching its cell group strategy, the church committed itself to 40 days of prayer individually and corporately for 40 consecutive nights from 7:30 P.M. to 9:30 P.M. with an average attendance of 100 members to consecrate this new effort. In addition to this extraordinary commitment to prayer, the church also gathers daily at 7:00 A.M. and 8:00 A.M., and every Tuesday night for prayer.[7]

As the church continues to raise several young spiritual leaders, many are now ready to lead small groups. Additional leadership is provided by the total team of ten full-time ministers and staff, along with four interns. The church's income has exceeded $1 million annually.

Evangelism and Community Service

The church sends out evangelistic teams weekly to draw people to the church, distributing more than 3,000 tracts. This type of outreach has been effective in introducing new immigrants to the church. A range of community services also draws people of all ages. Offering summer day camps (with up to 300 children), afterschool programs, art and painting classes, a Chinese language school, piano lessons, English tutoring, and medical checkups has attracted hundreds to the church.[8]

In April 2004, a Christian café and bookstore opened. Designated as a "pre-evangelism" ministry, it provides an avenue for people to come to church. The Faith Bookstore and Café are licensed by the New York City Health Department and serve both Chinese and US cuisine. The restaurant has become an important place to congregate for immigrants who have no familiarity with Christianity.

One young customer who worked the night shift in a computer company became a regular customer, intrigued by the Christian music and the service. He converted to Christianity after hearing the testimony of a café employee.[9]

The church plans to establish the Hope Center, an 18,000-square-foot facility a little farther east in Flushing, near Murray Street. The center will enable the church to expand its community programs to reach Chinese living farther away from Main Street.

Planting Training and Missionary Centers and Churches Worldwide

Faith Bible Seminary began simultaneously with Faith Bible Church in 1995. Courses were initially offered in a rented apartment, taught by a few highly respected Chinese pastors. Within ten years, 60 Christian workers were trained and sent out as pastors, church workers, missionaries, and church planters. Branch seminaries were planted in Taiwan, Montreal, Sao Paulo, Johannesburg, and in house churches in China. The house churches connected to Faith Bible Church have 400,000 members. Due to a lack of workers, house church pastors shepherd as many as ten churches at a time.

The church has sent out missions teams to Paris, Spain, Suriname, Taiwan, South Africa, Greece, and Brazil, as the Chinese population has scattered across the globe. When

Chinese immigrants arrive in a new place, they often rapidly aggregate. As the fruit of the trips to Taiwan, Faith Bible Church has planted four churches there.

Faith Bible Church

Year	Services	Church Plants	Community Service	Seminaries Planted
1995	Cantonese Mandarin		Afterschool Program (30)	Correspondence Students (20)
1996	English Youth		Summer Day Camp (300) Chinese School (100)	
1997			English Class (50)	
1998		Corona, Queens (100)		
2000	Wenzhou			
2001	Second Cantonese	New Hyde Park, Long Island (10)		Taipei, Taiwan (100)
2002	Mandarin for Working Class			
2003		Taipei, Taiwan (40)		
2004		Brazil (30) Taiteng, Taiwan (40)	Piano Tae Kwan Do Arts and Painting Decorating	Brazil (30) Montreal
2005	Fuzhou	Kaohsiung, Taiwan (30)		
2006		Taichung, Taiwan (200)		Inland China
Summary	**7 services = 950**	**8 church plants= 450**	**8 offerings**	**5 Seminaries**

The first local church planted in New York City is in Corona, Queens. It is now an independent church. The second church plant is in New Hyde Park, Long Island. Patterned after the mother church, the church plants also offer afterschool programs and summer day camps.

In Sao Paulo, Brazil, Chinese immigrants, steeped in Communist culture and predominantly from mainland China, have no religious background. Reaching the atheist worldview of the 100,000 Chinese in San Paulo is daunting, but teaching Chinese immigrants Portuguese has opened doors to their lives and resulted in many faith commitments. Faith Bible Church sends annual missions teams to support the work of evangelism and discipleship training.

An Informed Theology and Prayer Life

John Hao draws his strategy from Paul's church planting methodology in Acts. Paul is seen as constantly taking short-term missions trips across Asia and Europe. He would plant churches and then visit them. Paul was also part of a team. Rev. Hao and his leadership travel to the major continents of the world to reach the rapidly expanding Chinese immigrant population. Whether to China, Taiwan, Paris, Sao Paulo, or Johannesburg, the church at home is strengthened as the result of its investment abroad.[10]

Observations

What has made Pastor John a remarkable leader is his radical ability to trust God to provide, to envision and train leaders, and to creatively innovate new outreach methodologies. This is a rare blend of leadership gifts, but he has maintained a posture of humility, working out of a modest-sized office in the church. Rosie Hao is also an incredibly important part of the growth of the church. She and Pastor John have made a great team with a tremendous breadth of gifts to serve the church. Rosie is a gifted preacher and has forged the English-speaking ministry of the church. Their life together as a couple has been an important magnet, drawing people to the church.

Leadership Reflection Questions

1. Are there any neighbor churches that are of a different culture you could visit in your community?

2. How does your church see the relationship between leadership development and outreach?

3. What is the role of corporate prayer in your church in seeking God to meet the needs of the community through creative programs?

Chapter 15

A HARVEST IN GREENWICH

"Open your eyes and look at the fields!"

JOHN 4:35

Glenn Harvison had been senior pastor of Harvest Time Church in Greenwich, Connecticut, for four months by fall 1999. Talking with a good friend, Gary Kellner, who was participating in the great spiritual revival taking place in the Ukraine, Kellner commented, "God doesn't love the people of Kiev any more than the people of Greenwich. He is willing to do right here what He has been doing in the Ukraine."[1]

That statement greatly affected Glenn Harvison. He had been hearing how difficult it was to reach the upper classes of Greenwich, but Gary's comment sparked a revolution in his heart. Glenn said to himself, *We don't have to accept things the way they are. If God can use a*

Gideon, He can use me and use this church. I am praying the prayer of Habakkuk 3 to God—renew Your deeds in our day.[2]

Named after Jesus' statements that the harvest is plentiful but the laborers are few—"I tell you, open your eyes and look at the fields! They are ripe for harvest" (John 4:35). Harvest Time's Pastor Harvison points out that many believers have a perception problem—the deficiency is not in the number of *hearers* but in the number of *laborers*.

The Journey of Harvest Time

Harvest Time had its inception in a YMCA in Greenwich, Connecticut, where the church met immediately following the local Alcoholics Anonymous meeting. That was in 1983, as Harvest Time grew to 100 during its first year before relocating to rented space in the Town Civic Center. They met in this location for almost 20 years and then moved into newly constructed space.

It was in 1996 that Pastor Harvison came to the church as associate pastor, stepping into the senior pastor role 3 years later. The church's growth, limited by its rented facilities for 16 years, numbered 275 people. When Pastor Harvison assumed the senior pastor role, he had only six months to raise $1.5 million for new property acquisition.

The church closed on its property in 1999 and launched a capital campaign. Harvest Time broke ground 2 years later and moved into the new facilities in 2003, on the church's 20th anniversary. The years leading up to this moment were full of uncertain moments; faith was tested at every step.

To build a church in Greenwich to seat 350 people would cost $7 million. Due to an unexpected heart attack suffered by the construction supervisor two weeks before breaking ground, Pastor Glenn became the general contractor for the project! There were moments when money simply ran out, and Pastor Glenn would gather his leaders and drive to the site where they would pray with their faces to the ground. Time and time again, God brought them through. In addition to the new sanctuary space, the church decided to build an air dome to accommodate an additional 500 people.

The Vision of Harvest Time

Harvest Time has a threefold vision:

1. *To be partners in the harvest with Jesus and to collaborate in this with other churches.* Harvest Time invests $500,000 annually in missions, both locally and around the world. Every year, the church sends teams to places around the globe that present great challenges. In 2007, 130 people went to assist in rebuilding communities devastated by Hurricane Katrina.

2. *To be an equipping center for believers.* Harvest Time has designed and launched a training program called e-cwip. This initiative takes members through a two-year curriculum focused on character development, Scripture-based instruction, and a practicum. The training covers the absolute essentials and includes coaching.

   Members are trained in the discipleship ladder of 2 Peter 1:5. The focus is on *faith*, *virtue*, and *knowledge*:

   Bringing people to faith is a core value for the church. The church experienced dramatic growth after it participated in 40 Days of Purpose, developed by pastor and author Rick Warren and Saddleback Church. Harvest Time has since more than doubled to 600. An additional 200 Hispanic congregants meet in a Spanish-language service. Seven hundred people are equally divided between midweek services and Sunday School. In 2008, the church began to launch 50 Alpha groups, in which participants share a meal and enjoy a safe environment to discuss faith.

   Virtue is an important commodity in a culture that has departed from biblical values. The church helps its members focus on lifestyle and character issues. In a relatively affluent area, modeling generosity and encouraging people to live generously is an important value.

   Knowledge is also an important training value. Every Tuesday and Wednesday night, family life programs allow people the opportunity to participate in age-appropriate activity. Youth programs and marriage-oriented sessions comprise the curriculum.

3. *To be a model community to Greenwich and the world.* In a desire to have an impact on the culture, it is important to introduce an alternative culture that is more appealing. The

new church property is built on a property that at one time was meant to be part of a United Nations village, designed to be a model for peace and justice.

The churches in Greenwich and Fairfield County are largely divided along ethnic and socioeconomic lines. Harvest Time has been deliberate in building a multiethnic church; the congregation is currently 50 percent Anglo, 20 percent Hispanic, and 30 percent African American, Caribbean, and Pacific Islanders.

Harvest Time attracts ethnically diverse people due in large part to its core value of honoring one another—every year a day is set aside where congregants participate in acts of service for one another. This vision of service is not only internal to the church but also external. This past year, the church served a Jewish nursing home. The church's good reputation is spreading into the neighborhood and town.

Harvest Time and Missions

As an Assembly of God church, Harvest Time has a strong commitment to global missions. The church has contributed to and participated in church planting in Senegal, Ukraine, Ecuador, and Poland. The church also has purchased land in Ukraine that is producing resources for the work in Senegal. Additionally, Harvest Time has invested in four church plants in New Jersey and New England.[3]

Harvest Time and the Broader Church

Concerts of Prayer Greater New York (COPGNY) began to connect with churches in Fairfield County, including Harvest Time, in 2000. Claudia and Pete Roux from Noroton Presbyterian Church were instrumental in organizing meetings for pastors to get acquainted with each other. For five years, we held semiannual concerts of prayer that ranged in participation from 250 to 600 attendees.

This network of churches grew to 60 and spanned from Greenwich to Norwalk. The church that had the largest participation was Macedonia Church, an African American church. Harvest Time hosted one of the concerts of prayer in a park in Greenwich. Leaders from Greenwich, Stamford, Darien, and Norwalk all participated. Quarterly meetings were held with local church representatives where we prayed together for the region of Fairfield County. The spiritual challenges are very significant. Like the North Shore of Long Island, Westchester County, and northern New Jersey, Fairfield County is experiencing the inverse relationship between spiritual openness and affluence. The more financial resources a community has, the less spiritually open it tends to be.

Greenwich is considered to be the second wealthiest community in the United States. The average home sells for $2 million. There are more CEOs per capita in the county where Greenwich is situated than in any other US county. People who live in Greenwich shape global economics. More than 60 percent of Greenwich residents have bachelor's degrees, and nearly 45 percent have master's degrees. Families with young children are the largest single demographic, according to Pastor Glenn.

Pastor Glenn has developed close relationships with other local churches, including Presbyterian and Pentecostal churches. A group of pastors meet on a regular basis to pray for and support one another. In another demonstration of gathering the body of Christ together, Harvest Time hosted the Leadership Summit for Fairfield County in 2007. In preparation for the conference, the church hosted a pastors' gathering in April with Bill Hybels, senior pastor of Willow Creek Community Church.

Slowly but surely, pastors are beginning to connect with one another across cultural and denominational lines. Harvest Time has been the perfect place for diverse churches to connect, as it models diversity so well. Another Connecticut leadership summit site in Danbury is under the leadership of Walnut Hill Community Church. The vision is to continue to expose dozens of new churches to models of leadership development, innovation, and church growth.

Part of the collaborative spirit that emerges under Pastor Glenn's leadership is networking his parishioners with the broader church. Allan Houston, two-time NBA All-Star, attends Harvest Time. Allan served as the chairman for the 2003 COPGNY Gala Dinner, and he also has joined the National Advisory Team of the New York City Leadership Center. Allan Houston is giving leadership to strengthen father-son relationships through his own foundation. My fondest memory of Allan was having lunch with him, Pastor Glenn, and my teenage son Jordan. In every subsequent conversation, Allan always inquired about Jordan, demonstrating his great heart and genuine concern for others.

The Role of Prayer

Pastor Glenn sees the church's prophetic role to become a house of prayer for all nations. The church participates regularly in the discipline of corporate fasting. He has a handpicked group of 12 intercessors he meets with every other Tuesday—they've been meeting for about a decade. The church also has different prayer groups that meet on a daily basis. During the 40 Days of Purpose campaign, the church had a focused, daily prayer mode.

Leadership Reflection Questions

1. Think back to the beginning of your church or organization. Can you remember a moment when you had to trust God for a significant change in direction or financial breakthrough?

2. What is your church or organization doing to purposely multiply laborers for the people God wants to reach through your team?

3. What is role of prayer in achieving this multiplication of impact?

Chapter 16

A New Wineskin on Long Island: Shelter Rock Church

"I am the vine; you are the branches."
JOHN 15:5

In 2002, Steve Tomlinson awoke to a realization about the challenges of growing his congregation in the Long Island context. The church he served on Long Island had grown to 435 people and needed a bigger facility. As he looked around, he realized that real-estate costs were soaring. A health club in Roslyn listed for $3 million, but another $1 to $2 million would be needed to make it habitable. Steve soon discovered that any land to build on near the church would sell for at least $1 million per small lot. Additionally, he faced the daunting prospect of securing permission from the town if the Shelter Rock Church were to build a new addition.

Long Island's spiritual demographics make it enormously challenging to build strong churches. One estimate is that 55 percent of Long Island is Catholic (with only 18 percent active); 25 percent is Jewish; and the other 20 percent is comprised of 5 to 7 percent evangelical and 8 to 15 percent mainline Protestant. The largest demographic group on Long Island is lapsed Catholics. Long Island has 2.7 million people: approximately 65 percent Anglo, 15 percent Hispanic, 12 percent African American/Caribbean, and 8 percent Asian.[1]

In Search of a Strategy

After his search for real estate turned up no promising results, Steve Tomlinson took his leadership team on a journey to visit several innovative models. They asked themselves, *Should we plant a church? What would be the best location?* The leadership looked at models in California and Illinois ranging from traditional, video café, to high school settings and contemporary worship.

In Naperville, Illinois, they studied Community Christian Church's model, with eight campuses linked together technologically. While visiting that church, they watched a video of how Community Christian had transformed a church near death into a vibrant campus of their church. Shelter Rock leadership watched the testimony of the last remaining elder of that dying church; the elder wept as he saw what was once an empty building filled to capacity on opening Sunday.

It was at this point that the Shelter Rock leadership team members set their hearts on seeking the very same thing. One of the Shelter Rock elders wept, too, as he thought about how this model they discovered might rescue dying churches on Long Island. The leadership at Shelter Rock concluded that building was simply too expensive and they didn't have the resources they needed to do the church planting necessary.

Shelter Rock leadership entered into a discussion with Bible Baptist Church in Syosset at the end of 2004. Bible Baptist had dwindled to just a few members, typical of many Long Island churches, and after discerning the way forward together with Shelter Rock, Bible Baptist suspended itself as a congregation. A funeral service was held for the church and it closed in June 2005.

The sanctuary reopened as a satellite campus for Shelter Rock on September 18; 270 people came to the initial service. The group was comprised of one-third former Bible Baptist members, one-third Shelter Rock members, and one-third new people mostly from the lapsed

Catholic community. This fact became evident when the pastor closed in prayer; he ended with the words "in the name of the Father, Son, and Holy Spirit" and at least one-third of the crowd made the sign of the cross. Shelter Rock's dream of reaching spiritually disconnected people seemed to have been realized. Steve Tomlinson recalled for me that two of the original members of Bible Baptist were weeping together because, for the first time, they had to sit in the balcony as there were no available seats on the main floor. Shelter Rock had promoted heavily by sending three communication pieces to a target audience of 5,000 people and placing posters at all of the nearby Long Island Rail Road stations.

Two years later, regular attendance reached 250 people at the Syosset campus of Shelter Rock, with its own dedicated campus pastors. This fresh innovation positions the church for significant growth. Church attendance over the past 32 years has grown as follows:

Shelter Rock Church
(formerly Manhasset Baptist)

Year	Attendance
1975	12
1980	60
1985	100
1990	250
1995	320
2000	400
2005	500
2007	700
Easter 2007	1,400
November 2007	725

In the 2 years between 2005 and 2007 the church grew 40 percent, or by 200 people. With the adoption of a multicampus strategy, Shelter Rock church is poised for exponential growth across the dry spiritual landscape of Long Island.

Shelter Rock is not alone in its innovative strategies. In Port Jefferson Station, the True

North Community Church congregation, led by Bert Crabbe, has grown from 300 to 700 people; the average age is 23. Beacon Church, led by Robert Kelly, is a young church plant that was given a building in Garden City by another struggling congregation. Beacon also has grown quickly with youth and young families. CenterPoint Church, located in Bellemore, is one more young church with a young and dynamic population of 300 attendees.

The thrust of this strategy is to use existing buildings that are no longer fully utilized due to aging, dwindling congregations. Steve Tomlinson's observation is that *pastors* like big churches but *congregants* enjoy small churches. Shelter Rock is looking at three other locations around Long Island and Bayside, Queens, where dying churches are eager to partner.

In addition to finding the right congregations and facilities to partner, Steve has hired a number of new staff members who reflect Long Island's younger demographic; the staff is also becoming multicultural. Shelter Rock's Asian demographic has quadrupled from 5 percent to 20 percent from 1995 to 2007, reflecting the large numbers of Asian Christians immigrating into the region.

The Vision and Mission of Shelter Rock Church

Simply put, the vision of Shelter Rock is to reach Long Island. The mission is to lead as many people as possible into a joyful and life-giving relationship with Christ. The strategy is subdivided into eight themes:

1. *Sunday services on multiple campuses.* This provides an opportunity for people to hear preaching from various staff. The church models a plurality of leadership in the context of a larger community.

2. *Easter outreach at the Tilles Center for the Performing Arts (Long Island's premier concert hall, seating 2,242).* The church recognizes this as the best opportunity annually to bring all of the people together from the campuses, as well as a chance to invite new people into a neutral setting.

3. *Host the Long Island Leadership Summit.* Shelter Rock is as committed to investing in other churches as it is to its own growth. In two years, more than 400 leaders from dozens of churches have participated in the Willow Creek event.

4. *Student and adult missions teams.* In 2007, 100 people participated in missions teams.

5. *International mission support.* Shelter Rock has a large missions family that it supports in countries around the world, including a partnership with World Vision in Malawi.

6. *Leadership for large evangelistic events.* Shelter Rock seeks to partner with national organizations that have islandwide meetings on Long Island. To this end, they have partnered with Billy Graham and Greg Laurie.

7. *Ministry community events.* Shelter Rock hosts multichurch events for Long Island, including events with speakers such as Kay Arthur.

8. *Assisting church plants on Long Island.* Shelter Rock has invested financially in churches that have been started in the past five years.[2]

Youth for Christ and Other Partnerships

Youth for Christ (YFC) was established on Long Island in 1959 under Dave Swanson; Chuck Rigby led the organization from 1962 to 1970. In 1971, Jack Crabtree and 25 other staff members were recruited from across the nation. They moved to Long Island from across the country, and the cultural adjustment and cost of living were so onerous, Jack was the only staff member that stayed more than a few years.

When he arrived in 1971, Jack noticed the poor relational climate between diverse church groups on Long Island. Denominational groups were leery of talking to churches that were independent.

Relationships began to thaw in the late 1980s and early 1990s with the emergence of the Billy Graham Crusade and the presence of Concerts of Prayer. The first concert of prayer took place at Cathedral Church of the Intercessor in Hempstead (formerly St. Thomas Episcopal Church) in the spring of 1989. Friendships were forged during preparations for the Billy Graham Crusade. Ron Hutchcraft, a senior leader with YFC at the time, said that many churches were more concerned about protecting the truth than reaching out with the truth. Under Jack Crabtree's sustained leadership, YFC has become perhaps the most widely recognized and respected missions agency in the region during the past 35 years. He was asked to be the Billy Graham Crusade chairperson for the 1991 crusade in Nassau Coliseum.

Youth for Christ is penetrating many of the public schools across Long Island. With its present staff of 12, it is reaching into more than 30 public schools. YFC has been a champion for racial reconciliation for the past two decades. For 15 years, YFC hosted a South African dance team modeling what a Black/White partnership can look like.[3] YFC staff members are training students to live for Jesus in their own contexts:

- Abide in Christ daily.
- Discover and tell their story.
- Care for friends and learn their story.
- Share God's story with their friends.
- Bring God's life-changing power into their school.

Every year, thousands of students participate in rallies in September, and in November thousands more students participate in a sports outreach event. The YFC budget neared $1 million this past year.

Youth for Christ has identified five essentials of fruitful and sustainable ministry sites:

1. Widespread prayer
2. Loving relationships
3. Faithful Bible teaching
4. Collaborative community strategy with churches and agencies to reach young people
5. Adults who empower[4]

As part of Shelter Rock's partnership with Youth for Christ, Jack Crabtree has served in the role as teaching pastor for the church. Jack's leadership provides important perspective and longevity for the growing church.

Increasingly across the metro area, leaders like Jack Crabtree serve as statesmen for a region, and are given the opportunity to contribute significantly to the life of local churches. In addition to YFC, groups like Youth Guidance and InterVarsity play an important role in linking young people to the local church. John Craig has led Youth Guidance for the past several years. Dan Brady arrived on Long Island in 1991 and gives oversight to InterVarsity Christian Fellowship's presence on area campuses.

When I arrived in 1984 at Stony Brook University, the largest two groups on campus were the Communist Group (known as Red Balloon) and the Gay/Lesbian Alliance (GALA). High school and college campuses can be exceedingly difficult places to penetrate spiritually. Intelligent partnerships between local churches and missions agencies have been an important part of the fabric of influencing Long Island spiritually.

Additional primary partners on Long Island have been the Suffolk County Evangelical Ministers Fellowship (SCEMF). SCEMF has been gathering for decades. In the past year it has grown to be a very vibrant group under the leadership of Pastor Scott Ingvaldsen of Grace Church in Smithtown. A May 2008 National Day of Prayer event at Smithtown Gospel Tabernacle hosted by the association was a very powerful experience. Hundreds gathered across denominational and racial lines to pray together. Pastor Scott said, "This was one of the most powerful prayer experiences I have ever had."

Leadership Reflection Questions

1. Can you identify one way that your church or organization has innovated in order to reach more people?

2. What are the unique cultural dimensions to your context that are necessary to understand in order to have significant impact (familiarity with the demography, socioeconomics)?

3. Are there senior leaders that can be met with to gain a greater understanding of the spiritual history of your community?

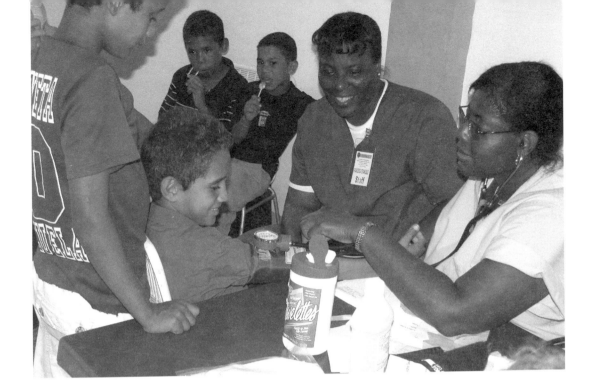

Chapter 17

BORN OUT OF REJECTION: BETHEL GOSPEL ASSEMBLY

"More are the children of the desolate woman than of her who has a husband."

ISAIAH 54:1

Two young African American women from Harlem were attending a Midtown Manhattan church. They came forward in response to the altar call, and were eager to become part of the church. Unfortunately, the leadership of the church told them they would not be welcome to join because of the color of their skin. It was 1916.

Lillian Kraeger—a young woman of German descent—followed the young women back to Harlem and offered to lead a Bible study with them. After discussing this with him, Lillian's fiancé gave her an ultimatum—she could suspend her plans to meet in Harlem with the young women or face a broken engagement. It was an awful decision to make. Lillian heard from God the words of Isaiah 54, that He would increase the tent of the barren if she were faithful. The engagement was broken. On November 18, 1917, at 11:00 A.M., Bethel Gospel Assembly was born. The DNA for a congregation committed to cross-cultural mission was sewn into its fabric.[1]

In its 90-year history, Bethel has had only three senior pastors: James Barzey, a young man from the West Indies became the pastor in 1924; Bishop Ezra Williams; and Pastor Carlton Brown. The fledgling Bethel Gospel Assembly grew to 100 members, until Pastor Barzey died in 1965.

Bishop Ezra Nehemiah Williams

Ezra Williams became pastor at the age of 37. His pastorate was off to a slow start, as the church receded to 30 members. However, over the course of his 34-year pastorate, he led Bethel into several remarkable frontiers of growth. From the expansion of the old church to the overseas crusades of the young people, Pastor Williams began to teach this new generation of believers about the mighty power of God. Young people began to learn how God could use even the unlikely to impact missions fields around the earth. According to Bishop Brown, "It has always been a part of the DNA of Bethel to sow abroad and reap at home. We have never done the predictable or the self-preserving."

Ezra Williams was an unlikely candidate to become a pastor. He grew up in Harlem and displayed a penchant for getting into trouble at school. He was taken to the principal's office so often that he was told he would never amount to much. God had different plans. In 1982, Bethel purchased and moved into its present location on the corner of Madison Avenue and 120th Street in Harlem. The building was a former junior high building, the very building that Ezra Williams had attended as a boy. In a wonderful irony, the principal's office that Williams visited so frequently as a young student in trouble was converted into his pastoral office.

The story of the purchasing of the property is a modern-day miracle. The building, in complete disrepair and occupying an entire city block, was purchased for $300,000. It would take two years of renovation before the church was able to open for worship.

The church grew quickly from the 200 in 1984 to an average attendance of 1,000 by 2000. The ministry expanded to include a 24/7 men's residential discipleship program; a prison ministry program; full-time Beth-Hark Christian Care Center; an active community youth program (with two gyms and a computer center); active Bible college; Harlem-wide and citywide evangelistic initiatives; and missions work in South Africa, India, Venezuela, Aruba, and St. Vincent.

Pastor Carlton Brown

Carlton Brown grew up in the church. He was one of those young people powerfully touched by Bishop Williams's leadership. He traces a straight line from his involvement in leadership at the age of 12 all the way into his current role as senior pastor. Consider the pathway of this indigenous leader raised up from within the church:

- Ages 12–14: Sunday School assistant
- Ages 15–19: Working with the mission board as a trainee
- Ages 20–22: Active with missions and teaching Sunday School
- Ages 23–24: Missions team leader and deacon
- Ages 28–33: Associate pastor
- Age 34: Full-time associate pastor overseeing the men's ministry, Christian education, youth, administration, van ministry, publications, missions program, and Beth Hark Christian Care Center

In 2000, on assuming the position of general overseer of the Bethel Ministry, Pastor Brown immediately established the Loving, Learning, Launching church motto to describe the threefold focus of the ministry. The motto underscores the commitment to the truths that each individual person is important, improving, and having an impact on others.

In addition, Bethel established four missionaries on the field between 2000 and 2007. The church also planted seven new churches in New York, New Jersey, Georgia, and Virginia during the same time period.

The Context of Harlem and Bethel

Bethel is in a community in transition. There is a convergence of Anglos (especially young families), Haitians, French-speaking Africans, and Mexicans and Central Americans. Bethel attracts people from many different walks of life. African and Caribbean Americans comprise 80 percent of the membership; Hispanic 15 percent; and 5 percent international. The church has 1,100 members on the roster with 1,500 regular attendees. The congregation's ages are spread over a wide range:

Bethel's Age Range

0–21	500	56–75	250
21–35	250	76–90	50
36–55	400		

Like other New York City neighborhoods, the church is grappling with how best to serve single mothers and the swelling senior population. The church also faces the challenges of caring for at-risk youth involved with gang violence and sexual experimentation.[2]

When a person joins Bethel, he or she is introduced to a detailed understanding of the principles and teachings that shape and form the ministry. First-time believers attend the New Converts Class and seasoned believers attend New Members Class. Christian education is arranged systematically to help students understand their purpose in Christ. Classes range from the Mind of Christ to MasterLife (an adapted Southern Baptist curriculum). Cross Trainers is an overview of the Bible. Graduates then move into MP3/WP3 classes (Purpose, Passion, and Promises) designed for men's and women's groups.

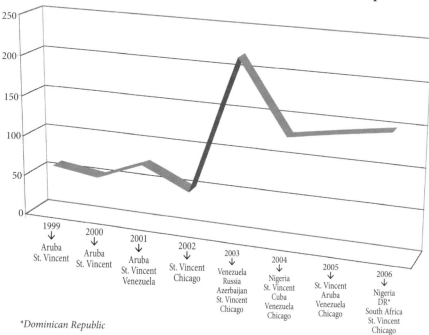

Member Involvement in Short-Term Missions Trips

*Dominican Republic

For those who believe they have a call to ministry, Bethel offers Minister in Training. This supplemental curriculum is taken in conjunction with their own Bible school and seminary pursuits. Pastor Carlton Brown is able to assist in the development of a philosophy of ministry that is relevant as well as reflective of the core values that propel Bethel into Christ-centered, Holy Ghost–empowered global evangelism.

Bethel's Reach from Harlem to the Globe

What differentiates Bethel from most churches is its raw passion for both local outreach and global mission. Twice a year, Bethel leads an outreach known as Operation Spiritual Thunder, involving 100 street preachers on 100 street corners throughout Harlem. Bethel has an incredible team of talent on staff and in the congregation. This supplements its year-round commitment to men's discipleship programs and youth outreach.

The Christ Community Action Initiative (CCAI) started in 2004. This ministry effectively advocates for those who have been disenfranchised and underserved by the various secular agencies. The CCAI resource team hails from various professions including education, law, health care, and mental health care. Together they serve as a tremendous resource to church and community residents with unique crisis conditions and no real sense of where to turn. The group also provides a forum for the exchange of critical information that empowers the participant in securing the support needed for quality of change.

Members on the pastoral team like Gordon Williams, Mark Williams, and Mimsie Robinson have tremendous talent as preachers and missionaries. All these individuals were trained from within the church. The pastoral staff, also including Joan Williams, Joyce Eady, Darren Hicks, Willie Jarrell, and Wendie Trott, anchors an exceptionally experienced church staff.

Over the past four years, Bethel has hosted the Northeast Regional Great Commission Conference in New York and two separate conferences in the Caribbean. The goal is to bring churches of color, as well as churches of all ethnic persuasions and denominations, into an understanding of God's design for churches within the context of world evangelism. Bethel gives leadership to six churches in South Africa's Transkei region, as well as the Harmony Estates ministry complex and Christian School in South Africa. Bethel has also planted three churches in St. Vincent. Since 1999 Bethel has sent over 800 people on short-term missions trips to the

Caribbean, South America, Africa, and Chicago. The annual missions giving has reached the $1 million mark with more than $4 million given since 1999.

BGA Missions Giving for the Past Eight Years

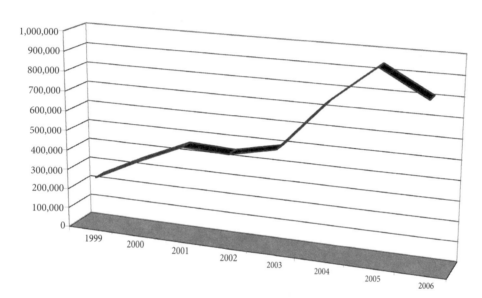

Innovation for the Future

To serve the expanding needs in the community and abroad, Bethel has forged an innovative partnership with a housing developer. Recognizing that it resides in a community with a large percentage of working poor who are living from paycheck to paycheck, the partnership is a creative way to generate resources. In exchange for Bethel's air rights, allowing the developer to build properties adjacent to the church, a new 2,000-seat sanctuary is under construction at Bethel. The church will also receive 47 apartments, which can be converted into an income stream. Additionally the church is looking to develop resources for members and the community:

• An upgraded bookstore
• On-site café

- Day-care center
- Fitness center
- Progressive youth center
- Conversion of the existing sanctuary into a ministry arts theater with a view to create long running plays, as an uptown Broadway.

Bethel sees the development and parallel income stream as an opportunity to create additional revenues to support missions both locally and abroad. The church is committed to become the center of activity, with offerings that are progressive and fulfilling.

Collaboration with the Broader Church

Because of its unique history, planted by a German woman in Harlem, Bethel is particularly effective in partnering with other churches across cultural and ethnic lines. Walter Wilson, a longtime staff member of Bethel, was a founding board member for Concerts of Prayer Greater New York (COPGNY), and the very first board meeting for COPGNY was held at Bethel. Bethel has partnered with Anglo churches across the country in joint outreach around the world. In 1999, the first national Gatekeeper's Consultation was held at Bethel, attracting 300 leaders from across the nation, representing dozens of cities. Walter Wilson was codirector of that event. Its facilities have made Bethel an incredible place to host large citywide or national events. Pastor Brown joined the COPGNY board a few years ago and has been an active participant in citywide initiatives. At the 2004 Concerts of Prayer Gala Dinner, COPGNY gave a lifetime achievement award to Pastor Brown's predecessor, Bethel's pastor emeritus Bishop Ezra Williams.

More Are the Children of the Barren

The original promise given to Lillian Kraeger has come true. Thousands have been drawn to faith by the outreach of Bethel in its Harlem neighborhood. Thousands more around the world in Asia, Africa, Europe, the Caribbean, and Latin America have been drawn to faith.

Ninety years of innovative thinking, taking risks, and radically trusting God have benefited Bethel. The team-leadership model that personifies Bethel has provided enormous stability in a rapidly growing congregation. Bethel models the great truth that the greatest experience this side of heaven is being radically loved by someone who is different.

Leadership Reflection Questions

1. Can you think of a moment in your personal or church history when a difficult experience shaped a future benefit for your church (loss of members, illness, financial difficulty)?

2. Has your church or organization ever adopted the "sow abroad to reap at home" philosophy? Why or why not?

3. Can you chart over the last five years your missions giving and sending patterns? What does that say about your church or organization?

4. How has your church done with a deliberate succession plan to leadership?

THE NEXT GENERATION OF SPIRITUAL LEADERSHIP ON STATEN ISLAND

"Be strong and courageous. Do not be terrified; do not be discouraged, for the
Lord your God will be with you wherever you go."
JOSHUA 1:9

Dan Mercaldo felt as though he were leading a congregation in the wilderness in 1976. He had started with a core group of 16 people in 1965. For 11 years, his congregation had been struggling to break the 100-member barrier, and Gateway Cathedral had no permanent building. There were few strong churches on Staten Island at the time.

As we sat across each other in the diner, Dan shared the history with me. "We had tried everything to grow. It seemed as though we were hitting our heads on a ceiling on

Staten Island. There were very few successful models that we could follow in the region."

The church had experienced a major theological shift in 1970—away from Pentecostalism to a more evangelical view of Scripture. Finally, two important developments took place. Gateway got connected to the Fuller Evangelistic Association, and was exposed to the church growth movement. Simultaneously, Gateway began participating in the Institute in Basic Life Principles founded by Bill Gothard, which turned the focus of the church to building strong families.

Pastor Mercaldo had been looking for families to help build the church. His assumption was there were healthy, intact families that could come right into the church and contribute to its growth. He realized that families just weren't there in large numbers.

He then decided to focus on the church's strategy to build families rather than the other way around. With this adjusted philosophy of ministry, the church began to grow rapidly. By the late 1970s and into the 1980s, the church saw an annual growth of 35 to 40 percent. *Moody Monthly* described Gateway as one of the fastest growing churches in America, and for 20 years Gateway was the only evangelical church on Staten Island that had more than 500 people.[1] Over Pastor Mercaldo's 43-year pastorate, Gateway has been featured in *Christianity Today, Moody Monthly,* and *Global Church Growth.*

Today the church has a congregation of more than 1,600 people, with Sunday worship attendance up to 1,000 people. Pastor Mercaldo has been described as a cross between Robert Schuller and Chuck Smith, and has gleaned lessons from such diverse consultants as John Wimber, Peter Wagner, Lyle Schaller, Carl George, and Conrad Lowe.

Gateway was able to relocate to new property in 1993. Its facility expansion played a critical role in its ability to offer new programs and creative outreach. Pastor Mercaldo's gifting as an administrator has been an important factor in its growth. The church places a strong value on families worshipping together and strives to develop a biblical worldview for children in their early development. Over the past 25 years, Gateway has continued to grow steadily and expand its programming, largely aimed at family ministry with these actions:

- Gateway Academy for children preschool through eighth grade
- Youth programming for both junior high and high school
- Children's Bible classes for prekindergarten through fifth grade

The Gateway Academy is located on the campus of beautifully kept buildings with expansive parking and rests on a 23-acre complex. Soon to be known as Church at the Gateway, its location at the very first entrance into New York City is strategic to the witness of Christ in the region.

The Creative Arts Department, developed under the leadership of Pastor Mercaldo's son Tim Mercaldo, provides year-round opportunities for children, parents, and the broader church to engage in musical productions. Every year, the Gateway Christmas pageant attracts nearly 8,000 people from the region, making it one of the largest of its type. In scope and excellence, it rivals a Broadway show, but at a fraction of the cost, and with delicious homemade cookies, coffee, and hot cider at intermission!

Gateway Looks to the Future

As Pastor Dan Mercaldo evaluated the trends of the church, he came to realize the significant challenge of growing a consistent worshipping body of thousands of people. He has made strategic staffing and programming decisions and implemented a radical restructuring toward the simple church model. This model narrows the focus of the church, and Gateway chose four key areas of ministry:

- Worship
- Children
- Youth
- Small groups

The mission of Gateway is "Connecting people to God and others—Transforming their lives, families, communities and world generationally."[2] The simple church model will help integrate the core values of *exalting* God through personal and corporate worship and cultivating intimacy with Him; *encountering* people who need Christ; *establishing* believers through a process of intentional discipleship; *encouraging* each other in nurturing relationships; *equipping* Christians to exercise their spiritual gifts; and *extending* the growth of the church both locally and abroad through culturally relevant ministries.[3]

The next strategic development of the church, according to Pastor Mercaldo, is hiring the right staff to multiply the number of lay leaders in the church. There are currently not enough lay leaders to respond to the kind of growth the church envisions for its future. Over the past 3 years, Gateway has been greatly aided by the Navigators organization's Church Discipleship Ministry, developing a pathway for people to become fully mature and devoted disciples of Jesus Christ.

Prayer and Mission

Gateway has emerged as one of the most committed praying churches in the region. The church has had a dedicated staff person coordinating the prayer life of the congregation. Every month, as many as 200 people participate in the Lord's Watch, the monthly prayer vigil coordinated by Concerts of Prayer Greater New York. The church also has a vast eprayer ministry, perhaps one of the best organized in the region. This is particularly important for emergency needs within the congregation.

When the Concerts of Prayer meetings began in 1989, Gateway was the original Staten Island host. Gateway also hosted the Staten Island Pastor's Concert of Prayer in 1994. Dan and Tim Mercaldo regularly attend the annual Pastors' Prayer Summit, from the time it was held at Tuscarora Inn in 1992.

At that first Tuscarora event, I will never forget Pastor Dan Mercaldo and Pastor Bob Johansson connecting with each other—two fellow spiritual fathers in our city. They had both begun their NYC pastorates in 1965 and in 27 years had not seen this level of united prayer over the city. Pastor Mercaldo, at Gateway Cathedral in his introduction to meeting with Staten Island leadership in April 2008, said, "For the first time in my lifetime I have seen the Evangelical and Pentecostal leaders come together in unprecedented unity. This has now been happening for more than 20 years."

Tim Mercaldo has also played an important leadership role. In the majority of these annual prayer gatherings that draw more than 300 pastors annually, he has led the worship. Consistently, the pastors who attend the Summit describe the worship experiences as some of the most powerful in their personal history. Tim has also led worship in citywide events, such as the Rekindling Citywide Spiritual Awakening: 150th Anniversary of the Fulton Street Revival.

Gateway also focuses outward, with an extensive missions outreach around the globe. In this season of his life, Pastor Dan Mercaldo has committed himself to participate in leadership training wherever he travels internationally. He has traveled to Eastern and Western Europe, Central America, India, and more recently to Africa. The church has started orphanages in India, Nicaragua, and Mozambique. Their burden to develop and minister to children and families began at home, but now extends globally.

On Another Side of the Island—International Christian Center

Russ Hodgins came to Staten Island in 1998 as a young pastor from Upstate New York. When he arrived, church attendance was 200. In ten years of his leadership, the church has grown exponentially—to more than 2,000 worshippers. In the interview, Russ said, "I came to Staten Island with a huge assignment to lead this church. I was unsure but have seen God move in extraordinary ways to grow our church."

Several factors have influenced the growth of the church:
- The centrality of preaching Jesus in a loving way
- Inspirational worship
- Launching of small groups that have grown to include 400 people
- Role of corporate prayer, which gave birth to the church vision

What is the vision for the church? During a 6:00 A.M. prayer meeting in June 2006, the vision of having one church in many locations came into focus—multiple preaching centers and bridge groups would infect all of Staten Island. When International Christian Center (ICC), affiliated with the Assemblies of God, established a second campus on Staten Island, the church found it was able to reach a different audience in the rapidly growing ethnic diversity of Staten Island.

One cannot underestimate the role of prayer in the rapid growth of ICC. Throughout every worship service, a team of intercessors prays. Every Friday night, there is a strong prayer expression. Hans and Lori Wiesner, who attend ICC, were the Pray New York! coordinators for Staten Island from 2004 through 2007.

Like Gateway, ICC has a strong missions commitment. It is particularly active in Bangladesh where a strong church planting movement has emerged. ICC plans to work with the Assemblies of God and plant a church in the capital of Liberia, Monrovia.[4]

The Leadership Role of Staten Island Association of Evangelicals

A Profile of Staten Island

The 2003 census for Staten Island listed the population at 459,737, or about 5 percent of all New York City residents. Of the total population, 78 percent are Anglo, 12 percent Hispanic, 10 percent African American, and 6 percent Asian. Although the smallest borough by population, Staten Island is growing three times more rapidly than the city as a whole.[5]

Geographically, the African American and Hispanic populations live on the north side of Staten Island, north of Interstate 278. The southern part of Staten Island traditionally has been Italian Catholic.[6]

Although the estimated population of evangelical believers across Staten Island is less than 5 percent, there is a growing camaraderie among the emerging church leadership. In the 1970s, there was a strong movement of leaders gathering from the charismatic movement under the leadership of Ben Crandall. Concerts of Prayer Greater New York began building some important trusting relationships in 1989.

Throughout the 1990s more and more churches began to participate in Staten Island-wide events. Pastor Dan Mercaldo made an important effort to go out and meet with more than 30 pastors from minority and immigrant backgrounds. Interestingly, the fastest growing immigrant groups on Staten Island are Mexicans and Liberians and the number of internationals on Staten Island increased by over 60 percent during the 1990s to 75,000.[7] Every year, on the third Sunday in January, Gateway features a prominent minority leader from the city who embodies the spirit of Martin Luther King Jr.

Groups like the Staten Island Association of Evangelicals (SIAE) desire to assist the struggling and often disconnected churches. Russ Hodgins served as president of the SIAE during the period his church was experiencing rapid growth. He brought great administrative skills to the assignment and organized several effective islandwide programs. His successor, Dave Beidel, has continued to knit the hearts of diverse leaders together across Staten Island.

Currently, with the nucleus of younger leaders like Russ Hodgins, Tim Mercaldo, Dave Beidel, Eddie Cole, and Lee Ka, there is optimism about translating spiritual unity into functional unity. The churches seem poised to do new things to grow their own congregations but also to stand as one voice across Staten Island. In one recent comment, Tim Mercaldo said,

"We are planning to have the pastors do 40 Days of Purpose as a pastoral community before leading our congregations through this in Lent 2009."

Carlos Ortiz, a longtime Staten Island pastor and staff member with Concerts of Prayer Greater New York, has helped to shepherd the unity effort. Carlos, born in Puerto Rico, has wonderful pastoral gifts and a strong contemplative spirituality. Together, he and Dan Mercaldo have been important spiritual father figures for Staten Island and the region.

Leadership Reflection Questions

1. Do the pastors of your church and community meet together on a regular basis?

2. What cooperative gatherings have your churches participated in over the past year? How would that help a sense of unity?

3. What are the fastest growing communities in your neighborhood? How should that affect how your church reaches out?

Chapter 19

Changing the World One Child at a Time: World Vision - New York

"Religion that God our Father accepts as pure and faultless is this: to look after orphans and widows in their distress and to keep oneself from being polluted by the world."

JAMES 1:27

"God is in the slums, and the cardboard boxes where the poor play house. God is in the silence of a mother who has infected her child with a virus that will end both of their lives. God is in the cries heard under the rubble of war. God is in the debris of a wasted opportunity and wasted lives. God is with us if we are with them."—Bono[1]

From the plaque hanging above John Clause's desk

John Clause graduated from law school in 1982. He went to work with his family in real-estate development on the east end of Long Island. In the late 1980s, the stock market crashed on Black Monday, major lenders were being taken over, and environmentalists created a moratorium endangering the real-estate market. In the midst of this tumultuous period, John Clause made a faith commitment—the year was 1986. The financial crisis drove his family's real-estate firm into bankruptcy by 1992.

John Clause was strangled out of business and entered a desert experience. What should he do next? After a long period of prayerful searching, he decided to explore ministry options. In the 1980s, he experienced the extremes of wealth and poverty at a profoundly personal level. The 1980s and 1990s were God's crucible for John, forging extraordinary leadership in him.

What emerged was an understanding of God's call. John was able to discern his own passion for children; World Vision provided him an opportunity to appropriate that calling.

An Emerging Pandemic

Halfway around the world, a pandemic was brewing in the 1980s. Many believe the geographic ground zero of the HIV/AIDS pandemic is southern Uganda. HIV/AIDS is rooted in poverty, cultural norms (such as serial relationships), and ignorance, all of which have converged to unleash a deadly virus. This virus is killing 8,000 people per day and leaving 6,000 orphans per day in its wake.

Globally there are now more than 40 million people infected and 25 million have already died—a majority of the victims are in Africa. The pandemic has become the largest of its kind in human history. By 2050, the projected number of deaths due to HIV/AIDS in 53 affected countries is expected to exceed 290 million people.[2]

Six months after joining World Vision, John traveled to Uganda and met 2 children—Charles and Gertrude—whose parents had died of AIDS. John Clause's purpose was to tell Charles and Gertrude they had not been forgotten. On that trip, whenever he held 1 child, he saw the eyes of another 50 children asking when it would be their turn.[3]

John also visited Ethiopia on that trip. He saw the Antsokia Valley in Ethiopia, ravaged by the famine that took 1 million lives. Now, through the resources and partnership of World Vision with local Ethiopians, the valley was flourishing and green. John said, "I had never seen anything like this before. The potential to transform a desert into a garden is huge." Like every vision trip, this provided the backdrop of hope against the reality of disease, poverty, and despair.[4]

Adult (aged 15-49 years) HIV prevalence in countries which have conducted population-based HIV surveys in recent years[5]

Countries	Population-based survey prevalence (%) (year)	2001 HIV prevalence (%) reported in 2002 Report on the global AIDS epidemic	2003 HIV prevalence (%) reported in 2004 Report on the global AIDS epidemic	200 HIV prevalence (%) reported in 2006 Report on the global AIDS epidemic
Sub-Saharan Africa				
Benin	1.2 (2006)	3.6	1.9	1.8
Botswana	25.2 (2004)	38.8	38.0	24.1
Burkina Faso	1.8 (2003)	6.5	4.2	2.0
Burundi	3.6 (2002)	8.3	6.0	3.3
Cameroon	5.5 (2004)	11.8	7.0	5.4
Central African Republic	6.2 (2006)	12.9	13.5	10.7
Chad	3.3 (2005)	3.6	4.8	3.5
Côte d'Ivoire	4.7 (2005)	9.7	7.0	7.1
Equatorial Guinea	3.2 (2004)	3.4	NA	3.2
Ethiopia	1.4 (2005)	6.4	4.4	(0.9–3.5)
Ghana	2.2 (2003)	3.0	3.1	2.3
Guinea	1.5 (2005	NA	2.8	1.5
Kenya	6.7 (2003)	15.0	6.7	6.1
Lesotho	23.5 (2004)	31.0	29.3	23.2
Malawi	12.7 (2004)	15.0	14.2	14.1
Mali	1.3 (2006) 1.7 (2001)	1.7	1.9	1.7
Niger	0.7 (2006) 0.9 (2002)	NA	1.2	1.1
Rwanda	3.0 (2005)	8.9	5.1	3.1
Senegal	0.7 (2005)	0.5	0.8	0.9
Sierra Leone	1.5 (2005)	7.0	NA	1.6
South Africa	16.2 (2005)	20.1	20.9	18.8
Swaziland	25.9 (2006-7)	33.4	38.8	33.4
Uganda	7.1 (2004-5)	5.0	4.1	6.7
United Republic of Tanzania	7.0 (2004)	7.8	9.0	6.5
Zambia	15.6 (2001-2)	21.5	16.5	17.0
Zimbabwe	18.1 (2005-6)	33.7	24.6	20.1

The Unfolding Vision

John Clause began his tenure with World Vision in 1997 as the only development representative for New York and New Jersey region. John was conflicted—opportunities abounded to assist children in the poorest countries of the world, but only $250,000 had been raised from the entire metro NYC region. John knew that the unrealized potential for donor development was astronomical. This realization led John Clause to draft a vision document for metro New York. The idea slowly began to take shape when Rich Stearns became the new president of World Vision. By 1999, John Clause had become manager of the Northeast development team. Finally, in 2000, a select group of World Vision leaders, including John, shaped and implemented the strategy of regionalization.

The thesis John held was that by decentralizing the efforts of World Vision into a grassroots organizational structure, the return on investment would grow geometrically. Donors and churches would be recruited through a relationship-based methodology that mass marketing could not create.

I met John Clause for the first time in December 2000 at First Baptist Church in Flushing. We immediately connected on how to advance World Vision's presence in the church community. My wife, Marya, and I had sponsored children since 1982 and were familiar with World Vision. Praying through Operation World and every country on the globe on a daily basis for three years, I saw the presence of World Vision in 100 nations.

In 2001, World Vision - New York launched with 9 staff members. Within a few months, 9/11 shocked the world as the attack struck just two miles south of the World Vision - New York offices. Within two weeks, under the leadership of John Clause, 45 staff members were added to serve the needs of the city. The American Families Assistance Fund was created to steer resources to assist victims of the attack. Victims were given assistance checks at churches in their neighborhoods, forging an important partnership with local churches and the ministry of World Vision. The fund was co-created and co-administrated with Concerts of Prayer leadership.

By the summer of 2002, the staff had been scaled back to 15, but grew again steadily over the next four years to 30, with leadership given to development, marketing, community relations, local programs, and church partnerships.

Engaging Churches

World Vision president Rich Stearns has stated that one of his top goals is to engage the US church with the needs of the HIV/AIDS pandemic. New York City has been one of the most responsive cities to that message. John Clause approached me in spring 2002 to attend a vision trip the following July. A small group of us traveled together, including my daughter Anna, co-worker Brian Considine, and ministry colleagues. We traveled to Uganda and Tanzania, seeing the pandemic firsthand. Similar to John Clause's first trip in 1997, the trip was a blend of overwhelming despair and joyful hope.

In Tanzania we saw two contrasting images. The first image was that of a woman who had been driven to prostitution by poverty. She had contracted HIV and was in her final days of life. She looked like she was in her 50s, but was only in her 20s. The other image was that of an entire community that had graduated from its partnership with World Vision and was now functioning independently with an educational, economic, and medical system in place to support the community.

Over the next five years, the World Vision/Concerts of Prayer partnership resulted in more than 100 leaders traveling to East Africa and the Dominican Republic and more than 8,000 children sponsored. As important, churches have begun to collaborate in common countries through sponsorship and special projects. Rwanda, Kenya, and Uganda are three of the common countries where churches have collaborated through child sponsorship and vision trips.

A Partnership Strategy

World Vision - New York is committed not only to working internationally, but also to having an impact on poverty locally. After partnering with several churches through its Youth Outreach Worker initiative, World Vision - New York decided to focus its efforts in the south Bronx— communities there are among the poorest in New York City and in the nation. Children are assisted through local mentorship programs and area retreat center programs.

Interventions include a 40,000-square-foot warehouse providing clothing, school supplies, building materials, and other products. The Storehouse solicits member churches and community organizations through whom the resources are made available to the broader community. Gifts in-kind are recruited from the corporate world and then passed through the Storehouse. Over the past five years, John's team has distributed more than $20 million worth of products throughout the local community. Storehouse events have included high-ranking politicians like Adolfo Carrion Jr., Bronx Borough president, and Congressman Charles B. Rangel. Over the past ten years, World Vision has expanded its primary partners—the local church, the donor community, mass media, agencies like Concerts of Prayer, and spokespersons like borough president Adolfo Carrion.

Ten Years Back and Ten Years Ahead

John Clause summarized the areas of greatest achievement:

- Partnering with Concerts of Prayer to engage the church. Churches have responded to the wake-up call to engage biblically and compassionately. The 9/11 response by the churches was very powerful. The idea of creating Hope Sundays was initiated in New York. The Hope Church Alliance was also birthed here in New York.
- Youth groups have been mobilized to participate in 30 Hour Famine. Hundreds of youth groups participate every year. Learn more on the worldvision.org Web site.
- In ten years since John introduced the idea of creating a stronger metro NYC presence, $30 million has been raised, multiplying the 1997 giving rate of $250,000 more than 100 times.
- There have been 12,000 children sponsored internationally from metro NYC donors and churches.
- The name awareness for World Vision in the region has more than tripled.
- Three metro ministry areas were birthed in New York, Chicago, and Seattle.
- Today 3 regions (East, Central, and West) have been designed, with 14 areas targeting 25 cities across the country.
- Organizationally, annual income has risen from $300 million to $1 billion under the leadership of Rich Stearns.
- Looking ahead, the desire is to replicate lessons learned in New York City across the United States by building a ministry to the poor and a ministry to the donor community.

A Call to Action

Given the desperate plight of the poorest of the poor around the world, World Vision will continue to challenge people to go beyond themselves in loving their neighbor as themselves.

The passion is to create a movement within the church to move outside our walls and adopt a community of AIDS orphans where homes can be built and lives can be rescued.

World Vision will continue to be a borderless, nondiscriminatory, child-focused Christian organization seeking to assist the poorest of the poor in more than 100 nations. World Vision looks for the most hopeless who would not survive without assistance. An empowerment model will be employed to teach, identify, engage the community, and create joint solutions. People will be taught how to lift themselves out of poverty.

Preparation for a New Decade of Leadership

In December 2005, John was diagnosed with head and neck cancer. He was aggressively treated over eight months of 2006, and thankfully survived the battle. He is now cancer free. The months of intensive chemotherapy and simultaneous radiation gave John an even greater level of identification with the poor and sick. During his season of recovery, John was able to prayerfully envision and plan for an even greater organizational structure over the next ten years, to connect communities of influence, affluence, and compassion along the eastern seaboard with the poorest of the poor across the globe.

Beginning in 2007, the work of World Vision was divided into three regions across the country. John Clause assumed responsibility over the East Coast, with work focused in the major metropolitan communities of Boston; New York; Washington, D.C.; Atlanta; Miami; and the Carolinas. The vision is to see an epidemic of compassion that will outpace the AIDS pandemic and root causes of poverty.

Leadership Reflection Questions

1. What is your church or organization currently doing to engage the HIV/AIDS pandemic?

2. What churches or organizations could you influence to do something together to impact children and communities in desperate need around the world?

3. What leadership lessons have you learned from your own experiences of suffering and trusting God over a long period?

Chapter 20

RESCUING CHILDREN IN RWANDA:
TRINITY BAPTIST CHURCH

"I praise you because I am fearfully and wonderfully made."

PSALM 139:14

Keith Boyd stood on the street corner of 5th Avenue and 34th Street on the morning of 9/11; he was in Midtown to attend the board meeting of Concerts of Prayer Greater New York (COPGNY) at the Empire State Building when two planes suddenly struck the twin towers of the World Trade Center. The Empire State Building was immediately evacuated. Keith Boyd, pastor of Trinity Baptist Church in Manhattan, was deeply moved by the tragedy, and thus fully engaged in the immediate relief efforts of 9/11, serving as a Red Cross chaplain at ground zero.

However, as the pages of the calendar turned, he found his heart returning to a state of uneasy unconcern. In the fall of 2003, Pastor Keith prayed that God would transform the hardness of his own heart and rekindle the compassion that had somehow waned. Unaware of his personal spiritual angst, I extended an invitation to Pastor Keith to join a vision trip hosted by World Vision to Rwanda.

We left for Rwanda in November 2004. The small team of New York leaders included Keith Boyd; Betsy Bond, a Trinity Baptist longtime member and a practicing veterinarian; and Allan Kemp and George Cox from Suffern Presbyterian in Rockland County, New York. On our way to Rwanda, we participated in an orientation at the Safari Park in Nairobi, Kenya. Pastor Keith remembers the first meal there, where we sat around a table with Nathan Gasatura, a World Vision leader in Rwanda. Viewing the picture folders of unsponsored children, Pastor Keith began to weep, moved by the plight of these children living in an AIDS-impacted country.

Before the trip, Trinity Baptist had already hosted two Hope Sundays, one on a Mother's Day and one on a Father's Day, and congregants had sponsored 100 children. Between the time Pastor Keith returned from the trip in November and Christmas, an additional 150 children were sponsored—from a congregation of 400 adults.[1]

For Pastor Keith's wife, Dee Ann Boyd, the journey took a little longer. When Pastor Keith took that first trip in November 2004, she was skeptical. Dee Ann realized it was a country recovering from genocide, but she still wondered about the real impact of child sponsorship. Could a few dollars a month really make a difference? How do we really know if the dollars even reach the intended children?

Dee Ann was in that state of mind one day when she went to pick up her youngest daughter, Claire, and bumped into a woman whose daughter was Claire's classmate. The woman was intimidating. She had her doctorate and authored textbooks; she had a career on Wall Street and sat on a White House committee. She was a Manhattan power mom.

The woman said to Dee Ann, "I hear that Keith is in Africa. What is he doing there?" Dee Ann told her that he was with a group of pastors to visit World Vision projects.

She asked, "The World Vision that sponsors children?"

"Yes," Dee Ann responded.

Then she said, "Dee Ann, do you know that when I was a little girl in the Philippines I was the youngest of six children when my mother left us? I was a sponsored child."

She went on to tell Dee Ann her story. Dee Ann's mind and heart forever changed that day.[2]

A 20-Year Journey with Trinity

My first contact with Trinity Baptist came in 1987 when I met Ted Gandy. Ted Gandy and Aida Force, with Here's Life Inner City, helped plan the first concert of prayer in June 1987. Ted has been a longtime member at Trinity Baptist. When I went away to study at Trinity Evangelical Divinity School, Ted gave me his computer so I could write training literature for the prayer movement.

Trinity, founded in December 1867 by Captain R. E. Jeanson of Gothenberg, Sweden, is a member of the Baptist General Conference (BGC) denomination. The BGC was a movement of Swedish Baptist churches begun in the nineteenth century. In 1931, the current location of Trinity Baptist was constructed using some of the finest Scandinavian architecture in North America. Located on 61st Street just off 2nd Avenue, it is a few blocks away from the United Nations and Central Park—part of an Upper East Side community whose residents are among the most influential and affluent in the world.

Trinity is located in a densely populated neighborhood with 7,000 people within one city block. The 500-member church is 50 percent Anglo and 50 percent international, including people from Asia, Brazil, Colombia, Africa, the Philippines, and many other nations. The relational lifeblood of the church is the 30 small groups that meet regularly.

The church experienced near fatal decline in the 1950s and 1960s. A core group of faithful parishioners maintained the vision for Trinity during the lean years; membership revived in the 1980s; and it grew during the pastorate of Gordon MacDonald in the late 1980s and early 1990s. Keith and Dee Ann Boyd came in 1992; Pastor Keith served in an associate role. Pastor Keith assumed the senior pastor role in 1993, when the church had 250 attendees.[3] Also in 1992, I was ordained into the Baptist General Conference. My home church, Central Baptist, located in Sioux Falls, South Dakota, sent my wife, Marya, and me to New York City in 1984.

Trinity Baptist became a primary supporting church of Concerts of Prayer Greater New York (COPGNY) in the 1990s. Pastor Keith Boyd joined the COPGNY Board of Directors upon its formation in 1998. The linkages between Trinity Baptist and COPGNY continued to mature in the new millennium.

The Vision of Trinity Baptist

Pastor Keith believes God has placed Trinity Baptist in an affluent, socially elite environment in order to be a window on the world of need. Leaders at Trinity Baptist attempt to get people from the Upper East Side in the door, and then show them a global worldview—acknowledging the reality most of the world faces. Rwanda provides the door people can go through to get outside of themselves. The Rwanda initiative has energized hundreds of people at Trinity. The vision of Trinity Baptist is:

> To **Encounter** God in all His mystery;
> **Engage** one another in meaningful community;
> **Explore** the questions of life in the context of a relationship with Jesus the Messiah;
> **Equip** one another for works of service; and
> **Empower** one another to become agents of transformation in our spheres of influence.[4]

A Rwandan Journey

Since 2004, the villages of Nyamagabe and Mudasomwa in southern Rwanda have been considered an extended family of Trinity Baptist Church. Each year, teams of volunteers travel to serve and personally connect to the people of these two villages. Part of the trip is always dedicated to building houses for some of the most needy—often child-headed households.

According to Nathan Gasatura of World Vision Rwanda, the orphan population has now climbed to 1.3 million, out of a national population of only 9 million.[5] The needs are enormous, and the rationale is not just to send money, but to also go and build *with* them, showing them how much they are loved. The team works alongside members of the community to roll mud, fetch water, carry rocks, and "get dirty" in order to build a home.

The local World Vision staff explained to the 2006 team how World Vision is set up locally. They gave an overview of specific ways people who have been devastated by genocide, poverty, and HIV/AIDS were being supported. They took a small group of the team for a day to see some of these efforts. It was a day to remember. The team was sitting on the grassy lawn of a church, under a beautiful canopy of trees. The group met 100 people living with HIV/AIDS. The team joined them as they met together to give and receive support, to pray, and to help relieve the isolation living with the stigma and hardship of HIV/AIDS brings.

That morning the group met John Mary, a nine-month-old baby boy who was quite sick and whose parents had recently died. One of the women in the group was asked if she had access to antiretroviral medication. She said the medicine was available and free. However, people did not take the medicine because it had to be taken with food. There wasn't enough food available to assist people dying of AIDS with lifesaving medicine.

At the end of the 2006 trip, team members were able to meet their sponsored children. The Boyd family sponsors Chantal. When I witnessed the first meeting between Keith Boyd and Chantal in 2004, it was supernatural. Pastor Keith said that he felt like Chantal had become their third daughter. While the sponsors and their children were playing games and having a feast, something happened. A large group of children formed along the fence of the youth center where the group was meeting. They were curious, hungry, and needy. They longed to come over the fence. Dee Ann and a few others were truly "wrecked" by this. They decided to do whatever was necessary to bring more of those children over the fence through child sponsorship.

Over the Fence

Upon their return from the trip, a team of 20 "storytellers" was organized to launch an Over the Fence campaign. Each storyteller was charged with the responsibility of sending 100 emails sharing their experiences, and asking their friends, family members, and co-workers to consider sponsoring a Rwandan child. For $35 a month, child sponsorship provides basic interventions such as food, clothing, education, medical care, and housing. Not only does the individual child benefit, but the entire family receives medical care. The community benefits by the creation of educational and economic development.

As a medium-sized church of 500 people, the campaign electrified the congregation. Over several weeks, an additional 400 children were sponsored. By early 2007, the cumulative number of children sponsored was 750.[6]

The success of the Rwandan partnership has been rooted in the leadership of Keith and Dee Ann Boyd. Additionally, Mike Whalen has become the deacon for Rwandan missions and the congregational champion. Robynne Bruckenstein, a longtime member of Trinity Baptist, was so moved by her participation on one of these trips that she joined the staff of World Vision in New York. She now helps coordinate the World Vision AIDS exhibit throughout the East Region of the US.

Trinity Baptist Church: Rwandan Ministry

Year	Sponsored Children	Community Development
2002–2003	100 children (through two Hope Sundays)	
2004	150 children	
2005	100 children	Constructed two homes.
2006	400 children (through Over the Fence Campaign)	Constructed two homes.
2007	750 children	Constructed two homes with Christ Tabernacle. Eight-day exploratory trip. Funded ten wells.
2008	Team World Vision sponsorship campaign with Chicago Marathon.	Pastor's vision and training trip. Construction trip.

A Vision for Leadership Development

Gordon and Gail MacDonald coached Keith and Dee Ann Boyd on developing leadership in the church. The MacDonalds counseled them to expect to wait three years to see growth. The intent was to grow kingdom leaders called to lead for the kingdom in whatever sphere of leadership God placed them.

The Boyds launched the Trinity Leadership Initiative (TLI) in 2002. TLI is an invitation-only opportunity to be mentored and trained for eight months, between October and May, meeting every Friday night for three hours. People were expected to participate every Friday, with the exception of two weeks off. In the first three years of TLI, 65 leaders participated. The TLI graduates have become many of the core members of the Rwandan outreach, as well as serving in various other leadership roles in the church.

As is the reality in most Manhattan churches, high turnover abounds. New York is a very transient city, and Trinity Baptist is no exception. Fifty percent of those that have attended TLI have already left the city. The Boyds are not discouraged by this, recognizing that their investment in these leaders is for the kingdom of God, not for Trinity Baptist. Thus, they are confident that most of these TLI graduates have assumed leadership roles in other places around the nation and the world, whether in churches or the marketplace.[7]

Trinity Baptist's passion for leadership development reaches beyond its own congregation. For three years, the church has hosted the Manhattan site for the Leadership Summit. More than 600 leaders have benefited in Manhattan, the world's most influential island. Prior to hosting, Trinity Baptist leaders would travel to New England or New Jersey for the summit. Trinity Baptist hosts the Leadership Summit because they see it as training tool and a unifying force for the cause of Christ in the city.

Keith Boyd believes strongly that all the churches have to be in this together to see the city changed for the cause of Christ. The need is to see all hands on deck. We can't just *do* church; to *be* the church, people need to go to the front lines, leading the cause for Christ.

Leadership Reflection Questions

1. Can you remember a time of asking God to completely break your heart over the suffering in the world?

2. Have you or people in the leadership of your church taken others on a firsthand immersion into the needs of other parts of the world?

3. What deliberate leadership development strategies have you put in place to mold those under your influence?

PART IV:
JESUS, CULTURE, AND COMMUNITY

Chapter 21

CHRIST IN CULTURE:
THE CHRISTIAN CULTURAL CENTER

"The kingdom of the world has become the kingdom of our Lord and of his Christ."
REVELATION 11:15

A. R. Bernard was working at Bankers Trust in the 1970s. He had been searching for truth in various places, including the Nation of Islam. The Nation of Islam provided discipline and identity, but not a personal relationship with God. While working at the bank as the unit head for the Student Loan Division, a secretary witnessed to him.

Her persistent and childlike faith in Jesus Christ disarmed him, so when Bernard was invited to a meeting at the Baptist Temple on January 11, 1975, he accepted the invitation. Nicky Cruz spoke that evening. At this meeting, Bernard heard God speak to his spirit as with the power of a blow torch through his chest, "I am the God you are looking for. I and My Word are one."

Up to this point Bernard had used church to attend activities and to participate in sports, but had viewed Christianity as a tool of oppression. However, at this point in his life, Rev. Bernard experienced the God that revealed Himself in Christ. He then dove into Scripture, making the salient observation that there is a distinction between the institution of Christianity and the person of Christ.

Growing in God at Brooklyn Tabernacle, Rev. Bernard discovered the Book of Romans and learned about the importance of memorizing Scripture. In 1976, he accepted God's call to ministry and by 1978 launched a storefront church that grew to 325 members by 1985. The church originally met in a storefront in the Williamsburg section of Brooklyn.[1]

A Turning Point

The growing church relocated in 1985 to a loft in Greenpoint, Brooklyn. In 1987, Rev. Bernard had a conversation at city hall with a New York City official, and he was informed that the Office of Clergy Liaison was being disbanded. The liaisons for the Jewish and Muslim communities were kept. When asked why, the official simply said that Judaism and Islam represented a culture, whereas Christianity was just a religion.

This conversation served as a catalyst in Rev. Bernard's thinking. He resolved to pursue the understanding of Christianity as culture and to understand the truth of Christ *in* culture. At the time of this revelation, the church was meeting in a loft with 450 members and 700 attendees. This new conviction of the culture of Christianity took years to study and manifest itself in the mind and life of Rev. Bernard. Convincing the congregation of this vital paradigm shift was a lengthy and deliberate process. Rev. Bernard felt the church had embraced a false view of church and state.

The church again relocated in 1989, to a renovated supermarket on Linden Boulevard in the Canarsie section of Brooklyn. The next ten years would include explosive growth—from 625 members to 11,000. On a typical Sunday morning in the 1990s, people would stand in line to get into one of four Sunday morning services.

Teaching the truth of Christ in culture, as well as teaching on the resolution of that identity as the key to growth, the church grew by 1,000 members per year. Scripture came alive for Rev. Bernard and for those who sat under his teaching. Passages in Daniel spoke to the potential of building relationships inside the political system and accepting the responsibility of leadership. Relationships and exercising leadership create the platform that speaks the language of culture.

Rev. Bernard found the relevance of his faith increased in this theological shift. Having been nurtured in a spiritual culture that made the *return of Christ* a focus with prophesy preceding that return, he now discovered the dynamic *presence of Christ* was creating immediate change in individuals and society. People were being changed in an instant, in a transforming moment in time.

Rev. Bernard's preaching encourages every listener to identify and pursue their vocation. Regardless of one's vocation—whether law, health, education, business—every aspect of one's work needs to be seen as a divine call. Rev. Bernard directs people toward their God-given gifting and aptitude. He found the Puritan definition of vocation to be powerfully true—that all the callings of God were gifted by God. Rev. Bernard paraphrased *Webster's* definition of vocation as a summons from God to individuals or a group to undertake a divine call to service to others; to serve the divine purposes in every condition, work, or relationship in life (it involves the total orientation of a human's life and work in terms of each person's ultimate sense of mission).

The Christian Cultural Center (CCC) mission is "to help spiritual seekers become transformed believers modeling Christ in culture and encouraging others to do the same."[2] Discipleship is understood as more than simply developing personal piety; it also involves having an impact on the society around each individual and the church collective. CCC seeks to transform and redeem family, church, education, politics, economics, the arts, and entertainment by empowering people to make a difference.[3]

This change is not effected primarily by protest. It is done by building relationships with and "whispering" into the ears of leaders. When a person visits the church and walks in through the South Administrative entrance, there is a pictorial witness to the impact of this model. Senators, mayors, and international leaders have visited the church out of respect for the leadership of Rev. Bernard. In February 2007, Rev. Bernard received the Martin Luther King Jr. Award from three of the most prominent Jewish organizations in New York City.

Another Decade of Growth

Currently there are 29,000 members at the Christian Cultural Center. The pattern of adding 1,000 new members per year continues. On an average Sunday, nearly 15,000 people attend worship. There is tremendous congruency of message between the teaching, the development of leaders, and the architecture of the space. The 11-acre church campus is currently located on Flatlands Avenue in Brooklyn. While predominantly African American, Latino, and Caribbean, the church is becoming increasingly diverse.

The sanctuary holds 3,900 people with overflow rooms that add another 700 worshippers. The large facility is breathtaking in its beauty. It is a unique architectural contribution on a global scale.

Consistent with its message regarding culture, the church also exhibits a mini art gallery. The walls throughout the building are filled with artwork from around the globe. The 3,000-gallon aquarium on the first floor has an exquisite array of 200 species of exotic saltwater fish from around the world. Having places of beauty to convene the body of Christ is an important contribution to the unity of the church. It creates a transcendent regionwide experience for many believers who are often limited in their own resources or the resources of their churches to gather in this way. Attention to design and detail is part of the legacy of Rev. Bernard. In addition to the sanctuary, there is a second-floor restaurant, Koinonia, that accommodates more than 100 people for special functions and gatherings. The restaurant provides first-class menu offerings and service.

Applying the strong teaching ministry, leadership development is a pivotal priority. The church is organized as an inverse pyramid. Rev. Bernard serves as the CEO and has an executive team of 7 leaders. There are 12 department heads who oversee 50 leadership teams. These teams consist of 1,200 team members. The church has 112 full-time employees.

This leadership model allows the church to effectively involve thousands of people in a range of ministries. On the Web site alone is a listing of more than 25 avenues for volunteer involvement. The second primary reason for the explosive growth of the church is the service experience it provides. Team members participate in monthly Saturday morning leadership training lasting from 9:00 A.M. to 11:15 A.M. This monthly gathering provides the opportunity to impart vision as well as to give team members a voice. Surveys are used to field the thinking and opinions of the leadership.

Skills are developed at each level of the organization. Each year, there is a four-day staff training event usually off-site. In 2006, the entire team traveled to Disney Training Center to study the model of staff development at Disney. The church routinely covers 50 percent of the cost for these training experiences. Staff members are constantly stretched to sharpen their customer service skills.

Another important dimension of team life is recognition. Every year at the Christmas staff dinner, one award per department is given. Two people are given an all-expenses-paid trip for their outstanding service to the church. In 2007, the two award recipients were sent to Spain.

The church has a broad range of programs and outreach. The performing arts department involves 300 people and major productions are a staple of the church. In December 2007, the Christian Cultural Center partnered with the American Bible Society to host a benefit concert for the Bowery Mission at Lincoln Center, featuring Natalie Cole. One of Rev. Bernard's sons, Jamaal Bernard, leads the youth ministry, involving several hundred youth. There are also multiple adult choirs, a youth choir, and two bands.

Every week, the elders lead the Tuesday night prayer service where between 1,800 to 2,000 people are regularly in attendance. The church has also served as a host for the National Day of Prayer broadcast seen around the world.

Christian Cultural Center: Organizational Struction

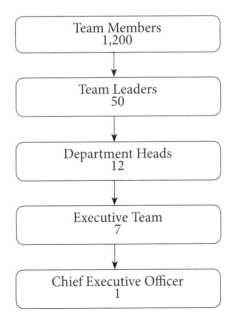

Citywide Leadership

Rev. Bernard has built a strong relationship with New York City mayor Michael Bloomberg and participated on the mayor's 2001 transition team. He has served on the New York City Economic Development Corporation Board. In 2008, he was elected president of the Council of Churches of the City of New York, representing approximately 1.5 million Protestants, Anglicans, and Orthodox Christians in New York City. Rev. Bernard's vision for the next ten years is to see a new level of partnership between the government and private sector to benefit local communities. He envisions a resurgence of the role of faith in the public square.

Rev. Bernard interfaces with numerous faith-based organizations. Since 2005, the Christian Cultural Center has been the Brooklyn site for the Willow Creek Leadership Summit. More than 1,500 leaders have participated. Rev. Bernard has hosted Bill Hybels on an annual basis, allowing him an excellent venue from which to speak to city leaders. Rev. Bernard himself was a plenary speaker at the 2004 Leadership Summit, and a keynote speaker at both the 2007 Fulton Street Revival Conference and the 2003 Gospel in the City Urban Consultation. Both events were cohosted by Concerts of Prayer Greater New York, and attracted leaders from 50 cities around the world. Rev. Bernard also serves as a National Advisory Team member of the New York City Leadership Center, incorporated in 2007, lending his expertise and experience in administration and leadership development.

The Council of Churches hosted an event at Christian Cultural Center on May 18, 2005, with Dr. David Yonggi Cho of Korea, pastor of the largest church in the world. Dr. Cho received the Family of Man Medallion from the council. Past recipients included John F. Kennedy, Dwight D. Eisenhower, Richard M. Nixon, and Jimmy Carter. Dr. Cho was the 25th person and the first Asian man to receive the award.[4]

Rev. Bernard has been passionate about bringing clarity to the central belief of Christianity in the public dialogue. He desires to see Christ become the main character in the cultural discussion.

Leadership Reflection Questions

1. Has your church or organization ever studied the engagement of culture by having its members utilize their vocational callings?

2. What type of investment is being made to grow the number of trained volunteers in your church and organization?

3. How have you persisted in your calling to see God's vision come to fruition through your leadership?

Chapter 22

CHRIST CROSSING CULTURE: CHRIST CHURCH

"How good and pleasant it is when brothers dwell together in unity."

PSALM 133:1

Jamaican-born David Ireland moved with his family to Rosedale, Queens, New York, when he was eight years old. They were one of the first black families to live in that area in the early 1970s. Two weeks after the Ireland family moved in, six teenage boys threw four Molotov cocktail bombs into their rear bedroom window.

Part of the home was burned, but thankfully no one was hurt. The attack was racially motivated, and the Irelands also received death threats and hate mail. For a time, police provided 24-hour-a-day surveillance around the house. Other racially motivated events followed, in successive attempts to drive the family away.

The Irelands did not move. The civil rights movement righted many wrongs, but it obviously did not eradicate racial prejudice. While the civil rights activism of the 1960s paved the way for improved relations across cultures, the work of reconciliation is far from over. Even in the twenty-first century, acceptance of cultural diversity is often not found in communities, schools, businesses, politics, and sadly even in churches across the country.

"My parents shielded me and my three other siblings from as much of the hate crime as possible," Pastor Ireland says. "When I turned 20 and became born again, the Lord healed me of my own pain of victimization, and I believe I became an authentic reconciler. An authentic reconciler is someone who's dealt with their pain to a point where they can be an advocate for someone who is different than themselves."[1]

Thirty-five years after the firebombing of the Ireland home, Dr. David Ireland's passion for multicultural ministry is alive and well at Christ Church in Montclair, New Jersey, affecting the value and strategies of this growing (and increasingly diverse) congregation.

A Defining Moment

In 1986, David Ireland and his wife, Marlinda, were invited to start a church. Pastor Ireland was already an accomplished engineering student, having completed degrees in mechanical and civil engineering. He continued in a consulting role in the engineering field for six years. The church plant began with the Ireland family and six others. The church plant was two weeks old when Pastor Ireland had a defining moment while in a grocery store aisle .

"'When I reached my hand on the shelf to put an item in my basket, . . . because I looked down the end of the aisle and I saw different kinds of people,' Ireland remembers. 'I saw white, African-American, Asian, Hispanic, biracial, and East Indians. I saw so many different kinds of people in that grocery store, all brought together by a common need. The Holy Spirit spoke to my heart and said, "David, why can't it be like that in My church?"

"'The need for the gospel and desire to worship are as universal as our common need for food. I started weeping, and I'm not a very emotional person. It was in that moment that the Lord chose to mess me up emotionally and to give me a vision for the rest of my life.'"[2]

Between 1986 and 1994, the church grew to 500 worshippers, even as it moved eight times. In 1994, an opportunity arose to purchase a dilapidated cathedral. The building had been used by Harry Fosdick in 1917. "Fosdick was the most prominent liberal Baptist minister of the early 20th Century. Although a Baptist, he was Pastor of the First Presbyterian Church on West Twelfth Street and then at the historic, interdenominational Riverside Church . . . in New York City."[3] In 1994, the building looked like it belonged to the Addams Family—10 to 12 different groups rented space in the multiroom, ancient structure.

Pastor Ireland was taken in by the beauty of the stained glass in the building. He made 700 color photocopies of the stained glass in order to persuade the congregation to invest in the purchase of the building. At a congregational meeting, people salivated at the opportunity to buy the property. Pastor Ireland challenged them to commit $100,000 before they left the meeting. They accepted the challenge, and the building was purchased for $1.25 million; an additional $1 million was given to renovate the property.

The church grew rapidly to the 1,000 attendance mark by the mid-1990s and to 2,000 by 1999. The church attendance doubled again by 2002 to 4,000 and reached 5,000 by 2004. Today the church has crossed over the 5,500 mark. See the chart below.[4]

Christ Church
Church Street and Trinity Place • Montclair, New Jersey 07042

ATTENDANCE SUMMARY

Sundays Prior 2003	In 2003	Saturday In 2006	As of Dec 31 1999	As of Dec 31 2000	As of Dec 31 2001	As of Jun 30 2002	As of Jun 30 2003	As of Jun 30 2004	As of Dec 31 2004	As of Dec 31 2005	As of Jul 31 2006	As of Jul 31 2007
7:30 AM	7:00 AM		573	688	825	866	676	743	781			
9:00 AM	8:30 AM		665	915	966	1121	953	1000	1050	1831	1648	1598
11:00 AM	10:00 AM		775	1008	1209	1463	1492	1537	1614	1630	1548	1471
1:00 PM	11:45 AM				492	556	1001	1051	1082	1093	1104	1115
	1:30 PM						750	773	796	804	723	738
		7:00 PM									500	575
TOTAL			2003	2514	3492	4006	4871	5104	5322	5357	5523	5497

Notes: Prior to April 2001, Christ Church had three morning services (8:00 AM, 10:00 AM, and 12:00 PM)
Prior to April 2003, Christ Church had four morning services (7:30 AM, 9:00 AM, 11:00 AM and 1:00 PM)
December 2003: Average of 4,891 and 5,104 = 4,988
December 2002: Average of 4,871 and 4,006 - 4,439
September 2005: Combined 7:00 a.m. and 8:30 a.m. service into new 8:00 AM service
March 2006: Added Saturday night service at 7:00 p.m.

Growth Factors

In addition to the dynamic teaching of Pastor Ireland and corporate worship experiences, the church entered into an important paradigm shift. Until 1999, trained pastors led each aspect of the church, including the strategic and administrative dimensions. Pastor Ireland decided to hire people with academic backgrounds in the areas of administration, education, and finance. He was challenged at a John Maxwell conference, during which he came to the realization that the church staff was working off of his energy.[5]

Staff persons need to begin to create their own energy spheres. One of Pastor Ireland's important hires was Rupert A. Hayles Jr., who arrived at Christ Church with training from the Wharton School of Management. Hayles, the chief operating officer, held senior-level positions with Prudential Insurance Company, Cytec Industries, and Merck and Company before joining the church staff in 2002. The seven-person executive team includes the senior pastor, chief financial officer, vice-president and chief of staff, chief operating officer, two associate pastors, and a senior associate pastor.[6]

The church realized that with five Sunday services, it maximized its space at the Montclair site and needed additional room to grow. After years of prayer and research, the church located property in Rockaway, New Jersey. The property is 100 acres and 30 minutes away from the Montclair property. A former office and industrial complex for Agilent Technologies, the property had been vacant since October 2002.

The property was offered at an asking price of $17 million; the leaders of Christ Church countered with an offer of $10.25 million; their offer was accepted at the end of 2003. The subsequent process of gaining approvals and raising funds has been an enormous challenge.

Meetings with the Rockaway Township Planning Board to gain zoning ordinance approval for the church to use the property started in December 2003. Initially, the mayor and city leaders welcomed Christ Church to the area. But when the information hit the newspapers that a multicultural megachurch was moving into Rockaway (which is 94 percent Anglo in the latest census data), a vocal group of residents began complaining that the increase in traffic would affect their quality of life.

This group, called Voices of Rockaway Township, Inc. (VORT), distributed literature to the homes of Rockaway residents designed to sway public opinion against the church's proposed move. It was remotely, yet eerily, reminiscent of Pastor Ireland's unwelcome reception in Rosedale, Queens, 30 years earlier. One handout erroneously stated that Christ Church's site plans included a nursing home and a prisoner rehabilitation facility.

By 2006, the church had attended its 30th planning board meeting. Rupert Hayles said, "In the very beginning, a group formed to find anything possible to not have us here. But we have all bought into the multicultural value, and we've been preparing for such a long time, which will be evident when we do get to Rockaway. Our hearts have been prepped. We realize this is a God thing for us."[7]

Despite the stiff community opposition and high expense, the plan is moving forward. The first $6.7 million raised, another campaign is scheduled to raise the necessary funding to prepare a sanctuary for worship by the end of 2008. The sanctuary will be 106,000 square feet. Buildings on the campus will total 263,000 square feet and include a family life center with a fitness center and gymnasium; educational building to expand Trinity Academy through grade 5; a performing arts school; a Bible training center for adults; and campus recreational areas. The new Rockaway campus positions Christ Church to have an impact on the five sectors of society as never before. The five sectors include education, politics and government, family, business and economic, and religious leadership.[8]

Another Vision

In 2005, Pastor Ireland had a dream that the President was sitting front and center at Christ Church. It challenged him to take on the mind-set that when he preaches, he needs to speak as if the President was in the audience—not because he's the President, but because in that role, his decisions impact the entire world.

"From this vision, we began to ask, 'How can our church impact society?' The Five Sectors Alliance developed from this dream. We are now asking ourselves, 'What are we doing as a church that will affect these five sectors?'" asks Hayles.[9]

The five sectors are basic to society:
• *Education.* This sector of society impacts the future by developing the minds and intellectual strength of its individuals.

- *Religious.* This sector serves the spiritual need of our society.

- *Family.* This sector is the fundamental building block of our society that influences the development of our children and communities.

- *Business and Economic.* This sector is where energies are expended for the continued growth and development of our economy in order to provide for and nurture our families and communities.

- *Government and Political.* This sector consists of society's will for the governance of interaction between individuals; federal, state, and local governments; and between nations around the world.

Launched at a gala award banquet in 2006, the Five Sectors Alliance will bring some of the best minds together from each sector to wrestle with major societal issues. Throughout 2007 and 2008, lawyers, politicians, CEOs, superintendent of schools, and presidents of family-oriented organizations came together to dialogue at the Five Sectors Plenary Summit. The topic of discussion was "A Response to the Economic and Social Impact of Absentee Fathers." The team has formulated strategies and is in the process of developing and implementing a program in a local city that will serve as an incubator to not only help the city, but to serve as a best-practice model for other nonprofits, governmental agencies, or individuals who would like to do something about this major challenge in society. Christ Church engages each of the five sectors in the following ways:

- *Education.* Launching Trinity Academy for children prekindergarten through grade 1. The Learning Center provides tutorial support to the local community. The Youth Leadership Institute serves as developmental program for young people to understand the key component of leadership as they develop into vibrant leaders of society.

- *Religious.* Christ Church has a global missions program including humanitarian work around the world, as well as leadership development. Countries benefited include the Dominican Republic, Jamaica, Mexico, Kenya, Nigeria, China, Zambia, Australia, and Guatemala. Regionally, Christ Church has planted five churches.

- *Family.* Through the Impact Community Development Corporation, a $1.3 million grant was awarded to establish Winners Wait and the Abigail Project. Winners Wait is a sexual abstinence program; the Abigail Project provides a safe haven for victims of domestic violence, and with a grant of $1.05 million from the state of New Jersey, a site consisting of three homes with the potential to house ten families was purchased in 2007.

- *Business and Economic.* Christ Church is a member of the Jones Center for Advanced Strategic Studies at the University of Philadelphia. The church sends key leaders to special gatherings of senior executives who, throughout the year, discuss business issues that impact society. The church launched the Center for Business Excellence in 2006 to address the growing need of the community entrepreneurs who needed help and assistance with the development of their businesses. The center brings in high-impact professionals to provide instruction, partner with governmental agencies to provide access to funding, and to collaborate with the Wharton School to have plans and business reviewed by high-caliber MBA students.

- *Government and Political.* Christ Church has established key relationships with both state and national legislators who effect the policies and laws affecting church members and the community as a whole on a regional, state, and national level. Both the Republican and Democratic New Jersey gubernatorial candidates were invited to speak to the members of Christ Church during the 2005 elections.[10]

Observations

I have come to know Christ Church and its leadership over the past several years. What has impressed me is the extraordinarily deliberate effort of a large church to maintain a multiethnic vision. The church is 75 percent African American and 25 percent Anglo, Hispanic, and Asian. I am very impressed that 50 percent of the church participates in LIFE Groups and Life Activity Groups. This requires four full-time staff members to coordinate pastoral care through these small groups. The passion of the church is to reach out beyond itself and to serve the broader church.

The church expresses its corporate prayer life with Wednesday night prayer from 6:00 P.M. to 7:00 P.M., a men's phone prayer chain, Upper Room Community of intercessors, and periodic 40-day journeys of focused prayer.

In 2005, Christ Church hosted the Willow Creek Leadership Summit for the first time. It was the third largest new site in the nation in terms of attendance. The minority involvement in the Leadership Summit in Greater New York in 2005 represented 20 percent of all minority involvement in North America. Christ Church has been a major educational influence for the Willow Creek Association as evidenced by Pastor Ireland's presentation at Willow Creek Association's 2006 Acts 2 Conference.

Three of the leaders from Christ Church joined me in Rwanda in 2003. The church has generously partnered by sponsoring 100 Rwandan children. Pastor Ireland has also joined the National Advisory Team for the New York City Leadership Center.

The accomplishments of the church over the past 20 years have simply been stunning. Christ Church; the leadership of Pastor Ireland; his wife, Marlinda Ireland; his team; and their future vision are a great sign of hope for metro New York City and the nation.

Leadership Reflection Questions

1. Can you identify a difficult moment in your life that turned out to be a turning point for your future?

2. How have you been challenged to deliberately cross denominational and cultural differences in your community?

3. What would be a place for you and your church/organization to start crossing these boundaries?

Chapter 23

REVIVAL FROM THE RUBBLE:
PRIMITIVE CHRISTIAN CHURCH

"The wall of Jerusalem is broken down."
NEHEMIAH 1:3

Marc Rivera's world came crashing down on 9/11—both philosophically and literally. He pastors a church a short walking distance from ground zero. Debris of the falling towers crushed his son's school. For most of that Tuesday, Marc didn't know if his son had survived. If the north tower had fallen north instead of south, it would have reached his church. Marc Rivera witnessed the unforgettable sight of people falling and jumping out of the south tower.

Primitive Christian Church became a ground zero church providing 24/7 care for the initial three months after 9/11. Of all the buildings in the immediate area, the church was the only one with functioning power lines. Dazed and dirty with soot, New Yorkers wandered eastward down East Broadway from the collapsing towers. Many of them ended up at the church, used as a rest station. The church dimmed the lights and played calm music; members set up phone banks to allow people to contact loved ones.

Marc Rivera and his leadership team, including his wife, Enid, as copastor, managed resources to assist victims. They unloaded trucks of food, water, and blankets. They provided a place for community training in the areas of pastoral care and follow-up with victims' families.

Immediately after the towers fell on 9/11, Pastor Rivera saw the need for the gospel to speak to terrorism, to his ecclesiology, and to his philosophy of urban ministry. The evil of the world was focused on New York.

The church provided counseling to healers. Primitive Christian Church gave birth to an organization, Northeast Clergy Association, that provided the training for pastors dealing with 9/11 trauma. More than 1,500 families were served through Primitive Church and its partners. An arena of extreme and ongoing importance was mental health. The terrorist acts shattered many New Yorkers' sense of security and stability. Fear was rampant. Pastor Rivera concluded that the gospel must change the heart and society. If souls are saved but society is not penetrated, then the church has failed in its mission.

Pastor Marc Rivera became a pastor to many of the political officials in the aftermath of 9/11, in both face-to-face and phone meetings. The relationships with politicians birthed during 9/11 continue to this day.

The aftershock of 9/11 resulted in the middle class leaving the immediate area around the Lower East Side. Those who stayed behind were the very rich and the very poor. This is yet another illustration of the impact of gentrification on the city, with particularly difficult consequences on the poor. The disappearance of the middle class is often accompanied with the disappearance of services benefiting the poor.

Primitive's Beginnings

The church had been founded in 1953 by Rev. Pablo Rodriguez as a Baptist church for Puerto Rican, Spanish-speaking immigrants. In 1960, the church operated as an independent congregation and bought its first building, followed by a second building in 1969. During construction on the church building in 1973, the buildings collapsed due to a structural integrity issue in the subway system near the F line. The congregation met and prayed over the rubble and banded together to raise money. In that first gathering in front of the debris, the congregation raised more than $17,000. After securing finances through the denomination, the church built the current building with $80,000 and uncountable sweat equity from its members. Today, the building is worth more than $7 million.

After having functioned independently since 1953, church leaders engaged in conversations with the Assemblies of God, and decided to join the denomination. Primitive Christian Church has maintained its relationship with the Spanish Assemblies of God for the past 30 years.

Dr. Juan R. Cortes became the next pastor in 1978. He was a progressive leader skilled at teaching and shepherding the congregation, and led the congregation from a legalistic Pentecostalism to a more balanced view of Scripture. Dr. Cortes helped guide the church from the view of the practice of the charismatic gifts as a condition of salvation. As the years went by, he noticed that the congregation was losing its children to English-speaking churches in areas throughout the city. To counter this exodus, Dr. Cortes established English Language Ministries.[1]

After Dr. Cortes had a heart attack in 1991, Marc Rivera became a full-time associate pastor. He had begun as a pastoral associate at Primitive Christian Church in 1977. Pastor Rivera assumed the senior pastor role in 1994. He had worked in the corporate world with IBM since 1974, and had never envisioned leaving that behind.

Primitive Church ministers on the Lower East Side in a historically Puerto Rican neighborhood. The community has been changing rapidly, not only socioeconomically but also ethnically. Along with the large Hispanic population, there is a large Jewish community. Chinatown continues to creep eastward with restaurants within a few blocks of the church. And Pastor Rivera projects that within ten years a large number of Anglo gays will continue to move into the neighborhood. Currently, 25 percent of Primitive Church's attendees are first-generation Hispanic. Today, Primitive Church has grown to 1,000 attendees, divided between the Spanish- and English-speaking congregations. Given the crowded conditions of the Lower East Side and poor parking, this is a miracle.

Community-wide and Citywide Engagement

Primitive Church was well-positioned to become the 9/11 church due to its history of partnership with the local community. Pastor Rivera oversees a local community development corporation called Vision Urbana that employs 20 staff members and is engaged in a variety of community services. Vision Urbana has raised public money to sustain its outreach.

Through the ministry of Vision Urbana, every day 165 young people participate in various programs, including afterschool offerings. Every week, 100 seniors are also served with program offerings. Pastor Rivera has rallied the community to address such important issues as housing, health care, education, and job creation.

Immediately after 9/11, Pastor Rivera and his network were able to gather 2,000 people to pray together in a local schoolyard on a Sunday afternoon. He also partnered with other local and some national leaders to host a citywide observance on the anniversary of 9/11 in Madison Square Garden. The Northeast Clergy Association hosted a luncheon in February 2002 with Anne Graham Lotz, Billy Graham's daughter, as a featured speaker.

Pastor Rivera has been an important mentor to many ministry leaders in New York City. He played an important role as a former board member of Concerts of Prayer. His insights into the growing and rapidly changing Hispanic community have provided an important lens to leaders from other cultures.

Pastor Rivera has also led Primitive Church into church planting. In recent years, the church has planted two other churches. Primitive Church has partnered with the Church Multiplication Alliance to access training and funding to help launch these new churches.

Pastor Rivera has said, "I have a lifelong commitment to the Lower East Side. I am committed to the welfare of my community and have invested time in developing relationships in all strata of the community."

Why has the church continued to grow? Pastor Rivera notes four reasons:
- The church has chosen leaders from within. Almost 100 percent of the leadership is from within.
- Longevity of leadership. There is no substitute for continuity of leadership.
- Consistency of preaching every Sunday.

- Living in community. The senior pastor knows the people of the community and has earned their respect. This has provided the credibility to rally people when important issues are discussed.[2]

Leadership Formation

Pastor Marc Rivera has identified the number one crisis facing churches and organizations today: effective leadership transition. It is particularly significant in this era of megachurches to ensure prominent leaders replace themselves intentionally. This has become particularly acute in a season with many of our most well-known leaders entering the winter season of their lives.

When Pastor Rivera joined the staff at Primitive Church, he did not have formal seminary training. Instead, he entered into a mentoring relationship with Dr. Cortes that has continued for more than 25 years. Remarkably, Pastor Rivera still meets with Dr. Cortes on a weekly basis, as he has since 1978, and they speak almost daily. Dr. Cortes has maintained his emeritus relationship with Primitive Church throughout Rev. Rivera's pastorate.

Following the model of Dr. Cortes, Pastor Rivera meets regularly with a young ministry leader 20 years younger. He seeks to live a transparent life before the younger leader. Pastor Rivera is committed to a careful and well-thought-out leadership succession plan. There are great challenges in leading a church like Primitive. Over the next two decades, the church will face exciting opportunities in a daunting environment.

In turn, Pastor Rivera also meets with his staff weekly, not only for administrative oversight, but also for their leadership development. He provides immediate feedback to staff members on their various assignments. Pastor Rivera believes that in order to develop a culture of leadership, there has to be a constant rhythm of critique and affirmation.

Pastor Rivera views delegation of authority as the key to leadership. He believes that the senior pastor only needs to make 5 percent of the decisions—but that 5 percent is the church's life-or-death decisions. In order to lead this way, the senior pastor needs to develop pastoral leaders to help shoulder the other 95 percent of the decisions.

Pastor Rivera sees his relationship with his mentor, his staff members, and leaders in the next generation as the critical success factor. He builds a strong enough reservoir of trust that allows him to be spoken to, as well as to speak into the lives of others. Pastor Rivera earned his master's degree at Alliance Theological Seminary, and finished his doctorate of ministry at Gordon-Conwell Theological Seminary in 2005. His dissertation focused on the needs of succession within Hispanic churches.

Observations

What has made Pastor Rivera such an effective leader at a local congregational, community-wide, and citywide level is his understanding of who he is himself. He is very clearly grounded in his lifelong calling to his church and community. He is conversant with the needs of the community and has the necessary relational currency with local and citywide officials to advocate effectively for his community. His compass is clearly the relationship he enjoys with his wife, Enid, and his mentor Dr. Cortes. This keeps him firmly rooted in the work that God has called him to do. He is creating an important template for leadership development for every church that takes its calling to its neighborhood seriously.

Leadership Reflection Questions

1. Can you identify three to five community leaders in your neighborhood who shape local policy?

2. What would be a practical way to benefit your community as modeled by Primitive Christian Church?

3. Is there an emerging leader in your congregation or organization that would be important to mentor over the next five years?

Chapter 24

A Preferred Future: The Life Christian Church

"I saw a new heaven and a new earth."

REVELATION 21:1

Terry Smith began speaking as an itinerant evangelist at age 16 in his home state of Indiana. Blessed with an unusual speaking gift, he crisscrossed the nation, speaking in 40 states by the time he was 29. Terry was speaking 250 times a year. He traveled to El Salvador, Ireland, England, Germany, Canada, Columbia, Israel, and Africa to speak on the topic of leadership.

Terry primarily addressed youth and revival meetings in his early career. He also spoke at various crusades on high school and college campuses under the banner of Take New Territories. Even at the beginning of his speaking career, Terry had a dream in his late teens that he would one day pastor a church in suburban New York City. Terry eventually came and spoke to a fledgling group of five or six people that included his friend of 20 years, who had planted a church in an upstairs apartment in Orange, New Jersey. Terry became well known as he also preached in larger venues during his 20s.

Every year, he came to metropolitan New York to speak to the little group in Orange, New Jersey. By 1991, the group had 54 voting members, but no building, money, and no leadership structure. When they called Terry to come as their senior pastor, he accepted.

Today the church has 900 active participants with a weekly attendance of more than 500. The Life Christian Church has become one of the most multiethnic churches in the region. The church also has some of the greatest socioeconomic diversity in the region. What happened?

The Journey of the Life Christian Church: A Timeline

Year	Accomplishment
1983	The original church was formed as New Life Church.
1991	Terry and Sharon Smith moved to West Orange, New Jersey, with their three children to begin the pastorate. The church began forming LIFE (Life in a Family Environment) Groups and moved into a school.
1993	The church rented space from a community house.
1995	The church bought a bowling alley in downtown West Orange and converted it into a worship center. They renamed themselves as the Life Christian Church.
1998	The church adopted a coffee bar model in the lobby of the worship center to become more welcoming to unchurched people.
1999	The church purchased the Ridgeway Campus—a 6.25-acre campus which was the site of a monastery. It was intended to be the future church site, and is now housing the offices of the church.
2002	Pastor Smith begins negotiating with the town of West Orange and developer Larry Pantirer for the exchange of the Ridgeway Campus with undeveloped Metzger farm on Northfield Avenue.
2004	Town of West Orange approves Northfield deal for the Life Christian Church.
2006	Northfield lot officially becomes 747 Northfield Avenue and is dedicated during the From Dirt to Destiny event.
2007	Groundbreaking occurs at 747 Northfield Avenue for new modular offices.
Spring 2008	Dedication of the new modular office complex.

The Texture of the Life Christian Church

The church has grown steadily 10 to 15 percent each year. Pastor Smith described the growth as not the spectacular, overnight type of growth, but the result of doing the little things to be a healthy church on a daily basis. The church is approximately 35 percent African American, 35 percent Anglo, 20 percent Latino, and 10 percent Asian or other; there are a number of internationals from Africa, Asia, and Europe.

The church's diversity is also seen not only in its ethnic makeup, but also in the *types* of people who have been attracted. A number of Ivy League graduates attend the church, particularly those from minority backgrounds. People come from both the wealthy communities such as Sparta, New Jersey, as well as from the inner-city communities of the surrounding townships.

East Orange is predominantly African American and Newark also has a large African American population. West Orange was settled by Irish and Italian Catholics, and is largely upper middle class. It is 30 percent Jewish also and is now a diverse community. The church draws from all of these communities, as well as from as far away as Manhattan and Brooklyn.

For many attendees, their experience at the Life Christian Church is the first time in their lives they have met others so remarkably different from themselves. In the context of the Life Christian Church, something extraordinary happens—people learn to love people who are radically different from themselves socioeconomically and culturally.

Carl George, noted author on church growth, made the observation that the one factor that all of these attendees have in common is that they are upwardly mobile. The church has created a leadership culture that helps people at whatever starting point they find themselves, and encourages and enables them to progress in all areas of their lives.

The mission of the Life Christian Church is "to inspire people to grow in their life with God and to learn, live, and lead as authentic followers of Jesus Christ." The vision of the church is:
- to be a church for the unchurched and spiritual seekers to explore the claims of Jesus Christ and find life's meaning through relationship with God and others;
- to encourage spiritual growth, through development of our relationship with God and others, and to encourage the pursuit of authenticity and excellence in each area of our lives;
- to be a church for people of all backgrounds, and to model reconciliation in every way, especially in relationships, and between races, cultures, and denominations;

- to facilitate ministry opportunities for every person joined to the local church;
- to be a church of leaders and a leading church.[1]

The Church's Strategic Programmatic Decisions

At the beginning of Terry and Sharon Smith's journey with the church in 1991, they decided to invest everything into small groups, great weekend experiences, and children's ministries. Their commitment was to provide a great weekend experience with culturally relevant worship, pregnant with the presence of God. The Smiths were equally committed to providing spectacular experiences for children and young people.

The church has always invested in the creative arts through music and drama. The intentional commitment to ethnic diversity is an important thread running through the church's life. At first they had been told they would not be able to grow a large church with so much diversity, but God has honored their deep unwavering conviction to this.

Today, 30 LIFE Groups meet three times per month. The groups are spread out in diverse geographic areas representing the members' addresses. These small groups provide the intimate setting for community, so desperately needed in the hurried, time-poor culture of the urban Northeast. In addition, the entire membership meets monthly for an evening of celebration and Communion service.

Having spoken several times at the church for the past ten years, I am always profoundly encouraged by this remarkable gathering of people. Terry and Sharon Smith have an unusual ability to attract and engage people from every walk of life, demonstrating an exceptional leadership skill that brings people together from diverse backgrounds.

The Influence of the Life Christian Church

Pastor Smith has always been very deliberate about engaging the broader community. The church has taken Christmas offerings and invested them in community projects with the Eagle Rock Civic Association. The civic association exists to provide practical service to the area.

To aid in health care in the community, the church purchased a defibrillator for the local volunteer first-aid squad. Pastor Smith is called upon for major civic functions, including the public relations commissions for the town of West Orange that grew out of the major crisis of corruption in government in the community.[2]

Pastor Smith participated in the inauguration of the mayor and received the first call from the mayor after 9/11. Pastor Smith interacts with Newark's current mayor, Cory Booker, and also interacted with former New Jersey governor, Richard Codey. This is what Governor Codey and Mayor Booker said about the church's impact at a banquet honoring the 15th anniversary of the church:

> *Governor Codey:* "I first heard of the reverend from my father who said that this young man was going to do a lot of great things for West Orange, and he was right. A lot of you obviously are not from town, but it's more than a town, it's a region. And what he and his wife and family bring to this town and to this region is why we celebrate this church."[3]

> *Mayor Booker:* "I'm here today because this church is not about four walls and just taking care of the congregation itself, but about bringing in the community and reaching out with love to be a conduit for the light and glory of God's love."[4]

Engagement in Mission

Besides its ability to connect with people of political influence, the church has a deep commitment to people in desperate need. The church has developed a partnership and financially supportive relationship with St. Bridget's house in Newark, a community where 1 out of every 63 African American men have AIDS. This has an impact on hundreds in the community.

Charles Valentine has emerged within the church to lead the PATH ministry (Peace over Addiction Through Healing). God enabled him to overcome a 20-year drug addiction and has a powerful testimony of how God can rescue the down-and-out. The outreach is a 12-step recovery program from a Christian paradigm and reaches out to people in jails and hospitals. It has been extraordinary to see the number of people with addictions, who are from all walks of life, who come forward for help. Since its inception, the PATH ministry has served hundreds of people.

Globally, the church has begun to partner in Rwanda with World Vision. After a 2007 vision trip, the church hosted Nathan Gasatura, a World Vision leader, who is also the national AIDS chairman for Rwanda. The Life Christian Church is now sponsoring more than 100 children as part of the Hope Church Alliance, the partnership between World Vision and Concerts of Prayer Greater New York. Dozens of leaders from the church have planned travel to Rwanda to visit sponsored children.

Another important partner is Touch the World. The church has sent more than 40 young people on summer missions trips to Uganda and Mexico with Touch the World. The Life Christian Church has been an excellent partner with other churches and agencies, drawing from regional expertise to strengthen its own outreach.

Pastor Smith was an early architect for the partnership with the Leadership Summit hosted by the Willow Creek Association (WCA). He and I made our first trip to WCA meetings in Florida in 2004. We thought carefully on how to bring the resources of the summit to our region in a different model. The ten sites that have emerged in the metropolitan area represent the greatest ethnic diversity of any city participating in the summit in North America.

A Preferred Future: The Church Looks Ahead

Pastor Smith has plans to build a facility—50,000 square feet in an initial phase. By phase two, it will expand to 111,000 square feet. The objective in the building program is to build an 1,100-seat auditorium. The church also plans to become a center for missions for years to come, with the new facility to include an arts center, leadership center, child-care center, recreation center, and bookstore.

As the new facilities emerge, they will be the first of their type for an English-speaking congregation in the West Orange community. It will represent a remarkable achievement for an ethnically and socioeconomically diverse congregation, pointing to a miracle-working God.

Pastor Smith believes, teaches, and practices the truth that God has a unique destiny for each of us from the promise of Ephesians 2:8–10. He says, "Our responsibility is to listen to God and then do our part in fulfilling the dream that God has for us individually and corporately as the body of Christ."

One of Pastor Smith's great strengths is his intentionality. I still remember the day when I got a phone call from Terry more than a decade ago. I was sitting in my attic office at home. Never having met, he knew enough about the work of Concerts of Prayer and its mission to seek out a meeting. He committed financial support for the organization over the phone—that was a first! Pastor Smith has become a very important part of the organizational culture of Concerts of Prayer, as well as a member of the board for the New York City Leadership Center. He articulates very clearly the possibilities of what God can do in our region through a community of like-minded leaders and churches.

Leadership Reflection Questions

1. Looking at your personal leadership journey, can you identify two or three experiences from your past that have prepared you for your present responsibilities?

2. Describe what a "preferred future" would look like for your church or organization in terms of its size and outreach.

3. Share your dream for your congregation or organization with another leader on your team. Note the similarities in your respective visions.

Chapter 25

FROM NEIGHBORHOODS TO THE NATIONS: RESURRECTION CHURCH

"And you will be my witnesses."

ACTS 1:8

Joseph and Joyce Mattera were married in 1980 in New York City. After their wedding, they traveled together as members of a missions team to Moscow, Kiev, and Leningrad, Russia. From the beginning of their union, their ministry has been both local and global. For nearly 30 years, they have worked closely to raise their family of five children, plant a church in Brooklyn, and incubate ministries that have had an impact on thousands of people around the world. Their first home group started in 1981; in 1982, the fellowship moved into rented space at Ebenezer Church.

A Woman in Leadership

Joyce Mattera founded Children of the City in 1982 after a Children's Crusade attracted 500 young people. Since then, she has nurtured this outreach to many of the most disadvantaged children of Brooklyn. Starting out as a children's prevention outreach, Children of the City evolved to "include trauma intervention, counseling, an afterschool and summer program, courtroom and legal advocacy, social work, guardianship, financial counseling, youth mentoring, and other as-needed services to help children and their families achieve success in education, social relationships, home," and in their finances and careers.[1]

The organization took on an important role after 9/11, identifying 200 children who were traumatized by the attacks. A grant from World Vision allowed Resurrection Church to hire administrative support and to begin grant writing to expand their programs for the children's growing needs.

Today, there are some 2,000 children on the roster with 1,000 actively visited by 50 volunteers. Children of the City offers counseling and afterschool programs. The program has resulted in measurable improvement in the children's school grades. College students serve as counselors, and current efforts focus on breaking the cycle of poverty through education. The assignment is challenging given the absence of strong families.

Every week, 300 to 500 children meet in this program. The organization also offers parenting solutions for up to 50 parents who attend seminars. Special programs are offered on the weekend of Valentine's Day, addressing the issues of sexual abuse. The church distributed 800 toys in December and 150 turkeys at a service for parents at Thanksgiving.

Joyce Mattera joined a citywide community of women leaders to host the Women's Prayer Summit in 1995 and 1996. Under the direction of Janet Broling, nearly 5,000 women gathered in at the Madison Square Garden theater. The planning team included a diverse group of women from African American, Anglo, and Hispanic backgrounds.

In 1995, the women gathered on the same day in Madison Square Garden that a million men gathered on the Mall in Washington, D.C. I remember the poignancy of returning home to Penn Station that day from Washington and realizing that just a short distance away, thousands of women had been meeting and praying.

A Church Is Born

It was the preaching of Ben Crandall, an important figure in the spiritual history of twentieth-century New York City, that deeply influenced Joe Mattera in the 1980s, along with many young leaders. The idea of reaching all of New York City with the gospel captivated Pastor Joe's thinking. The methodology that emerged for Pastor Joe is a strategy of church unity through multiple partnerships.

Resurrection Church was founded in 1984 as a multiethnic congregation. It now attracts more than 40 nationalities and almost ten languages are spoken by its congregants. For more than 24 years, it has served as a leadership incubator. Leaders from Resurrection Church have moved on to assignments in the Dominican Republic and diverse contexts throughout the United States. For example, Lenny Weston trained at Resurrection Church and launched Vision Ministries International

When the church was started, a high crime rate plagued their Sunset Park, Brooklyn, neighborhood. More than half of the attendees were lower-income welfare recipients with only one home owner in the entire church. In the past 30 years, the crime rate has dropped dramatically, many members have purchased homes, and the church has built up entrepreneurs, businesspeople, and community leaders.

The church now owns its own property and attracts attendees from throughout the tristate region. Part of the church's vision is "to prepare and place godly leadership into every facet of society for biblical justice and reformation; to teach and demonstrate biblical principles of stewardship to break poverty so believers can prosper and effect positive change in their communities."[2] The vision manifests itself both internally and externally through a number of new initiatives birthed under Joe Mattera's leadership.

A Defining Moment

Pastor Joe attended the first GateKeeper's Urban Consultation in 1995 in Manhattan, with 95 New York City leaders. Urbanologist, missiologist, and noted Bible teacher Ray Bakke taught about the interrelatedness of urban theology, history, and sociology. Joe Mattera said, "This was the most salient moment I had ever experienced in ministry. Bakke's teaching gave me permission to use my intellect and apply other disciplines in ministry, in addition to theology." Bakke helped give birth to Joe's commitment to holistic theology and ministry.[3]

Wedding the conviction of uniting the church with a holistic view of ministry, Pastor Joe has incubated several important initiatives over the past 25 years. In 1991, he initiated the All City Prayer meetings. Thousands gathered in multiple churches around the city to cry out to God. This prayer stream connected with Concerts of Prayer in the early 1990s. Eventually Pastor Joe joined the Concerts of Prayer Greater New York Board of Directors and was a pivotal leader in the Brooklyn Concerts of Prayer events throughout the 1990s. Many of the meetings were held at Bay Ridge Christian Center in collaboration with Luciano Padilla.

Building on the commitment to unify the body of Christ, Pastor Joe organized and hosted several unity communion events. One such gathering was held at Bedford Central Presbyterian Church in Brooklyn, pastored by Clive Neil. The spirit of these gatherings was to build relationship and awareness across racial lines in the body of Christ. This culminated in a Building Bridges Reconciliation Summit in 1996.

That same year, Pastor Joe hosted John Perkins of the Christian Community Development Association in the American Cities campaign. The Brooklyn Borough president, Howard Golden, presented a formal proclamation to the event.

International Ministry to Leaders

In 1994, Pastor Joe Mattera began traveling to the Dominican Republic to network pastors and leaders. This trip resulted in him forming a network of churches under the leadership of a local pastor he was mentoring. Today, that network has hundreds of churches and has had an impact on both the Dominican Republic as well as numerous Latin American nations, and beyond. From Puerto Rican ancestry, Pastor Joe's leadership has attracted a large number of people from Puerto Rican and Dominican backgrounds. In 1997, he initiated leadership training in Honduras, and during the following decade, leadership training travels would take him to Cuba, Holland, and Eastern Europe.

Christ Covenant Coalition and City Action Coalition
Pastor Joe felt led to consolidate ten years of networking and bridge building in the body of

Christ with the formation of the Christ Covenant Coalition. Along with Bishop Roderick Caesar Jr., this newly formed entity began to host monthly pastors' meetings. The vision of Christ Covenant Coalition is to:

- strengthen and affirm each member through relational development;
- strengthen and establish the local church through equipping ministries;
- help establish churches and ministries through covenant partnerships;
- help establish the city church in various regions through covenant partnerships;
- work with key spiritual leaders and other coalitions (or networks) to identify and establish and strengthen apostolic ministry in cities nationally and internationally.[4] These meetings became one of the largest of their type in the city.

Christ Covenant Coalition provided coaching, mentoring, and accountability relationships for pastors. Christ Covenant Coalition has continued to network nationally with other networks of like-minded pastoral groups. Approximately 150 to 200 pastors are connected to the vision through the affiliation of eight pastoral associations in the Greater NY Region (many more are connected through leadership affiliation beyond the Greater NY Region). In April 2006, a multiethnic group of 50 bishops and apostolic leaders consecrated Pastor Joe Mattera as bishop of this group.

City Action Coalition was created "to effect moral and social change in our nation by encouraging strategic partnerships to represent and advocate for the Judeo-Christian values of mainstream America to media, elected and public officials, the New York region, and to the nation at large."[5] One of the primary issues addressed by the coalition is promotion of traditional marriage; press conferences and rallies have convened to give voice to spiritual leaders on such important topics. In 2004, the coalition hosted a press conference in which 250 bishops, pastors, and clergy converged on the steps of city hall to speak on behalf of traditional marriage. Another event at city hall gathered thousands of citizens in renewal of their traditional marriage vows.

A Leadership Journey

One of Pastor Joe's leadership strengths has been his commitment to the life of the mind. He studied under Ray Bakke and graduated from Bakke Graduate University in 2006 with a doctor of ministry in biblical worldview. The program allowed Pastor Joe to travel to China and get even more exposure to the international church.

Joe Mattera is a prolific thinker and writer. He has hosted his own radio show, *Light Your City*, and weekly cable television program, *The Ekklesia*. He contributes regularly to local Christian newspapers, has a Web site with regular postings (josephmattera.org), and is the author of *Ruling in the Gates* (Creation House Publishing, 2003).

Through engaging diverse organizations and civic efforts, Pastor Joe has allowed himself to be molded as a leader. He has sat on the boards in an advisory capacity with Concerts of Prayer Greater New York, World Vision, CURE (Community Understanding for Racial Reconciliation), Brooklyn Community Board 7, and a vice-chair for the 2005 Billy Graham Crusade. He has also worked as a consultant and mentor to numerous political, business, and church leaders, including the New York City Police Department.

One of his early organizing efforts took place in 1989 when he formed a grassroots organization that successfully closed down a pornographic store. The organization, Communities Against Porn, successfully led the charge against the proliferation of pornography.

Leadership Reflection Questions

1. Can you identify and affirm three women in leadership in your church, organization, and community?

2. What can you do to grow the "life of the mind" in your leadership? Who should you pursue to study under or be mentored by?

3. Is there a cultural issue that your church or organization is called to address with the broader body of Christ?

Chapter 26

SEEKING THE WELFARE OF THE CITY:
LOVE GOSPEL ASSEMBLY

"Seek the peace and prosperity of the city."
JEREMIAH 29:7

Gerald Kaufman came from a good Jewish family. His family held to the Orthodox Jewish traditions, so at age 13, he experienced his Bar Mitzvah. Thinking himself a man at that age, Gerald began to drink wine. Two years later, at age 15, he started to use heroin. At first he began sniffing the drug, then injecting it into his veins. During the next 12 years of his life, police arrested Gerry and jailed him six different times.

In December 1962, he walked into a Puerto Rican Pentecostal church and accepted

Jesus Christ as his personal Savior. At the time of his conversion, he experienced a miraculous healing from drug addiction. The person chiefly responsible for his conversion was Rev. Leoncia Rosado, affectionately called Mama Leo, a petite, green-eyed woman from Puerto Rico. (This is same Mama Leo referred to in chap. 5.)

A few weeks after his salvation experience, Kaufman was sent to Zion Bible Institute in Rhode Island where he graduated with high honors in 1965. He later continued his education at Logos Graduate School, receiving his doctor of ministry degree with a major in urban studies. Churches generously supported Kaufman financially.

When Kaufman graduated, he came back to the Hispanic church John 3:16 in the Bronx under the leadership of Rev. Ricardo Tañón. In the late 1950s, John 3:16 was the largest Hispanic church in New York City—with 3,000 people. Kaufman's emergence and his leadership within the church caused Rev. Tañón to consider establishing an English-speaking congregation.

The 1970s were a time of upheaval in the Bronx. The construction of the Cross Bronx Expressway contributed to the destruction of whole neighborhoods, leading to the dislocation of 300,000 Bronx residents. The population loss resulted in 40 percent of the Bronx being burned to the ground through arson, as landlords tried to recover their investments through insurance claims. It was this context that helped to give birth to Love Gospel Assembly under the leadership of Gerry Kaufman.

A Protégé Is Formed

Ronald Bailey relocated from New York City to Ohio, where he lived from 1978 to 1982. While in Ohio, he began to serve God more fully. He was told by friend Sammy Cuestar to look up Pastor Gerry Kaufman on his return to New York. For several months, Bailey was unable to find Kaufman because the Spanish services were held in the morning and Kaufman was leading the English service at 3:00 P.M., which was an untraditional time.

In 1982, they finally met in Poe Park in the Bronx at a rally Bishop Kaufman was hosting. Bailey joined the church and slowly began to get involved. Over an 11-year period, his leadership unfolded slowly until the time he was named senior pastor in 1997, after Kaufman's sudden and tragic death. Bailey's leadership trajectory looked like this:

Trajectory of Bishop Ronald Bailey's Leadership

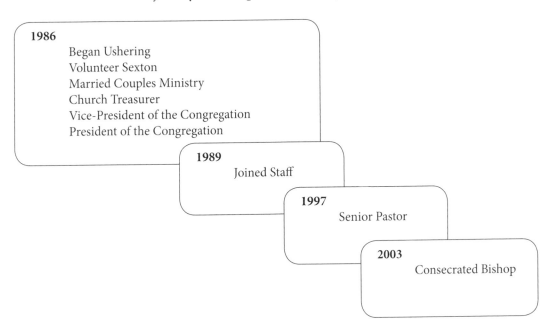

During the 11-year period between ushering and becoming a full-time pastor, Bailey worked full time as an electrical foreman from 10:00 P.M. to 6:00 A.M. each night. Concurrent with his work and church responsibilities, he attended Logos Bible Institute, where he earned an undergraduate degree. Bailey eventually earned both a master's degree and a doctor of ministry degree.

The friendship and partnership between Gerry Kaufman and Ron Bailey is an important and poignant story. A converted Jew became bishop and was succeeded by an African American who also became a bishop. As the result of their multicultural spiritual journey, a passion for the entire body of Christ has been pivotal to their combined spiritual legacy.

Love Gospel Today

The church is located on the major thoroughfare of the Bronx, the Grand Concourse, on the corner of 183rd Street, in what has been a notoriously dangerous community; historically it has been one of the leading neighborhoods for violence. Today, 600 people regularly attend Love Gospel

Assembly each Sunday; on Friday nights an additional 250 to 300 people attend the service. Due to their schedules, there are many who are only able to attend one of the weekend services.

The current leadership of the church includes 15 staff members; they oversee their most well-known outreach, the Love Kitchen. Having experienced the ravages of hunger during his 12-year drug addiction, Bishop Kaufman established the Love Kitchen as a way to assist people who were hungry.

Bishop Bailey says, "We were feeding the poor before it became fashionable." On holidays, the meal is accompanied by music or a message from the Word of God. On Thanksgiving, as many as 800 people are fed and given coats, hats, gloves, and a gift pack that includes toiletries, socks, and blankets.

Feeding the poor and clothing the homeless are "biblical mandates" for Bishop Bailey and his multicultural congregation. "'The Bible speaks more about the poor than it does about prosperity,' he said. 'According to Luke 4:18, we have a commitment to the poor and disenfranchised to not only feed them, but also to be a voice for the voiceless, and an advocate for the rejected and the marginalized.'"[1]

Since its inception 23 years ago, the Love Kitchen has provided 4 million meals. Every day, 300 to 400 meals are served. Between 11:00 A.M. and 1:00 P.M. families arrive, and at 3:00 P.M. children arrive. The commitment is to provide a meal in a way that ensures the dignity of those being served. The church has funded the Love Kitchen primarily out of its own tithes and offerings.

The church also has an extensive compassion ministry. Love Gospel reaches out to the addicted and the abused. This takes the form of a detoxification program for the addicted. They also provide nonperishable items to families in need. To meet medical needs in light of the exorbitant costs of health care and health insurance, Love Gospel partners with Montefiore Hospital to provide free medical attention. Staff members of the hospital hold examinations at the church for those unable to travel to and pay for medical attention. The church also provides legal representation for people who may need immigration assistance or other forms of representation. Church leadership also takes teams to local prisons. In its relationship to the community, Bishop Bailey has served as a chaplain to the 46th precinct police department and as chaplain to the Jewish Nursing Home and Hospital. Their myriad ministries are holistic—reaching every aspect of life and ministering to true needs.

Under Bishop Kaufman's leadership, the Antioch School of Urban Ministry launched 21 years ago. Today there is a student body of 50 to 60 who are studying for certificates and diplomas. Gifted teacher Rev. Dr. Dorothy Lewis is the school's dean.

A Citywide Influence

During the tumultuous 1970s, Bishop Kaufman challenged churches to stay in the Bronx (see chap. 4). His commitment ran so deep that he required all of his staff members to live in the Bronx if they planned to serve the church.

I first heard Bishop Kaufman speak at a Bronx gathering for a pastors' concert of prayer. He reflected on Nehemiah 1 and made the following comments:

> "You will never learn how to pray until you have learned how to weep. You will never learn how to pray until you are honest enough to confess. You will never learn how to pray until you are bold enough to take life-threatening risks for God."

Bishop Kaufman embodied the sentiments of those words in his compassionate leadership, since passed on to Bishop Bailey and his team.

The leadership of Bishop Bailey and Minister Pura Coniglio in the citywide prayer movement is foundational to the movement's influence. For the Bronx, Love Gospel is the church at the forefront of Pray New York!, involving more than 100 other churches. Bishop Bailey has been a member of the Concerts of Prayer Greater New York Board of Directors for several years.

A Vision for the Future

In preparation for future expansion, the church purchased all of the property between its building and the end of the block. Bishop Bailey envisions building a Promised Land Campus. This new structure will be a partnership between the church and the business community. Together, he wants that partnership to reach out to the poor and outcast as well as reach middle and upper classes.

In its current design, the project will include a five-story building with underground parking, retail space, 15 classrooms, a chapel for 200 people, and a multipurpose venue called Kaufman Hall. This will offer a full dining room with a full-size commercial kitchen to seat 700.

The second phase of the strategy is to build condominiums on the Grand Concourse. This would provide a funding stream to sustain the campus. Increasingly around New York City, churches are using innovative strategies, exchanging air rights to commercial developers to build space for church purposes. This development strategy also creates a significant income stream for the local church.

Challenging Times

Not only is it challenging to work among the chronically poor but also a concerning trend is taking place among Bronx neighborhoods. Historically, the Bronx was a place for the Irish, Jewish, and African American communities. In the past several decades, the borough has become increasingly Hispanic. What Bishop Bailey sees now is a large Muslim population that is systematically buying property and taking over neighborhoods. Churches are increasingly ceding the culture of the borough over to the Muslim community. This phenomenon is happening across the borough. Real estate is less expensive in the Bronx than in the other four boroughs, so it has become a natural landing place for many immigrants. The challenge to the church is to become strategic in assisting existing churches and church plants to take up residence in these neighborhoods that have many new and receptive populations.[2]

Leadership Reflection Questions

1. Can you trace the spiritual lineage of your church or organizational founder?

2. What would it mean for you to have a radical, long-term commitment to a specific geographic community?

3. How do you express your commitment to the poor in your leadership?

Epilogue

GREATER NEW YORK AND THE CHOREOGRAPHY OF GOD

This book began by describing God's determination to bless all the nations of the earth in the church's modern expression in Greater New York. The balance of the book told the story of how God has choreographed that determination through the stories of His people. The book serves as a modest attempt to tell part of the story of what God is doing in Greater New York. He is doing far more than what the book suggests. In the words of Paul's prayer in Ephesians 3, God is doing immeasurably more than we can possibly think or imagine.

All of the good things that have happened in our lives and the spiritual lessons we have learned have been the result of God's choreography. He is mysteriously involved in the cosmic movements of history, as well as immersed in the details and conversations of our individual lives. God is a God who pays attention to us. In fact, the final verse of Psalm 23 reminds us that God is chasing us with His goodness and mercy all the way into eternity. This book describes something of that chase.

The themes that have tied all of these stories together are these—God has raised up leaders who have interceded, innovated, and collaborated with the broader body of Christ. The leaders described in this book come from every imaginable walk of life, ethnic background, homeland, and economic status. All of this uniqueness is being used by God to change our region and the world.

God desires to make us like Himself. John Stott, in his final sermon in 2007, stated that the goal of our lives is to become Christlike. Throughout the stories of this book, we have read how people are a mirror to the image of Christ. Leaders have mirrored God in their creativity—making something from nothing. Leaders have mirrored God in their sacrifice—leaving home and stability to go into the great unknown to reach people otherwise unreached. Leaders have mirrored God in their stubborn persistence toward an unfulfilled goal, even after 50 years.

Jesus is committed to the city. As humanity has been drawn by the hundreds of millions to our urban centers, He is committed to build up a people and a witness in the most difficult places. Our participation with Him shapes our character to become like Him.

Jesus is committed to the unity of His people. Division in the church breeds atheism in the world. We become like Him when we make every effort to keep the unity of the church in our respective cities and communities.

Jesus is committed to children and youth. He came as an Asian-born baby and became an African refugee. This is not accidental—it is part of our becoming like Him in our identification with and service toward the most vulnerable on the planet. Children may be in our backyard or they may be in the barrios in the Third World; our responsibility is to all of them.

Jesus is committed to the mission of the church. We become like Christ in our leadership when we articulate the truth that the world is divided ultimately into two groups—people who know Jesus and people who don't. We are not ultimately divided into male and female, African, Asian, Latino, or European; Baptist, Episcopalian, or Catholic—we are divided into people who know Jesus and those who don't. We reach out in creativity and determination.

Jesus is committed to the relevance of His people. We become like Christ when we can relate to the full range of society—whether it be in city hall or to those who have no resources. We become like Christ in crossing culture and by manifesting a Christian culture in the midst of our cities. We become like Christ when we recognize the full worth of every person and extend ourselves in generous compassion toward the least of these.

Progression Toward Transformation of Life and Community

Steps toward transformation	Impact
United Prayer	We experience the spiritual power of being together in one place. We see walls of division and misunderstanding broken down.
Networking	We intentionally connect with diverse groups of leaders, groups, and churches to create the relational environment to do things together.
Knowledge	We intentionally work at getting to know people across cultural and denominational lines. We understand that people can only love that which they know. We study one another's church histories and journeys.
Agreement	We decide together what God wants us to do together. There is nothing more powerful than being in spiritual and practical agreement together.

My prayer for this book is that it will stimulate each of us to see the larger work that God is doing. I also pray that we will intentionally connect with the leaders, churches, and organizations who are working with similar passions. Finally, my prayer is that we will seek to become the kind of leaders that others will follow in leaving a legacy for the generations behind us.

Notes

Foreword by Terry Smith

[1]David Bryant, introduction to *The Power of a City at Prayer*, by Mac Pier and Katie Sweeting (Downers Grove, IL: InterVarsity Press, 2002), 19.

[2]David McCullough, *John Adams* (New York: Simon and Schuster, 2001), 1.

[3]Ibid., 7.

[4]Ibid.

Introduction

[1]Ray Bakke, foreword to *The Power of a City at Prayer*, by Mac Pier and Katie Sweeting (Downers Grove, IL: InterVarsity Press, 2002), 9.

[2]Mac Pier and Katie Sweeting, *The Power of a City at Prayer* (Downers Grove, IL: InterVarsity Press, 2002), 37.

[3]Ralph Winter, *Perspectives on the World Christian Movement* (Pasadena: Paternoster Publishing, 1999), 152–62.

[4]Bakke, foreword to *The Power of a City at Prayer*, 9.

[5]Tim Keller, Lecture on the Church and Cultural Influence (Hilton Hotel, New York City, February 2004).

[6]Jim Mellado, Lecture to New York City Pastoral Leadership (Bowery Mission House, Manhattan, April 2005).

Chapter 1

[1]Richard F. Lovelace, *Dynamics of Spiritual Life* (Downers Grove, IL: InterVarsity Press, 1979), 166.

[2]Norris Magnuson, *Salvation in the Slums* (Grand Rapids: Baker Books, 1977), 79.

[3]"New York Law Enforcement Agency Uniform Crime Reports 1965–2006," http://www.disastercenter.com/crime/nycrime.htm.

Chapter 2

[1]Amanda M. Burden, *The Newest New Yorkers 2000* (New York: New York City Department of City Planning, October 2004), 4, 12.

[2]Ibid., 8.

[3]Laird W. Bergad, *Latino Data Project: New York City's Latino Population in 2006* (New York: Center for Latin American, Caribbean, and Latino Studies, City University of New York, November 2007), 5, http://web.gc.cuny.edu/lastudies.

[4]Ibid., 6.

[5]Ibid., 8.

[6]Ibid., 4.

[7]Ibid., 6.

[8]US Census Bureau, *Major Asian Subgroups* (New York: New York City Department of City Planning), 2000 Census SF1 File, Table 21, 44.

[9]Pei-te Lien and Tony Carnes, "The Religious Demography of Asian American Border Crossing," in Tony Carnes and Fenggang Yang, eds., *Asian American Religions: The Making and Remaking of Borders and Boundaries* (New York: New York University Press, 2004), 38–54.

[10]Daniel J. Wakin, "In New York, Gospel Resounds in African Tongues," *New York Times*, April 18, 2004.

[11]*Russian Jewish Immigrants in New York City* (New York: The American Jewish Committee/Research Institute for New Americans, 2000), 5.

[12]Columbia News, "Columbia Presents First-Ever Study on Muslim Political, Social, Religious Identity in NYC," September 30, 2004.

[13]Association of Religion Data Archives, "Muslim Counties 2000," http://www.thearda.com/QuickLists/QuickList_57.asp.

[14]UCLA High Education Research Institute, *The Born-Again College Students of NYC* (New York: Values Research Institute, 2001).

Chapter 3

[1]Bill Hybels, Address at 2006 Concerts of Prayer Greater New York Gala Dinner (Hilton Hotel, New York City, October 20, 2006).

[2]Edward Hart, "Remonstrance of the Inhabitants of the Town of Flushing to Governor Stuyvesant, December 27, 1657," http://www.nyym.org/flushing/remons.html (accessed January 14, 2008).

[3]Mac Pier, *A New York City Leadership Center* (New York City, January 2006), 2.

[4]Tony Carnes, *Report on Church and Ministry Leaders of New York City Area* (New York: Values Research Institute, October 15, 2007), 13.

[5]Ibid., 29.

Chapter 4

[1]Robert Worth, "Guess Who Saved the South Bronx?" *Washington Monthly*, April 1999.

[2]Jonathon Kozol, *Amazing Grace* (New York: Crown Publishers, 1995), 143.

[3]Ibid.

[4]Pura Coniglio, interview by Mac Pier, December 18, 2007.

[5]Gateway City Church, http://www.gatewaycitychurch.net (accessed December 21, 2007).

[6]Charles Simpson, interview by Mac Pier, December 18, 2007.

[7]Joel Sadaphal, interview by Mac Pier, December 18, 2007.

[8]Hans Wiesner, "Staten Island Summary Report—Pray New York! 2004–2007."

Chapter 5

[1]Howard Caro-Lopez, *Latino Data Project: Socio-Economic and Cost of Living Indicators Among Foreign and Domestic-Born Latino Nationalities in the New York Metropolitan Area, 2005* (New York: Center for Latin American, Caribbean, and Latino Studies, City University of New York, 2005), 14.

[2]Ibid., 7.

[3]Ibid., 7, 17.

[4]Bishop Hector Bonano, interview by Mac Pier, December 20, 2007.

[5]Manuel Ortiz, *The Hispanic Challenge* (Downers Grove, IL: InterVarsity Press, 1994), 35.

[6]Andrew White, *Hardship in Many Languages* (Milano Graduate School Center for New York City Affairs, January 2004), 1–2, http://www.newschool.edu/milano/nycaffairs/immigrant/hardship.pdf.

[7]The Bronx Borough President's Office, "Biography of Adolfo Carrion Jr.," http://bronxboropres.nyc.gov (accessed June 17, 2008).

[8]Rev. Raymond Rivera, "Address to the Lived Theology and Power Workgroup" (Bronx, New York; April 20, 2002).
[9]Bishop Hector Bonano interview.

Chapter 6

[1]Rev. Roderick Caesar Jr., interview by Mac Pier, December 20, 2007.
[2]Mac Pier and Katie Sweeting, *The Power of a City at Prayer* (Downers Grove, IL: InterVarsity Press, 2002), 92.
[3]Robert D. Carle and Louis A. Decaro Jr., eds., *Signs of Hope in the City* (Valley Forge: Judson Press, 1999), 81.
[4]Stephen McGuire, "Rev. Floyd Flake & The Allen AME Church: Helping Southeast Queens Keep the Faith and Grow Economically," *Queens Press,* 2001, http://www.queenspress.com/anniversary2001-flake.htm.
[5]Greater Allen AME Cathedral of New York, "Professional Profile—Rev. Dr. Floyd Flake, http://www.allencathedral .org/allen/home.aspx?nid=250&idv=209&sbnav=237&shc=0 (accessed April 18, 2008).
[6]McGuire, "Rev. Floyd Flake & The Allen AME Church," 3.
[7]Kelly Hudson, reporter, Religion & Ethics, *Profile: Floyd Flake,* September 24, 2004, Episode no. 804, http://www.pbs .org/wnet/religionandethics/week804/profile.html.
[8]Greater Allen AME Cathedral of New York, "Shekinah," http://www.allencathedral.org/shekinah/default2.aspx (accessed April 18, 2008).

Chapter 7

[1]Kenneth O. Brown, *Inskip, McDonald, Fowler: Wholly and Forever Thine, Early Leadership in the National Camp Meeting Association for the Promotion of Holiness* (Hazelton: Holiness Archives, 1999).
[2]Scott Hoffman, interview by Mac Pier, December 17, 2007.
[3]Carl Ellis, *Beyond Liberation* (Downers Grove, IL: InterVarsity Press, 1983).
[4]Kathryn Long, *The Revival of 1857–58* (New York: Oxford Press, 1998), 48.
[5]Dr. Fish, *It Began with One* (Alpharetta, GA: North American Mission Board, 2007) (documentary on the 1857 Revival).
[6]Scott Hoffman interview.
[7]Scott Rasmussen, interview by Mac Pier, December 18, 2007.
[8]Scott Hoffman interview.
[9]Scott Hoffman, "The Discipleship Center at Ocean Grove" (Ocean Grove, NJ: n.p., 2007) (brochure).

Chapter 8

[1]Gary Frost, interview by Mac Pier, November 19, 2007.
[2]Mac Pier and Katie Sweeting, *The Power of a City at Prayer* (Downers Grove, IL: InterVarsity Press, 2002), 27.
[3]Ibid., 131–33.
[4]Jeremy Del Rio, "20/20 Vision for Schools: Transforming Public Education Within a Single Generation of Students," http://2020.coalitionnyc.com/page/3 (accessed April 25, 2008).
[5]Tony Carnes, Address to Denominational Leaders (First Baptist Church of Flushing, New York, September 2004).
[6]Ibid.
[7]David R. Jones, "Saving Children of Prisoners," *New York Amsterdam News,* May 4, 2006.
[8]Dr. Jawanza Kunjufu, *Raising Black Boys* (Chicago: African American Images, 2007), 18.
[9]New York State, *Kids' Well-Being Indicators Clearinghouse,* 2003–2007.
[10]Del Rio, "20/20 Vision for Schools."
[11]Ibid..
[12]Ibid.
[13]20/20 Vision for Schools, http://2020.coalitionnyc.com/?page_id=2 (accessed April 25, 2008).

[14]Gary Frost interview.
[15]Ibid.
[16]Ibid.
[17]Jeremy Del Rio interview.
[18]Ibid.
[19]*Amachi* DVD, Wilson Goode, Public Private Ventures.

Chapter 9

[1]Aimee Cortese, "A Monologue" (Bronx, New York; Crossroads Tabernacle, 1982), 1.
[2]Joseph and Melissa Cortese, interview by Mac Pier, November 21, 2007.
[3]Aimee Cortese, "Monologue."
[4]Emily Faucher, "Crossroads Tabernacle Pastor Envisions a Bright Future ," *Bronx Times*, January 10, 2002.
[5]Joseph and Melissa Cortese interview.
[6]"History of Crossroads Tabernacle, Inc.," 1–7 (brochure).
[7]Tom Campisi, "Boden Center Opens with a Higher Standard," *Tri-State Voice*, February 2005, 1, 13.

Chapter 10

[1]Robert Johansson, interview by Mac Pier, November 20, 2007.
[2]Robert Johansson, Lecture to Bakke Graduate University Students (Evangel Church, June 20, 2007).
[3]Robert Johansson interview.
[4]Ibid.

Chapter 11

[1]Nancy Gavilanes, "Christ Tabernacle Releases Powerful DVDs," *Tri-State Voice*, January 2005, http://www
.tristatevoice.com/Archives_1_2005.htm (accessed April 29, 2008).
[2]Ibid.
[3]Michael and Adam Durso, interview by Mac Pier, November 20, 2007.
[4]Ibid.

Chapter 12

[1]Jeff Boucher, interview by Mac Pier, November 29, 2007.
[2]Ibid.
[3]Fred Provencher, interview by Mac Pier, November 29, 2007.
[4]Cornerstone Christian Church, "Building Faith with the Word of God," 2007. (brochure)
[5]Fred Provencher interview.
[6]Jeff Boucher interview.

Chapter 13

[1]Redeemer Presbyterian Church, "Redeemer's History," http://www.redeemer.com/about_us/vision_and_values/
history.html (accessed April 30, 2008).
[2]Terry Gyger, interview by Mac Pier, November 19, 2007.
[3]Redeemer Presbyterian Church, "Redeemer's Vision," http://www.redeemer.com/about_us/vision_campaign/
(accessed April 30, 2008).
[4]Terry Gyger interview.

[5]Tim Keller, "Ministry in the Global City: Basic Principles in the Book of Acts" (National Leadership Forum, New York, October 2003).

[6]Mark Reynolds, interview by Mac Pier, November 19, 2007.

Chapter 14

[1]John Hao, interview by Mac Pier, November 20, 2007.

[2]Amanda M. Burden, *The Newest New Yorkers 2000* (New York: New York City Department of City Planning, October 2004), 8.

[3]John Hao, "The Setting: The Growth of Faith Bible Church" (diss., Palmer Seminary, 2007), 4.

[4]Ibid., 4.

[5]Ibid., 6–7.

[6]Michael Luo, "In New York, Billy Graham Will Find an Evangelical Force," *New York Times,* June 21, 2005, http://www.nytimes.com/2005/06/21/nyregion/21evangelical.html?scp=2&sq=&st=ny+ (accessed May 1, 2008).

[7]John Hao interview.

[8]Ibid.

[9]John Hao, "The Setting," 15–17.

[10]Ibid., 23–25.

Chapter 15

[1]Glenn Harvison, interview by Mac Pier, November 21, 2007.

[2]Ibid.

[3]Ibid.

Chapter 16

[1]Jack Crabtree, interview by Mac Pier, November 26, 2007.

[2]Steve Tomlinson, interview by Mac Pier, November 26, 2007.

[3]Ibid.

[4]Long Island Youth for Christ, *Yesterday, Today, Tomorrow,* Annual Report 2007–2008 (Huntington Station, New York).

Chapter 17

[1]Carlton Brown, interview by Mac Pier, November 21, 2007.

[2]Ibid.

Chapter 18

[1]Dan Mercaldo, interview by Mac Pier, December 18, 2007.

[2]Gateway Cathedral, http://www.gatewaycathedral.org/cms/page.aspx?pageid=205 (accessed December 22, 2007).

[3]Ibid.

[4]Russell Hodgins, interview by Mac Pier, December 18, 2007.

[5]US Census Bureau, *State & County Quick Facts—Staten Island, New York,* 2003 Estimate, http://quickfacts.census.gov/qfd/states/36/3651005.html (accessed May 7, 2008).

[6]Wikipedia, "Demographics of Staten Island," http://en.wikipedia.org/wiki/Staten_Island (accessed July 6, 2007).

[7]Amanda M. Burden, *The Newest New Yorkers 2000* (New York: New York City Department of City Planning, October 2004), 12.

Chapter 19

[1]Bono, Address at the National Prayer Breakfast (Hilton Washington Hotel, February 6, 2006).
[2]UN Secretariat, Workshop on HIV/AIDS and Adult Mortality in Developing Countries. Department of Economic and Social Affairs (New York, September 8-13, 2003), Table 6, 22.
[3]World Vision Report, "Serving God's Children" (Federal Way, Washington: Winter 1998–1999).
[4]John Clause, interview by Mac Pier, November 19, 2007.
[5]2007 AIDS Epidemic Update (Joint United Nations Programme on HIV/AIDS and World Health Organization, 2007), Table 2, 17, http://data.unaids.org/pub/EPISlides/2007/2007_epiupdate_en.pdf (accessed June 17, 2008).

Chapter 20

[1]Keith Boyd, interview by Mac Pier, November 20, 2007.
[2]Dee Ann Boyd, interview by Mac Pier, November 20, 2007.
[3]Trinity Baptist Church, "Story of Our Church," http://www.trinityny.org (accessed December 2007).
[4]Trinity Baptist Church, "Mission/Vision," http://www.trinityny.org/templates/custrinitybc/details .asp?id=27325&PID=155067 (accessed June 17, 2008).
[5]Nathan Gasatura, interview by Mac Pier, November 28, 2007.
[6]Dee Ann Boyd, "Courageous Leadership Award Proposal" (New York, Trinity Baptist Church, March 2007).
[7]Keith Boyd interview.

Chapter 21

[1]Garret Rain, Lecture by Dr. A. R. Bernard to Bakke Graduate University Students (Brooklyn, New York; Christian Cultural Center, June 20, 2007).
[2]Christian Cultural Center, http://cccinfo.org/AboutUs/tabid/242/Default.aspx (accessed January 25, 2008).
[3]Rain, Lecture by Dr. A. R. Bernard to Bakke Graduate University Students.
[4]"Dr. Cho Awarded the Family of Man Medallion," http://www.davidcho.com/journal/jbody.asp?id=729 (accessed June 17, 2008).
[5]Dr. A. R. Bernard, interview by Mac Pier, December 19, 2007.

Chapter 22

[1]Kim Anderson, *A2 Case Study: Christ Church, Montclair, NJ* (South Barrington, IL: Willow Creek Association, October 2006), 8.
[2]Ibid., 11, 12.
[3]Wikipedia, "Harry Emerson Fosdick," http://en.wikipedia.org/wiki/Harry_Emerson_Fosdick (accessed January 30, 2008).
[4]Anderson, *A2 Case Study*, 59.
[5]David Ireland and Rupert Hayles, interview by Mac Pier, November 29, 2007.
[6]Anderson, *A2 Case Study*, 52.
[7]Rupert Hayles interview.
[8]Anderson, *A2 Case Study*, 39–41.
[9]Rupert Hayles interview.
[10]Anderson, *A2 Case Study*, 28–34.

Chapter 23

[1]Garret Rain, Marcos Rivera Lecture to Bakke Graduate University Students (New York, New York; June 20, 2007).
[2]Marc Rivera, interview by Mac Pier, November 19, 2007.

Chapter 24

[1]The Life Christian Church, "Our Mission," http://www.tlcc.org/OurMission.html (accessed May 15, 2008).
[2]Terry Smith, interview by Mac Pier, January 18, 2008.
[3]Governor Richard Codey, "Celebrating the Past" (address at the Life Christian Church's 15-year celebration, October 2006).
[4]Mayor Cory Booker, "Celebrating the Past" (address at the Life Christian Church's 15-year celebration, October 2006).

Chapter 25

[1]Children of the City, "About Us," http://www.childrenofthecity.org/aboutus.html (accessed January 25, 2008).
[2]Resurrection Church, "Our Vision," http://www.resurrectionchurchofny.com/vision.htm (accessed January 25, 2008).
[3]Joseph Mattera, interview by Mac Pier, December 18, 2007.
[4]Christ Covenant Coalition, "Our Vision," http://christcovenantcoalition.org/index.php (accessed May 15, 2008).
[5]City Action Coalition, "About CAC," http://www.cityactioncoalition.com/about.html (accessed January 5, 2008).

Chapter 26

[1]Tom Campisi, "A Love Kitchen Legacy in the Bronx," *Tri-State Voice,* August 2001.
[2]Ronald Bailey, interview by Mac Pier, November 27, 2007.

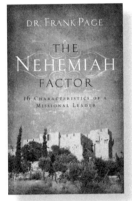
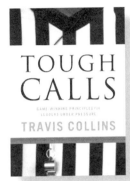

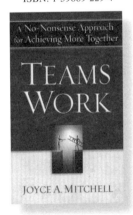

New Hope Publishers® is a division of WMU,®
an international organization that challenges Christian believers
to understand and be radically involved in God's mission.
For more information about WMU, go to www.wmu.com.
More information about New Hope books may be found at
www.newhopepublishers.com.
New Hope books may be purchased at your local bookstore.